D0938494

The Jack Bank

THE Jack Bank

A Memoir of a South African Childhood

Glen Retief

ST. MARTIN'S PRESS ✿ NEW YORK

Sections of the chapter "The Jack Bank" were first published in *Virginia Quarterly Review.*

Frontispiece: The author at age twelve, in his high school uniform.

Cover photograph and frontispiece courtesy of Peter Retief, the author's father.

www.stmartins.com

Book design by James Sinclair

Library of Congress Cataloging-in-Publication Data

Retief, Glen.
  The jack bank : a memoir of a South African childhood / Glen Retief.—1st ed.
      p. cm.
  ISBN 978-0-312-59093-2
  1. Retief, Glen—Childhood and youth.   2. Boarding school students—South Africa—Biography.   3. Boarding school students—South Africa—Conduct of life.   4. Hazing—South Africa.   5. South Africa—Race relations.   6. South Africa—Social conditions—1961–1994.   7. Young gay men—South Africa—Biography.   8. South Africa—Biography.
I. Title.
  CT1928.R47A3 2011
  920.68—dc22

                              2010042301

First Edition: April 2011

10 9 8 7 6 5 4 3 2 1

For my parents

Contents

Acknowledgments

This book would not have been possible without the support, both practical and moral, of many people. Thanks, of course, to Elizabeth Beier from St. Martin's and Michael Bourret of Dystel and Goderich, for their faith in me. Elizabeth, this book would be so much less than it is without your thoughtful and thorough feedback. My appreciation to all the great teachers along the way who encouraged me in my writing: Melissa Bank, who first told me I could be a writer; Fred D'Aguiar, who taught me about language; Mark Winegardner and Robert Olen Butler, who guided me in writing character-driven narratives; and Bob Shacochis, who made me realize I had something to say to the world. My tremendous appreciation to all my colleagues at Susquehanna University for supporting me with encouragement, ideas, and course releases.

My appreciation to all the people who helped me with fact-checking: Anthony Manion and Kamohelo Malinga of the Gay and Lesbian Archives in Johannesburg; Hein Kleinbooi, who read early versions of the chapters about my participation in the campaign to ban homophobic discrimination in the South African Bill of Rights.

Thanks to all the friends and allies along the way who invested time, energy, and emotional support in backing the project. Nina Herzog: on the long-ago day you first read my notes about my boarding school experiences, you leaned back in your office chair, shook your head, and said, "*This* is the kind of writing you should be doing." Carolyn Forché, having read only the seed essay for this memoir published in *VQR,* grabbed Michael Bourret in the hallways of the *Desert Nights* Writing Conference and asked him to pay special attention to the young South African memoirist with a story about race, sexuality, and violence. And while writing this manuscript, what would I have done without my three loyal critic-readers? My partner, Peterson Toscano—joy of my life. Barry Stopfel, who reassured me when I was stumbling. James Stroud—still my best reader and best friend.

Finally, Mom and Dad: thank you for caring for me. You made mistakes while raising your kids, just like any human beings would have. But in the end, it's your love and guidance that kept me going.

The Jack Bank

The Weight of Elephants

"We live," says Miss Jeanette, leaning forward and lowering her voice the way she does when she wants to impress us, "in one of the largest unspoiled wildernesses in the world. Aren't we lucky, children? Just look around."

She throws her arms wide open, like a prophetess presenting her tribe with a fulfilled promise. The entire class—all twelve or so of us Standard Threes, or fifth-graders—are standing in the school backyard, along the perimeter fence. Tall green ficus, marula, and jackal berry trees reach up towards the pale African noonday sky. Masked weaver nests, lumpy, wheelbarrow-sized hay sculptures, dangle from a spindly fever tree. Birds hop, chirp, and chatter around us—black-eyed bulbuls, tiny brown manikins, and bright blue glossy starlings; bee-eaters sipping at coral tree blossoms; hadedah ibises cawing and chuckling as they rise from their stick nests. From biology class we know there are 517 species of birds in our Kruger National Park—almost as many as in the entire continent of North America. Two thousand different kinds of plants populate our plains and gullies. A hundred and fifty mammals, more than in any other national park in the world, wander around our neighborhood: leopards, elephants, and aardvarks; sable antelope, giraffes, and monkeys. Could the Garden of Eden have been so abundant?

None of us nine-year-olds bother to look at any of this, though. We have heard this lecture from Miss Jeanette before, on how fortunate we are to live here; on what a great treasure for humanity all of this is—this sliver of land, shaped like a thin, pregnant amputee, lodged up in the northeastern corner of South Africa. We have heard how the entire state of Israel could fit inside this wilderness; we've heard how Wales could squeeze snugly into its swollen underbelly. Mr. Flip, the Standard Four teacher, has explained in assembly that it would take two million rugby fields to cover the entire expanse—one for every person living in Johannesburg. Who cares? When is the bell going to ring for the end of school? More importantly, what will my mother have cooked today for lunch?

Then, at last, the bell jangles, and instantly we fly, helter-skelter, in the glaring white sunlight, back into the classroom to grab our books. I pull my bike from the rack. On the way home, I speed past the Dutch Reformed church with its flying buttresses; the cricket and rugby field, with its family of warthogs playing in the sprinklers; and the house on the corner where my Auntie Merle, my Uncle Ian, and my cousins Lorna and Neil live. I head down the main street, Soenie Street, and tear downhill on Grysbok. I dash across the low water bridge—this is where I've seen hyenas and jackals; once I flew off this bridge on the way to school and skinned my palms and knees on the river sand, but today I fly gracefully across, a bee-eater diving for a sawfly, a kingfisher darting nestwards. Left again, and uphill: now I follow the course of the dry stream bed we call the *spruitjie,* which runs right in front of my family's home and winds its way through the village until it joins the wide Nwatswishaka. This *spruitjie* of ours is lined with bushwillows and silverleafs. On cloudy days the silverleafs glint a dull nickel color, the shade of twenty-cent coins coated with dust.

And now, here I am; I'm home, huffing and panting, by the newly built ranch house on the right, the one with the single knob thorn tree on the front corner by the barbecue and the lone appleleaf bush in the front yard, with the hollowed-out rock that serves as a birdbath. Corrugated zinc roofing slopes upward. I enter the wide wire gate, the one my parents keep closed at night against animals. I drop my bike on the lawn, next to my sister's and brother's—they must be home from school already. The impala grazing the lawn take no notice of me. I open the back kitchen screen door. Through the kitchen, with the linoleum-patterned floor and the pine breakfast set in front of fridges and chest freezers; through the TV room, with the kudu paintings and recliners; down the dark passageway, to my bedroom, where I drop my schoolbag next to the headboard with the Rand McNally globe and the *Illustrated Children's Bible*.

In the dining room, back at the other end of the house, the rest of the family is already seated, and Mommy's dishing up macaroni and cheese. The room smells rich and savory. Thick tubes of egg-filled rigatoni steam on my plate. Salad lies alongside the pasta: iceberg lettuce and red medallions of tomato and neatly peeled wedges of cucumber.

"What did you learn in school today?" Mommy asks. Mommy is auburn and tanned; shorter than Daddy, or most of the other women in the village—she likes to wear apricot-colored blouses and neat, white shorts. Her skin is the sorrel hue of river sand when you splash water on it; her eyes brown, like bark. Love radiates out from her like the heat in her hair, like her perfume, which smells of roses, or is it lavender?

"Nothing," I tell Mommy. School might as well not exist for me; all I can think of is the food. "I don't remember."

"*Nothing?*" This is Daddy. Daddy is taller, much lighter-complexioned than Mommy, and he has a small belly from beer and barbecues. He has a mole growing out the left side of his nose and lots of tiny dark hairs on his arms and legs. On his head, his hair is thick and brown, but he is starting to go bald in the middle: Mommy says soon he'll be a *kaalkop,* a barehead, like Kojak, her favorite police detective. Daddy's official job here in the Kruger National Park is "quantitative biologist," meaning he programs computers for the research department. Sometimes he also gets to help out his brother-in-law, Uncle Ian, a biologist, with field research.

Daddy loves us, too, but in a different way: he loves to tease and play with us, and to ask us questions about the world.

"Who just became the first female British prime minister?" he'll ask us.

Margaret Thatcher!

"Who sings 'Love You Inside and Out'?" The Bee Gees! Now, around the dining room table, he lowers his spectacles and stares at me, wide-eyed and blinking.

"All day long, Glennie? Six hours with Miss Jeanette—*nothing*?"

Lisa—two years younger than me; blond, skinny, and pale—now begins to softly guffaw. David, who just recently turned four—stocky and brown-haired, he's still a baby; Lisa often carries him around, spread-eagled, in a blanket on her back, like a Swazi mother—picks up Lisa's thread of laughter and starts to splutter, with his mouth still full of macaroni. I can see it: soon he's going to mess food. At this age I have little time for David. He runs inside with mud on his arms and ants crawling on his chest. Right now, for example, I know he has no idea why he's giggling.

But Daddy's still looking at me. "Just something about rugby fields, Daddy," I say, now, ladling a second helping of macaroni and cheese onto my plate. "Two million of them. The size of the park. It's the same story Mr. Louis always tells. I've explained to Daddy before."

We kids are cavalier like this. As far as we are concerned, children everywhere have parents who work for the National Parks

Board; uncles who are global elephant experts—Uncle Ian is one of the people with the responsibility for deciding how many elephant breeding herds need to get shot annually to preserve the vegetation. Why wouldn't other kids have houses like ours, filled with wildlife memorabilia? Mommy and Daddy's rhino ashtrays, with kidney-shaped depressions in their backs; Merle and Ian's end table sewn out of a stuffed elephant leg.

If you ask us, "What does watching a movie mean?" we'll say: "Oh, those boring flicks!"—meaning the nature documentaries that get screened over and over again outdoors in the tourist camp. If you query us about restaurants, we'll say something about buffalo pies with gravy on the verandah of the camp cafeteria—or, only on the most special occasions, Sunday prix-fixe menus in the tourist restaurant: impala steaks, stuffed guinea fowl.

Not a single thing is strange or different to us. Once a month or so, on a Saturday morning, Lisa, David, and I, and our cousins Lorna and Neil, clamber on the back of a *bakkie,* a pickup truck. We ride down rutted gravel firebreaks through red bush scrub into rhino territory and stop by dried dung heaps. Here, we clamber out in a hurry—"Last one there is a rotten old maid!" We gather whole armfuls of rhino dung, which smells of dry leaves and grass and has the consistency of caked dirt. As the morning passes the pile of dung on the back of the truck grows higher, until at last the five of us sit like kings and queens on our throne of feces, pointing at the ridges, kopjes, and coves of our domain—the green marulas and the dry brown mud pans. Back home, we help spread the excrement in our parents' flower beds, as fertilizer. Surely this isn't exotic? Three or so years ago, when our family still lived in Durban—this was when Daddy still worked as a computer programmer for the company in the skyscraper and I attended a suburban convent—I remember we were always picking up dog pooh in plastic bags.

True, that wasn't for fertilizer: "The people were supposed to pick up after themselves," Mommy always says when she talks about that time. And she shudders.

But now, on weekday afternoons, when we kids spot a giant monitor lizard, for fun we corner it against the house wall. Monitor lizards, which we call *lekkewaans,* are reptiles big as a child's leg, with black tongues that shoot out a third of their body length, and dark brown diamond patches on their scaly backs. When they get frightened and angry, they blow themselves up, and their eyes start to bulge. We throw small sticks, pebbles, and sand at these things until they snap, hiss, and frighten us away. How deliciously weird these creatures are! How fabulously monstrous! Yet these, too, do not strike us as altogether extraordinary—don't children everywhere get to play with these miniature brontosaurs from a *National Geographic* illustration?

Or still one more instance: the Friday and Saturday night backyard *braais,* which are such a social staple in this village. At these barbecues, we children run around in the front yard on the lawn, while the grown-ups talk about boring things like politics and taxes. Jackals cry nearby in the darkness: a soulful, bewildering cacophony of yelps that reminds me of babies' howling. Fireflies dart around the shadowy sausage tree with its dark, pendulous salamis; tambotie beans warm in our palms and then jump around of their own accord, animated by the microscopic worms that burrow into them. When we look up, we see a sparkling spillage of stars— the Milky Way, wide and luminous, covering half the heavens, the Southern Cross perched above the treeline like a skew-spun kite. What if someone told us only a tiny minority of humanity—nobody in the star-deprived Northern Hemisphere, to begin with, and nobody living in dense, humid rainforests or neon-lit metropolises— ever got to see stars like these?

"What's a Northern Hemisphere?" we'd probably ask. "What's the purpose of a galaxy?"

One evening, when my sister, brother, and I are sitting in the living room doing homework, our phone rings. It is Mr. Louis, the school principal, saying a journalist from the South African Broadcasting Corporation is staying in the tourist camp and has asked to interview an English-speaking kid about what it's like to grow up in the game reserve. Would my parents mind bringing me over to his house so the journalist can meet me?

In Mr. Louis's book-lined study, the tall, blond woman is dressed in a plain, pleated red jacket and skirt. Instantly I sense something different about her—something powerful and citified. The adult women I am used to encountering either dress in long white floral dresses, like the Afrikaner aunties, or in casual, fashionable modern clothes, like Mommy and Auntie Merle.

"So what's it *like* to be a kid in the Kruger National Park?" the journalist asks now, her voice all syrupy and expectant, her blue eyes thoughtful, friendly, interested.

I have no idea what she wants to know. Is she asking me how school is going?

"It's nice," I reply. "I like it."

"What are some of your favorite games and hobbies?"

"Monopoly. I also like playing *vroteier*." *Vroteier* is a game where we sit in a circle and an outside runner drops a clump of tissue paper behind an unsuspecting player.

"How about on the weekends? What does a game reserve kid do in his spare time?"

"Ride my bike! I have a BMX Powerline!" She shifts in her seat, looks down at some notes. I have a feeling I'm saying something wrong, but it's hard to figure out exactly what.

"Have you ever run into a wild animal in the village?"

"*Ja*. Impala." Perhaps I am thinking merely of the animals I saw that day, because inexplicably I decline to mention the lone elephant bull I once saw ambling down the road towards the low-water bridge, or the hippopotamus that came into our yard one night when I left the gate open, and that my father had to scare off by banging pots and pans together.

On the evening the interview is supposed to be featured on the English service's *Radio Today* program, the extended family gathers at my aunt and uncle's house, beside the Kenwood hi-fi set, with my aunt pouring all the grown-ups gin-and-tonics and the kids passion fruit squash. A political segment plays. The American president, Jimmy Carter, is having some kind of trouble with people in Iran: there are students misbehaving there, shouting and demonstrating. There are updates about rugby and cricket. Then they play the jangly melody that signals the end of the program.

"Not quite the radio star yet, hey?" asks my Aunt Merle. She rumples my hair. "Don't worry. They have so many interviews—they can't possibly run them all. Maybe they'll play it next time, Glennie."

But deep inside my chest I know differently. There, under my ribs, a truth niggles: I said the wrong things. I missed the whole point of the conversation, and there is no reason to play back my responses. I am supposed to proclaim, like Miss Jeanette does: *We are so privileged to live in the majesty of creation.* I am supposed to state: *This is like heaven for a kid to grow up in.*

It is not that we have complete freedom in this paradise. A web of rules and regulations exists to protect us from the risks of living in an unfenced settlement. We are not allowed to play in the storm pipes near the house—mysterious, fascinating, concrete cylinders laden with river sand and pebbles. Warthogs are said to nest there, and a mother warthog protecting its young is easily capable of tusking open a child's intestines. We are not allowed to leave the village limits: here, among the streets and houses, it is assumed that the human hubbub will keep away the really dangerous animals, but in the neighboring veld, buffalo, elephant, and lions all roam freely. We are to avoid sitting on logs or stumps for fear of disturbing a black mamba, whose bite can kill a grown man in half an hour, or a puffadder, whose toxins can rot away your flesh and turn a leg black as charcoal. Every evening, the minute the sun begins to set, we are to head back indoors. At night only a fool would be about on foot. Harry Wolhuter, the first game ranger here, got mauled by a pride of lions and then had to strap himself with his belt to a tree branch he had climbed to escape them, so he wouldn't fall out when he lost consciousness.

Pythons, they say, swallowed unattended toddlers here in the early days. A child's foot sinking into a muddy pool along a path can lead to infection with bilharzia—a disease where parasites slowly eat the liver and vital organs. Mosquito bites, especially those suffered in the early evening, can lead to cerebral malaria, where infected red blood cells stop up the brain. Spitting cobras can rear up and deliver streams of blinding cytotoxin straight into wide, transfixed eyes. The button spider, smaller than the surface of a lapel pin, can deliver enough neurotoxin to a child's sleeping neck to land her in hospital.

Examples abound of the consequences of recklessness. Tom Yssel, the game ranger from Nwanedzi who stops by our house when he's in the village to stock up on groceries, has a misshapen left leg and gets around on crutches. He was fishing in the Sabie River with some friends when a crocodile grabbed his leg and began to pull him under. He would have drowned if not for the courage and skill of his buddies, who jammed their pocket knives into the reptile's eyes. A maid crossed the Nwatswishaka riverbed on a footpath instead of over the low-water bridge. A buffalo charged her, tossed her, and trampled her. Four days later, in hospital, she died.

It is not exactly that we children are impervious to this ever-present peril. On languid afternoons sitting together baking mud pies behind my cousins' house, we regale each other with stories of *boomslangs* dropping out of trees and delivering their deadly poison, of hippos biting tourist rowboats in two below Victoria Falls. We older kids—Lisa and Lorna and me—share with the younger ones what we learned in biology class about how if our maids forget to iron our clothes, larvae will burrow from the cotton fibers under our skins, and one day *putsi* flies will break out of raised pink spots on our stomachs.

"A crocodile's jaws are stronger than the metal ones they use to pull people out of car wrecks, hey," I'll say, repeating something I've probably heard on the playground. "Elephants, when they trample you, weigh more than a car—more than the whole house."

But this all seems unreal to us, like witches in fairy tales. Nothing specifically bad will befall us. Even our teachers suggest as much: when I ask Miss Jeanette if a child has been killed in the village since she moved here, she replies that no, if we just follow all our parents' instructions, there is nothing to worry about.

"You shouldn't fret," she says, stooping down to kiss me on the forehead. In her presence, as in Mommy's, it is impossible to even think of the weight of elephants.

One day my siblings, my cousins, and I are walking down the shortcut through the bush to the swimming pool. I see the grass move ahead of us; I am almost certain it's the wind, but I decide to play a prank on the other kids.

"I think—wait—something's moving in the grass—a leopard!" I yell at the others. Lisa and Lorna do not believe me, but Neil and David begin to cry and run back towards my parents' house. "Just playing!" I shout, running after them, realizing they are truly upset. But now it is too late; the younger kids are screaming and trembling, and when I get back home my mother washes out my mouth with soap for telling a fib.

"This isn't a game, Glen," she tells me firmly, placing her hand on my knee. "Can you understand that, my love? Can you see this is real?"

I nod and tell her I'm sorry. But really, in my heart, I still don't register anything.

Miss Jeanette overhears me telling another kid about an old man who gets bitten all over by *putsis* and releases so many baby flies that the blue-green buzzing cloud produces an artificial night.

"What an imagination you have!" she says. "You should write these stories down instead of scaring the others!" I have written stories for fun before. In first grade, at the Durban convent, one of the nuns, Sister Jacqueline, encouraged me to come in early and write down tales of fairies, pixies, and goblins. Miss Jeanette has heard my parents talk about this, so now she suggests a revival of that tradition: I will come in a quarter an hour or so early and write extra tales in my notebook. Now, the pixies in my literary imagination have been replaced by orphaned jackal pups and marabou storks who get blown to Mauritius on jet streams.

It's for this reason that, one crisp winter dawn, I arrive early at the gates of Skukuza Primary School. My thin green uniform sweater is pulled over my khaki shirt. My bare feet and legs are red from the cold, and my breath puffs out ahead of me. I immediately notice something strange is going on. The gate opening onto the concrete driveway that leads to the bicycle rack is bolted shut. Beside it lie a couple of abandoned bikes. Where did these riders go? Why not just open the gate, which has no padlock on it?

So I do so, and I enter the school. I certainly do not think of what I am doing as defying authority: usually I am a rule-abiding child. It is more that I don't understand the gate. I take barely a step or two, and then arms sweep me up from behind: *whoosh*. I want to scream, but a hand covers my mouth. I am lifted, bookbag and all, off the ground, and then, before I even realize it, I've been whisked back out of the gate.

"Quiet, Retief," whispers a deep-timbered voice I recognize as that of Mr. Flip. He lets me down, puts a finger on his lips to show me I must keep silent, and then points to the church.

"Get in there now! *Run!*"

I do as he says. Out of the corner of my eye I see that to my left, Miss Jeanette's white minivan is pulling up at the front gate. Miss Dalie, the first-grade teacher, holds the door open to the church. Inside, the church is empty except for a handful of children, including another boy from my grade, Jannie de Vos.

"What's going on?" I ask Miss Dalie.

"Lions," she replies. "Four of them, on the basketball courts. Three females and one male. Now, get inside and stay there. We've called Nature Conservation."

Inside, I work out the details: the basketball courts are merely a hundred yards or so from the bicycle rack, at the far end of the athletics track sprint line. Even if it was just for a second or two, they would have smelt me at that front gate, been aware of me. I can picture them quite clearly, lying on the black asphalt. They roll over, yawn, and swat each other, as lions do. Perhaps, one of them even crouches, alert, her tail flicking, ready to charge me.

"Were you scared?" Jannie asks me. "I saw them, hey—on the basketball courts. They looked at me with their yellow eyes. *Yissis!*"

I cannot bring myself to confess that I was so stupid as to open a latched gate. So I say, "*Ja,*" playing up the drama of my encounter. "They were walking around right near the bicycle rack. One of them roared at me, hey! I almost fell over and had a heart attack."

But still I don't understand. In the days and weeks after this incident, I concoct several different theories as to why the lions never charged me, roared at me, or ran away.

"They were far, hey," says my uncle. "Also, they were probably full and sluggish from a recent kill." He was one of the Nature Conservation officials who helped dart the lions that morning and cart them away—a process that, to our disappointment, seemed to happen in just a few minutes, allowing the teachers to order us back to our classes. "I bet they were so comfortable on that warm tar they couldn't be bothered with a pipsqueak like you!"

But I can't quite get my head around this thought. On the one hand, it seems simply dull: it isn't worthy of a story in my class notebook. On the other hand—to the extent I'm able, at age nine, to consciously formulate this thought—there's something fundamentally terrifying about my uncle's statement. For a moment, in the hubbub of the teachers' early response to the lions, the bicycle gate was left unguarded. I opened it, took several steps towards the lions. If just one small thing about this scenario had been different—if Mr. Flip hadn't been nearby; if the lions had truly been around the bicycle rack; if they hadn't been so sluggish—then bam! I would have been all blood and skin, like one of the kills we see by the roadside, shimmering with famished flies.

Mortality: the thought is still too much for me. So instead, half for fun and half in earnest, I wonder to myself if these were real lions. Perhaps they were Swazi magicians who had adopted the shapes of lions, as in the fairy tales that Sarah, my parents' housekeeper, sometimes tells me when I sit next to her by her garden room as she eats her lunch after ours. Or perhaps, I speculate, a satellite was passing overhead. Last year, Miss Elsa, a teacher who has now left the school, told us that the communists had spacecraft in orbit around the earth, broadcasting political propaganda at inaudible frequencies that corresponded to those of the human brain. My father, when I told him this story, scoffed at it; take it from a computer scientist, he said—there is no machine capable of changing a human mind. But now, I wonder again: if Miss Elsa was right, and Daddy is wrong, could satellites like those have confused the lions and distracted them?

A superior solution presents itself to me a week or two later, though, when I pick up my *Illustrated Children's Bible* and open it at the Old Testament Book of Daniel. Here, right on the opening page, a vivid color drawing presents a gray-bearded old man at the bottom of a well. Four lions—it does not escape my notice that this is precisely the number that came in to lie on the basketball courts—eye Daniel warily. But there are also two translucent angels drawn in the picture: supple, winged young men wearing tunics. One of the angels holds closed the mouth of the male lion and pushes the head of one of the females away from Daniel. The other angel is seated cross-legged between two lionesses; he has his hand between one's shoulder blades and seems to be scratching the other on her forehead.

The Bible chapter explains: Daniel was a God-fearing Israelite, whom the Persian king threw into the lions' den because he would not worship false gods. The next morning, Daniel got pulled out of the den without a scratch; however, when some scheming courtiers got thrown in after Daniel, the lions tore their flesh from their bodies. The moral of the story was to trust in the power of the Lord, who could work any miracle to save his loyal followers.

Was it possible that God had done something similar for me that day?

I find my mother in the kitchen, preparing supper. "Mommy, could God have sent guardian angels to protect me on the day I walked by the lions?" She pauses in her cooking.

"God can do anything, my love," she says, reaching down to embrace me. "How exactly his power works, that's not for us to understand. But if there's one thing I'm sure of, it's that God loves you and doesn't want you to be harmed."

The answer is the one I was hoping for. That evening, as I lie in bed falling asleep, I half-close my eyes and try to sense any presences in the room besides my own. A branch rustles against the window: perhaps it is God, trying to tell me he is close to me. A shadow moves on the bedroom floor—leaves in the wind, or a phantom's attempts at writing. Now—this comes upon me unexpected and inevitable as a sneeze—I feel completely certain, first, that God is with me in the room, and, second, that I have nothing to fear.

It wakes me before dawn: a clatter of hooves like a thunderstorm, a live creature tripping over the guy rope near my tent, unsteadying the standing pole. Something tumbles off its feet. A bone-chilling growl rips through the night as meat gets torn out of a throat—the astonishingly loud rasping saw as a ruptured windpipe hauls its last breath. The hoof patter, dying away like rain; silence returning—even the tree frogs seem to have been stilled.

"Mommy?"

The three of us—Lisa, David, and I—are sleeping alone in this small blue A-frame tent, perhaps fifty yards or so downstream from the research trailer where my parents are staying. I am older than before, probably around ten. Here, at this camp, my father is helping out with a study of the hunting and mating habits of lions. For the past five days, we have driven around in a Land Rover, getting out every five or ten minutes and sweeping around an antenna that signals the proximity and direction of collared lions and then carefully jotting down information when we saw them.

Now, in the tent, a vague fear begins to rise in me. It is all too silent. I cannot even hear any cicadas, crickets, or night birds. Beside me, in the nylon pods of their sleeping bags, Lisa and David continue breathing smoothly, evenly. David has his face pushed into the far corner of the tent. I wonder if I imagined the sawing and thundering. But no—there is the front tent pole leaning slightly over to the right as a result of whatever foundered over the guy rope.

"Mommy?" I ask again, louder this time, projecting my voice back towards the trailer.

"Glen," comes back my father's voice, "three lions have killed a kudu right outside your tent. There's no need to be scared, okay? I have the gun right here, and I'm ready to shoot if I have to. But they don't know what a tent is, so you're safe as long as you stay inside and don't make a noise. Okay, son? I mean it. Still now—not a word."

"Everything will be fine, darling," my mother adds. While my father's voice was calm and authoritative, though—a teacher giving instructions to his pupils—my mother's has a tremble in it: she does not completely believe her own words. *Mommy's scared.* Her anxiety ignites apprehension in my own chest.

"Mommy—" I am about to ask how far away the lions are when I remember my father's orders: no sounds at all. I lie back and listen to the quiet. At first I hear nothing. I could be underground. But then the sound comes to me, unmistakable: *chewing.* Saliva sucking and popping inside cheeks. Teeth gnawing against each other. A sharp cracking sound, as if of a bone breaking.

I snuggle deeper into my sleeping bag. Daddy said the tent would confuse the lions, and so, I tell myself, I am actually perfectly safe inside here. Probably the sleeping bags will confuse them, too. If I get right inside and wedge the cotton fabric of the bag under my head, then I will essentially be incomprehensible to them, an inedible lump. I lie still like this in the darkness, feeling the warmth of my sister's body against my left shoulder. I try to picture angels among these lions, holding their jaws shut. But now a lion snarls and grunts, at what seems like no distance at all; another lion, also close but on the other side of the tent, calls out into the night—a short, low, repetitive series of grunts: the sound that, in some corner of my brain, I remember is used to call other members of the pride. These lions are powerful and enormous. My mouth is dry.

"Glen," comes my father's voice again. "I can't move now, because the lions have just killed, and it's night, and they're hungry. If I get out now they'll take it as a threat. But if we all just stay still for a little while, they'll fill their stomachs, and then I'll be able to chase them off. So stay quiet, son."

Which I do. I continue to listen to the chewing sounds, punctuated with an occasional growl or snarl. Miraculously, or so it seems to me, my brother and sister stay asleep. Perhaps the moon comes out behind a cloud: at some point, at any rate, my head is out of my sleeping bag again, and the canvas of the tent beside me is now pale blue and luminous. A shadow pops up on it, something black, vast, and shapeless.

"Daddy!" the words choke up in my throat. No sound actually comes out of my mouth, though. Something warm runs down my leg: I must have peed into my sleeping shorts.

"*Still,* Glennie," says my father.

The shadow moves away again, and quiet returns. Even the chewing sounds are gone, now; instead I hear the chirp of tree frogs and the high-pitched scraping call of franklins.

And then I must somehow have fallen asleep, for now I wake to the clamor of the Land Rover's engine and a gunshot. Before I can even gather myself, the tent flap is open and my mother is there.

"Now!" she screams at the three of us, somehow hauling all of us out of bed at the same time. My brother is first in her arms, through the entrance to the tent and into the open door of the Land Rover. With both arms she pulls my sister to safety. I follow, jumping into the backseat of the vehicle. The door is slammed before I can blink; then my mother is in the front seat and my father is driving away with his right hand on the wheel while his left hand passes his revolver to my mother, who sticks it in the glove compartment. I look back. Immediately next to the tent, on the side on which I was sleeping, is a dead kudu. The lions have vanished. As I watch, vultures, temporarily scared off, settle back down on the kudu and begin pecking at it.

My mother is crying now. She moves from the front of the car to the back and hugs the three of us. She is bawling so much she can't really articulate any words; between her sobs she gulps down air in short quick gasps.

"Why is Mommy crying so much?" I ask my father, and it is only then that I realize he has been weeping, too: at least his eyes are moist behind his glasses.

"Your mommy just loves you very much, Glen, and she wouldn't want to lose you."

"That was very, very scary for Mommy," my mother adds.

I try to absorb this: Mommy and Daddy, despite what they shouted to me from the trailer, really did believe we could easily have been killed. An icy vacuum opens up in my chest. The savannah seems emptier.

"I need to pee-pee," says my brother.

"Wait till Satara," replies my father. Satara is the nearby tourist camp where we go to eat hot meals, to buy ice and groceries, and to bathe and shower. "We'll have a *boerewors* breakfast there, and I'll buy you all a carton of condensed milk."

"Yay!" we cry. "Condensed milk!" Condensed milk is our favorite treat while camping; we like to suck it, sweet and gooey, right out of the can or carton, and let it cover our lips and drip off the ends of our chins, a viscous delight.

We drive down the bumpy firebreak and up the tarred tourist road. At Satara camp, first we use the bathrooms. Then we all sit on the verandah and eat full bacon-and-egg breakfasts, with *boerewors* sausages and fresh-brewed coffee. For dessert, we three kids indeed get our small triangular cartons of condensed milk, which we drain through tiny straws. It is every bit as sugary and smooth

THE JACK BANK · 19

as we expected it to be. If heaven has milk cows, their udders will produce liquid that tastes like this.

"Glen peed in his pants," Lisa announces to our parents, after I confide in her about the lion shadow.

"It's dry now," I say, and it is: all the dampness has evaporated.

"It doesn't matter," says Mommy. "I really love you. The only thing I care about is that you're okay."

We are sitting on the lawn in front of the cafeteria verandah. Plates and cutlery clatter on the tables behind us. Tourists stand at the boards showing sightings of buffalo, rhino, and cheetah.

"Lisa and David just slept like stupid rocks," I say, perhaps to soften my embarrassment about peeing.

"He says I'm stupid!" says Lisa. "He says I'm like a rock!"

"Stop it, kids!" Mommy says. "Can't we just enjoy this moment together?"

Behind us, someone starts up a lawn sprinkler. A tourist argues with the cafeteria cashier over the cost of a pastry. I pick up my condensed milk carton and suck a final droplet out of it, so good it makes my eyes pinch shut. Above us, the sun is clear, golden, and luminous; the sky wide, azure, and infinite—as if for the moment, death and suffering are just illusions.

Them and Me

Here is a memory of Afrikaners, the foursquare, bigoted, marvelously large-hearted country folk with whom I grew up:

I'm eight years old, and I'm sitting in a prefabricated classroom in our Kruger National Park staff village, along the side wall closest to the backyard. The class is quiet. We are drawing in our exercise books. Saffron sunshine floods in the windows. Starlings, crickets, and cicadas trill and chirrup in the outside yard; our coloring crayons, when they collectively scratch on the white drawing paper, sound like leaves rustling. Miss Elsa, who is plump and brunette and wears round glasses that give her the wide-eyed look of an owl, paces up and down in the paths between the rows of desks, stooping to admire different students' artistry, cooing over Liesl's flower beds and over Danie's palm trees and ocean.

I am drawing a crucifix. Why am I doing such a thing on a glorious summer morning, in a peaceful African hamlet far from the world of Gothic cathedrals and Romanesque chapels? Perhaps I am thinking of my mother, who has a crucifix over her dressing table and says the rosary at night before she goes to bed. Perhaps I recently visited my maternal grandparents, at the nearby citrus estate where they work. They have a tormented porcelain Jesus mounted above the wild teak liquor cabinet in their living room and a framed print of the crucified savior in their bedroom. My own crucifix—a bright scarlet scribble—looks nothing like these. Still, it is unmistakable: I have even drawn purple lines radiating outward to show Jesus' holiness.

Miss Elsa stops behind my chair. I wait for her to say something in praise of my piety—this woman who talks all the time about how important it is to read the Bible and pray. She picks up the exercise book and frowns.

"Is this—?"

She seems at a loss. Something is wrong. She is staring at my picture and saying nothing at all. I stumble out: "It's Jesus. Miss Elsa knows, doesn't she?"

A vague murmur rises in the class. Miss Elsa continues to look at my picture and blink. Then she closes the book. "There's something you need to know, Glen. But I can't explain it to you now. So please take this to Mr. Louis and show him."

As I stand up to leave, she adds: "You're not in trouble, Glen. I just want you to see Mr. Louis, okay?"

Still, I am petrified. Mr. Louis is the school principal, to whom you get sent only when you're in serious trouble. Most times when students go there, Mr. Louis makes them bend over and hits them on the backside with a board compass; sometimes he enters their offence in a thick black notebook and sends a letter to their parents. In Mr. Louis's office, with its curtains showing wildlife under a cheerful, jungly pastiche of banana leaves and its polished trophies lining the bookshelves, I tremble as Mr. Louis examines my drawing, peering, frowning, and tapping his pen on the wide wooden desk.

"You English," Mr. Louis says. He sighs. Like Miss Elsa, he seems hesitant; he scratches the long furrows running down his drawn cheeks. Generally speaking, he is a kind man. He rumples my hair when he passes me in the passageway; he calls me *bulletjie,* meaning little bull, one who will some day conquer the world. "You English—you don't have the same beliefs we Afrikaners do, about not drawing pictures of Our Blessed Lord?"

I don't know how to answer this. There are only three English families in Skukuza village: my own family; my Auntie Merle and Uncle Ian and my cousins Lorna and Neil; and the Dearloves, who only occasionally socialize with the rest of us. What do we believe about drawing Jesus?

"I don't know, Mr. Louis," I reply, confused. Will he cane me for this? "My mother likes crucifixes. Sometimes we draw pictures of Mary and Joseph."

Mr. Louis exhales again—a great heave of a sigh. "Listen," he says. "Son." He puts down the pen, and then laces his fingers with his two thumbs pressed against each other. "This is an Afrikaans school." Why is he mentioning the obvious? Then his face brightens. "Say, son, do you believe Jesus is in heaven?"

I nod. Mr. Louis turns and points to the laminated poster behind his desk, which lists the Ten Commandments.

"Can you read number two there?"

I read it aloud to him, using accentuated phrasing the way Miss Elsa has taught us to do: "Thou shalt not make unto thee a graven image, nor any manner of likeness, of anything that is in heaven above."

"In heaven above," Mr. Louis repeats, raising his eyebrows.

I stare at him, uncomprehending.

"Well, son, if Jesus is in heaven, and we are forbidden to make a likeness of anything there—well, that's why we Afrikaners believe it's wrong to draw Our Blessed Savior."

In a flash I picture our English Catholic church in Nelspruit with the statues of Jesus and Mary in front and the stained-glass windows showing the lives of the saints. All of this is wrong—a violation of God's commandment. It is Afrikaners, with their plain brown church windows and their empty cross at the front of the church—it is they who live in accordance with God's will. A vague shame rises in me, and I wish I were Afrikaans.

"Sorry, Mr. Louis. I didn't know."

"Don't worry about it, *bulletjie*. It's just that people are different, hey?"

On the way back to class I all but skip for joy: it is the first time I can think of that a child has been sent to Mr. Louis's office and not received a punishment. When I get home, though, and tell my parents what happened, my mother flies into a rage such as I have rarely seen.

"How dare they? We have as much right to our beliefs as they do!"

My father shoots her a warning glance, which I already know means, *Not in front of the kids*. But my mother is undaunted. "It's on days like this," she fumes, "I think Merle might have a point." Merle, my father's sister, regularly gripes about Afrikaners. Although she has Afrikaans friends, and in some ways seems really fond of them—she runs a home catering business and regularly cooks for their gatherings and conferences—she also loves to poke fun at them: at their flavorless *rooibos* tea, which she refuses to drink; at the way their men comb their hair back with greasy Brylcreem.

"Humph," says Daddy. "I don't know."

They begin to argue. The shape of this debate is a familiar one: Mommy complains about the Afrikaans people and how they impose their will on everyone else—no one in the village is allowed to swim, bike, or play sports on Sundays, for example; when she and Merle suntan in their bikinis, the fat Afrikaans aunties look at them and cluck their cheeks. My father tells her to be more tolerant. He says Afrikaners are in the majority here, so we must conform to their norms. My mother, on the other hand, says it is not she who is intolerant. *We* don't tell the Afrikaner kids they are not members of the one true Catholic Church, so why would they tell her son it's a sin to draw a crucifix? Today, as usual, the fight ends in a compromise. My mother will call the school to complain about what Mr. Louis said. I, however, will try not to offend the Afrikaners' religious sensibilities; from now on I will stick to sketching honey badgers sniffing around marula trees; knob thorns bedecked in chiffon-white flowers; and Land Rovers kicking up dust on pebble-strewn firebreaks.

We and they. Afrikaans versus English is not the only cultural dissimilarity that I know in that staff village, but it is the difference that presses upon my consciousness and squeezes it. Black people, for example, appear in the mornings to make our beds and work in our gardens. They are different from us, there is no doubt about it: they like to listen to pennywhistle and mouth organ music on the radio, and once when we gave Sarah, our maid, a lift back to her home in the tribal area outside the game reserve, I noticed that she slept on a bed raised on bricks—Daddy told me this was because she feared the *tokoloshe,* a mischievous goblin who spirits black people away. But by afternoon, here in the village, black people disappear from my world, back to their compound more than a mile away, on the far side of the tourist camp. They are not permitted to use our village store, tennis courts, swimming pool, or golf course, so they exist only in the background of my childish world. There is something essentially flimsy or ephemeral about them: like the cicadas or crickets, they are more heard than seen.

Not so with Afrikaners. These, by contrast, surround me, pale, tanned, or freckled in their khaki uniforms or green-checkered dresses. They yell at me to come play soccer, rugby, or volleyball on the straggly grass oval in the center of the athletics track. They join me for afternoon swimming lessons in the municipal pool; stand at the neighboring courts playing tennis on weekday evenings; and fill the village grocery store with chatter in their language, which has so many more guttural and plosive consonants than English—*g*s that sound like a child clearing her throat to spit, *r*s that roll like toy car engines. It is their church that stands in the center of the village, sprawling, powerful, intimidating, its flying buttresses like ships' rigging, its sloping red-tile roof taut as sails. Their newspaper and magazines—*Transvaler, Beeld,* and *Huisgenoot*—line the shelves next to the checkout counter and get delivered on porch steps in the afternoons; we English people, by contrast, have to receive our publications weeks late in the mail if we get them at all.

They are distinct from us. If the first lesson of life in this game reserve staff village is that nature is dangerous, then this is the second lesson: human beings vary from each other. Afrikaners are descended from hardscrabble Dutch *trekboers,* nomadic cattle herders. We English, on the other hand, are descended from landed farmers, from soldiers who came out to fight for Queen Victoria in the Anglo-Boer War, from prospectors searching for diamonds or gold. Now, while Afrikaners and English may have stopped fighting—occasionally the Afrikaans boys and girls may still tease us in a good-natured way for being *soutpiele,* salt dicks with one foot in England, one in South Africa, and our genitalia dangling into the brackish Atlantic—there is still this sense of dissimilar manners.

To begin with, they dress differently. While we all wear the same Afrikaner-style school uniforms, with everyone barefoot, my cousins and I will ditch our uniforms sooner than they do and change into boxer shorts, T-shirts, and, if we wear any shoes at all, rubber-and-plastic flip-flops. We will never wear casual khakis—those farmer-style outfits that the Afrikaner boys sometimes put on. *Velskoens*—big, flat sturdy shoes of untanned hide—are for us about as cool as putting a comb in your sock, the way the older Afrikaans-speaking men do. On Sundays the contrast is clearest. If the five of us—Mommy, Daddy, Lisa, David, and I—drive through to Catholic mass in Nelspruit, an hour and a half away, we'll wear our normal shorts, T-shirts, and sandals. If we pass the Dutch Reformed congregation gathering, it will be a vista out of a history textbook: the men and boys all dressed like Dutch colonists, in black three-piece suits with suspenders. The women and girls wearing flowing white floral dresses, with straw hats laden with plastic fruits and flowers—a cornucopia of plums, grapes, peaches, and bananas, carnations, fuchsias, and hibiscus.

"Like walking produce stands," says Auntie Merle. "I'm tempted to offer them a rand for a bunch of grapes!" Auntie Merle never wears hats except when she's hiking. She, like Mommy, wears fashionable short-sleeved blouses.

Television and music highlight further discordances. Partly as a result of their Calvinist religion they are a stricter people than we are, more buttoned-down. While Mommy, Daddy, Uncle Ian, and Auntie Merle like listening to foreign pop music, to ABBA and Boney M, Afrikaners have their own favorite TV shows and singers. The number one TV show in the village is *Nommer Asseblief,* which means "Number, please"—about a telephone operator who listens in on people's gossip. The current megahit of the Afrikaans music scene is Sonja Heroldt's "Waterblommetjies in die Boland," a song about water lilies.

"Water lilies in the Cape!" the Afrikaners sing along at their barbecues, with the women, children, and men milling around the backyard tables bedecked with curried kebabs. "Tell me you love me before you go to sleep!" When Auntie Merle's neighbors start doing *langarm* to this song—a stilted folk dance where the couples stretch their right arms out and up, like ostrich plumes—Merle puts ABBA on the hi-fi set, turning up "Fernando" to top volume: *Since many years I haven't seen a rifle in your hand.* On the front lawn we children loll and shake in the meshed amber light falling from the screened verandah, giggling as we cock and shoot at each other with our imaginary rifles and laughing at the Afrikaans children who stop their ears when they notice what we're playing and run to the far side of their yard. Or we listen to "Honey, Honey" and blow each other kisses. When we go inside to watch television, it is never a program like *Heidi,* the dubbed Swiss cartoon about children living in the Alps and drinking goat's milk. From our parents we take the lead and gravitate towards edgier American fare, like *The A-Team.*

Afrikaners dislike black people: there is some bad blood there I do not altogether comprehend. Miss Jeanette, when she talked to us once about the tensions between the races, said it had to do with the fact that both the blacks and the Afrikaners love land and cattle—hence the battles of circled wagons against the spear-throwing warriors. But my own hunch is that there must be more to it than that. In the way some of the playground boys joke about dropping an atom bomb on Mozambique or putting poison in the Soweto water tower, I sense a vast, toxic reservoir of superiority and contempt.

What do you call an 80-year-old kaffir? *Broken farm equipment.*

What do you call a thousand kaffirs *at the bottom of the sea?*

"I never want to hear you say *kaffir,*" Mommy says to me, even though this is the standard term for black people on the elementary school playground and even with some of my teachers. "We Catholics believe all people are children of God and should be treated well."

Daddy, when he shaves, listens to the BBC World Service on the shortwave radio. He doesn't trust the South African Broadcasting Corporation, which he says is an Afrikaner Nationalist propaganda tool.

"Bloody nonsense and lies," he says. "Pure paranoia."

And Gogo, my maternal grandmother, is always warning me about the Voortrekkers, the Afrikaner equivalent to the Boy Scouts that meets on Friday nights in the big hall next to the grocery store, and which counts most of the kids of the village among its members.

"Only a step or two away from the Hitler Youth," she once muttered when the issue came up in some story or other she was reading me. "Pa almost died in the Sahara fighting against that kind of thing." What kind of thing does she mean? When I press her on the details, she demurs, saying that Mommy and Daddy wouldn't like her badmouthing people I go to school with.

If the Afrikaners are racist, what does that make us English? We also have maids and gardeners. Uncle Ian also talks about *muntus,* an only slightly less derogatory word than *kaffir.* We even vote much the way the Afrikaners do, as far as I know, at least the moderate Afrikaners Mommy and Daddy like to socialize with, like Uncle Johan and Auntie Jeanette Verhoef, my fifth-grade teacher. At the last election my parents voted for the liberal opposition Progressive Federal Party, but from the way Uncle Ian and Auntie Merle talked to the Dearloves, I think they may have voted for the ruling Nationalists.

So what exactly do the grown-ups mean when they sit in their living-room armchairs with their beers and cocktails and worry about whether we children are absorbing too much Afrikaner influence?

"I wonder sometimes what they're teaching them," Auntie Merle remarks.

"Just like little Afrikaners," Mommy says, when she sees us speaking Afrikaans to each other while playing *vroteier.*

And when we sit down to eat lunch or supper, Auntie Merle makes us practice our English pronunciation.

"Che-uh," she says, pointing to the wooden contraption we sit on. "Just like the queen would say it."

"He-uh," she says then, holding onto her bouncy, full-bodied brunette locks.

"Chê," we reply, as we seat ourselves around the table, pronouncing the vowel flat as a footstep. "Hê," pointing at each other's heads. Then we giggle in the hope of vaguely aggravating her: Auntie Merle has a Union Jack in her bathroom and a London Underground sign salvaged from a long-ago tourist trip she and Uncle Ian took. Every year she organizes Wimbledon parties with cucumber sandwiches, strawberries, and tea.

The truth is, I feel this difference, this Englishness, right in the core of my body, in the pit of my chest, where my teacher, Miss Jeanette says my heart is supposed to be: this heart that, incidentally, looks nothing at all like the double curvy shape the boys draw on the notes they send to the girls when they are asking them the *kys*. Rather, the real human heart is all blood and pulp. Miss Jeanette has shown us pictures: in one of them it looks like a skinned raw chicken. If you had to cut it up and fry it, Miss Jeanette says it would taste like kidneys or liver—I think kidneys in gravy on toast. I have never eaten even an animal's heart: apparently it is a black people's dish, along with chicken feet stew and mopani worms. But even at seven or eight years old, I find that image of a heart on a chopping board resonates. I can imagine the prick of the knife into tissue: like the sharp needlepoint of a maths compass when you press it under your fingernail. I can sense how it would be to experience open-heart surgery, like Dr. Chris Barnard performed for the first time ever in Groote Schuur Hospital back in the 1960s, when Miss Jeanette was still a teenager: to be all open.

"*Ai*, children," Miss Jeanette says to us, holding up a picture of a blond bespectacled young man next to the diagram of the ventricles and arteries. "We were so proud of ourselves that day, we

Afrikaners. For a moment we were the world's most special nation."

It is not that I am actually heartsore or unhappy. Probably if you
had to ask Mommy or Daddy they would say, "Our Glennie, he's
such a cheerful, well-adjusted child, not demanding at all." Much of
the time I am indeed contented. At home I often have my head in a
book: having been taught to read by Gogo even before I entered
first grade, I love adventure stories and fairy narratives, Enid Blyton's Famous Five series and Willard Price's *South Sea Adventure*.
When I get antsy from all of this, I run around outside, in the front
or back garden, waving a broken twig or a bent piece of honey-
suckle creeper, and telling myself stories aloud, continuations of
what I've been reading: winged chairs performing crash landings
with bell-capped pixies on them; Hal and Roger trying to catch an
escaped boa constrictor on their ship. If the neighbors laugh or
comment—"*Hau,* what are you doing, *kleinbaas*?" Sarah, our
Swazi maid, always wants to know—or if this generates a reputation for eccentricity, well, at home, in the cocoon of Mommy, Daddy,
and the cousins, I am blissfully unaware of it. I jump and wave and
talk to ghosts.

Things are different during recess on the school playground.
Here, I am forced into a group of forty or more Afrikaner boys, all
of us required to play on the far side of the classrooms, along the
edge of the school hall, and on the rugby field inside the athletics
track. Lisa and Lorna, my main playmates from home, hang out
with the other girls on the front lawn. There, they play the games I
sometimes watch with envy from the steps by the bicycle rack: hop-
scotch and rope-skipping, cards and mock tea. Something in me
feels I should perhaps be with them, although that isn't it exactly,
either: what I really want is to be able to participate in the other
boys' games—but I feel I cannot.

The first problem is that I don't like rugby. Rugby: this is the
Afrikaners' second religion, the national obsession. It is another

core cultural difference: Afrikaners like rugby, the English prefer cricket and tennis. The Skukuza boys collect rugby cards and post pictures of Springbok players on the brown paper covers of their exercise books. On Monday mornings they talk about rugby games that took place over the weekend: Western Province versus Northern Transvaal at Loftus Versveld. In these conversations I stand around, confused and helpless, tongue-tied—irredeemably dissimilar.

"Which team do you support, Glen?" Danie might ask. He is one of the nicer boys in Standard Three: he has dark hair and freckles and is a little on the plump side.

"Nobody," I'll say, and the boys titter.

"The English don't like rugby, hey," someone else will note.

"They are weird."

"Cricket, then?" That's Danie again.

I'll name a team—say, Northern Transvaal. But the fact is, I don't really like cricket either: not like, say, my cousin Neil. I'm strange even for an Englishman. What other boy in the world is so crazy about telling stories to himself about Middle Earth wizards?

"*Yissis,* but why don't you at least *try* rugby, hey?"

So I do—for a month or two. What is so awful about it, that I so quickly drop it? I hate the scrums, where we all have to push and groan and try to scoop at the bouncing ball with our feet—sweat, pain, and muscle ache. I dislike tackling: I am afraid to go in for the kill, to throw my whole body against the charging knees and legs—a potential bone cap slamming the teeth out of my mouth, a shoulder that can be jolted out of its socket. Being tackled is just as rough and uncomfortable: sometimes I leave practice with scrapes and cuts that need Mercurochrome and a chest full of bright scarlet bruises.

"Don't worry, my love, you can drop the sport," my mother says.

But the other guys at school tease me: "You're just a *bangbroek,*" they say, a scaredy-cat. "No guts."

Which is also how I am with fist fights—the second problem that stops me from leaving the playground steps, where I sit alone with my lunch box or along the wall of the hall, where I'll read a book or perhaps talk to the younger kids, like Hannes or Nico Verhoef. What is it about the Afrikaner boys and fighting? I may occasionally get in scraps with my cousins or siblings. But for the majority of the older boys, belligerence seems to be a rite of passage.

The preludes to these battles are highly stylized. During a game at break, a boy might deftly steal a ball from another. "You're a *doos*," the injured party will say. This is one of those astonishingly vulgar Afrikaans words that no child would ever say in front of a grown-up. It literally means "box" or "cunt"; it explodes in the mouth with a foul, tangy turbulence magnified by its linguistic incongruity among all those water lily songs. In the context of a playground spat, its intention is unmistakable: a no-holds-barred altercation is desired.

"Three o'clock this afternoon below the rugby field," says the first boy. Their fights are always this way: timed like aristocrats' duels.

At the appointed hour the antagonists arrive in the sandy hollow between the trees below the rugby field, along with perhaps one or two dozen other boys. Overhead the sun beats down. The shadows of the tambotie leaves embroider a fine but uneven tulle on the pale brown earth. At three on the dot, the two boys begin to hop up and down on the shadows and dance around each other, Gerrie Coetzee and Kallie Knoetze style, fists balled in front of their faces, jabs and hooks shooting outward. Once someone lands the first punch, the orgy begins in earnest—punches, kicks, head slams, knocks that dislodge teeth: there are no referees or ground rules here, only the incantatory chants of the spectators: "Get him!" On the edge of the gathering, a boy stands watch for grown-ups.

But no adult ever interrupts these fights. Cars drive by and their occupants look the other way, towards the lawns and houses. While both their fathers will probably lash them this evening with army belts, this is all pretence: few Afrikaans parents seem really serious about stopping a son fighting. Tomorrow at school, both boys will brag about their black eyes, fractured ribs, and tanned backsides, while at the golf club, their fathers will joke over Castle lagers about which of their sons is the better boxer.

The thought of these fights fills me with terror. When I think of myself there, with my clumsy arms and my weak, skinny legs, trying to punch, kick, and dance to save my eyes, face, and stomach, an icy vacuum of dread forms in my solar plexus. I feel dizzy, un-steady. My throat clenches. In my desire to avoid battle, I am fully supported by the English-speaking grown-ups. My mother says it's wrong to fight. Daddy and Uncle Ian both claim they never got into any fights at school. "An English boy is a gentleman," my Aun-tie Merle says. "If I ever hear of you slugging it out like those Afri-kaners, you'll be sorry."

My unwillingness to do battle is a bit of a joke at elementary school: whenever any kid shows the slightest inclination to pick a fight with me, I walk away or threaten to call a teacher. "Sissy," say several of the other boys, and this somehow links, in ways I cannot yet clearly understand but that some of the other boys seem to di-vine, to the third peculiarity that sheaths me—that gives me an air of solitude as I sit at my desk listening to Miss Jeanette talk about, say, Lord Kitchener's brutal scorched-earth policy against the Afri-kaners during the Anglo-Boer War: I don't really like girls, at least not in the way the other boys seem to—not with kisses stolen in the swimming pool when none of the grown-ups are looking, or with hand-holding and love poems and little folded letters left in trees.

"Sissy," say the older boys in particular—and some of them

even tease me, saying that the only girl who'll marry me is my cousin Lorna.

"*Moffie*," says Albert, in the grade ahead of me. *Moffie*—faggot— what does this word mean? When I ask Albert he guffaws and whispers something to another guy.

True, I don't seem to really notice which girls are pretty, which ones get the most love messages scratched out for them in the dust below the jackalberry trees next to the asphalt basketball courts.

True, as I get older I increasingly become aware that I find some of the older boys attractive: Albert himself, for example, with his honey-brown skin, his muscular body, and his penis which, like all the Afrikaner boys', has a fold of skin on the end of it that mine doesn't: just one more difference between them and me that draws my gaze when one of them comes and stands next to me at the urinal trough.

True, I find myself glancing at these Afrikaner boys more and more whenever I get the opportunity. I enjoy the sight of them when they peel off their shirts to play rugby. But if all of this amounts to anything beyond the obvious—something more than Boer versus British—I am still unable to see it.

One sunny weekday morning, though, all of these different issues come to a head. I'm playing hand tennis with a boy named Neels. Now a squabble develops over a ball that was, from my point of view, clearly and unambiguously out, but that he regards as good. He accuses me of being a cheat and a spoilsport; I tell him he's the one who is trying to swindle. Then, irritated at me, he escalates the accusations.

"You're a total *sissy*," he says. "You like boys, not girls. My pa says some boys turn into these weird, sick perverts—I bet you're one of them."

I simply don't comprehend the content of this allegation. In my family I have never heard of these exotic deviates. What does he even mean? Nevertheless, his intent is clear enough. He hates me and ladles insult after insult. I must stand up for myself. At a certain point in my life I must move beyond weakness; I must be something other than the brunt of jokes.

"I'm not a sissy," I reply.

"Oh yes?" Neels asks. "If so, prove it. Three o'clock below the rugby field." He shakes his fist at me. "I'm going to *moer* you so bad your ma won't even recognize you. I'm going to *donner* you until you can't see out of your eyes." He is one year younger than me, but he is lithe, strong, and compact and moves with a cheetah's fluidity. He has a blond fringe that hangs across his eyes so you cannot see them. He has already won two fights against boys older and stronger than me: one of them got a mild concussion; the other lost two teeth. The cocky confidence in Neels's voice, the anger that seethes when he spits out the word *moer* with a toss of his fringe—all of this now causes my stomach to buckle and list. The rest of the day in class the boys nudge me and whisper, asking if it's true, if I'm really going to fight Neels. I nod. I am plagued, though, by a green nausea, a fear that causes my hands to tremble as I try to hold my writing pencil.

That afternoon at lunch I am so visibly upset I cannot eat anything. Eventually Mommy and Daddy pull the truth out of me. Mommy is outraged. She insists that Daddy do something. He calls Mr. Louis. Behind his bedroom door I hear, "Not our family. We didn't bring him up like that." All afternoon Mommy watches me, wide-eyed, sorrowful, guard dog–like. When someone asks for me on the phone she says I'm not in. Shortly after three, a bunch of boys from the school knock on our front door.

"Is Glen here?" someone asks. "He made an appointment to play with us." My heart flails in my ribs—a rat struggling to escape from a cage.

"Sorry," Mommy says. "He went into town with his father. He'll only be back late." It is the first time I have known Mommy to lie. During catechism lessons she always says being truthful is the most important thing in the world—that we can do anything wrong and still tell her about it. But some foreign menace has now suddenly entered our lives, and duplicity has become required. If I notice this subtle shift in my nine-year-old moral universe, though, I do not consciously register it.

At school the next day I expect the others to tease me, asking how my father managed to be at work in the Nature Conservation offices and shopping with me at the same time. But nobody says anything, at least not until Neels comes up to me at break with his friends.

"You English people are *all* sissies," he says. "Being English is being a woman, a poofter. Even my dad says so. You don't know how to fight—that's why even hundreds of thousands of you couldn't defeat us in the war without locking our women and children in concentration camps."

I shrug. The Afrikaner kids mentioned this to me after the lesson about Kitchener—this story about how we English ground up glass in the Boers' food so their women and children died in agony hunched over outhouse toilets. But to me it seems other-worldly. Surely one would feel or notice glass in mashed potatoes?

"I don't care. I am what I am." The words explode out of me now with a sudden and unexpected vehemence. It is true: at that moment I am simply tired of all this English-Afrikaans tension. I am fed up with Neels and his belligerence. I am weary of changing in the municipal bathrooms after swimming practice and having the Afrikaner boys point at my penis; I am fed up with throwing a tennis ball like a girl, with my wrist flopping over my shoulder. I want there to be no differences anymore.

I stoop to gulp down the cool water. When I finish drinking

I half expect Neels to still be standing there. But he is gone. Starlings chatter in the jackalberries along the perimeter fence, with squawks and flutters.

Soon after this I decide to join the Voortrekkers. Regardless of what Gogo says about them, I want to be a part of this group with their khaki uniforms and their scarves twisted together in different combinations of red, blue, yellow, and green. I want to be present at their gatherings where they sport flame torches, which flicker in the high frosted windows of the hall building—trembling, shimmering rectangles of ruddy orange that, viewed from the outside, from the swimming pool on a blue-gray summer's evening, seem somehow magical. I want to be part of the Monday morning playground conversations where the boys talk of knot-tying contests and fire-building competitions. In gym class, when we practice rope-climbing, everyone uses words like "brake" and "squat" and wraps the ropes around their knees and calves; I, on the other hand, sway helpless and clumsy, a fly fluttering on a spider's thread.

Jacques, another boy in my grade, slaps me on the back and confirms: "You should join the Voortrekkers. They'll teach you how to do this."

One Saturday night, when my parents and aunt and uncle are all barbecuing at the Verhoef family's house, for a lark Hannes and Nico dress up for the English kids in their Voortrekker uniforms. In the front yard, on the opposite side of the house to where the grown-ups are *braai*ing their meat, they construct two mock flame torches by dousing dry log tips with the gasoline their father, Johan Verhoef, keeps in the garage. With the five of us English children seated in front of them, they stand at attention holding these flickering logs and singing us a ditty we know from music class at school, called "The Song of Young South Africa." Except this is a rendition of the tune unlike any I'm familiar with, a melody in two-part harmony, their voices sonorous and subtle as the flames play on their freckled faces:

> *And do you hear the mighty thundering?*
> *Over the veld it comes hovering wide*
> *The song of a nation's awakening*
> *That makes hearts shiver and shake.*

At the end they both salute, then laugh, run off, and squelch the flames in the soil of the nearby flower bed. The smoke issuing from the extinguished logs is unpleasantly reminiscent of an unkempt petrol station: I pinch my nose. Still, I am smitten. The song was beautiful, with its lilting, wistful theme and its soaring, repeating, crescendo. Hannes and Nico looked magnificent in their uniforms: could being a Voortrekker affect in me a similar transformation?

Later that evening, as I am saying my good-nights, I ask Daddy if he will pay the membership fee for me to join the Voortrekkers. He frowns. "You're not an Afrikaner, Glen," he says. "We've told you before—you get enough of that propaganda at school."

"I won't listen to the political speeches. I just want to learn about the fires and camping." But Daddy won't budge. Nor is my mother amenable to working on Daddy, the way she sometimes does, securing us cartons of condensed milk on wildlife-viewing expeditions.

"We don't like Voortrekkers," she reminds me—"we" being her, Daddy, Merle, Ian, and Gogo and Pa. Nothing to be done: I am as English as baked beans.

The following Friday evening, though, my curiosity gets the better of me, and, under the pretext of buying sweets from the village store, I ride my bike out to the municipal hall shortly after sunset. At the front entrance, which is located directly across from the store, two Standard Five (seventh-grade) boys stand in their uniforms, guarding the glass door leading to the hall lobby. Behind me, VW minibuses and station wagons are pulling up and discharging gaggles of chattering children, whom the boys on duty point to the right. I lean my bike against the wall of the store; then I walk toward the hall entrance.

"Hey," says one boy, leaning forward and grabbing me by the arm. "You can't come in here. This is for Voortrekkers."

This boy's name is Kobus. He is in my class at school, and his dad, Peet, is one of the Voortrekker commandants. "Can I just quickly use the toilets?" I ask him, pointing to the facilities at the left of the hall lobby.

"Use the outside ones," he says, and of course I cannot argue with this; there are perfectly good public toilets a mere dozen or so yards away, back in the direction of the swimming pool. Should I charge past Kobus? Pretend to have lost money or a watch in the hall and insist on looking for it? Yet even in the urgency of my desire to see the Voortrekkers, I sense the transparency of any such tricks or maneuvers.

But then, a few months later, I get a break. Miss Jeanette Verhoef organizes a school play to commemorate the 150th birthday of C. Louis Leipoldt, a brilliant poet, intellectual, and botanist, and one of the first writers to use colloquial Afrikaans instead of high Dutch. To celebrate this anniversary, different classes at school memorize various Leipoldt poems and act them out with props—haystacks, paper streamers, and plows; rugby balls, pellet guns, and colored-paper birds.

For my part, I am given a significant solo in this play. I am to recite one of Leipoldt's shortest, most popular, and most evocative poems, "Viooltjies," about the blue and red African violets that blossom in the spring along the dry Western Cape coast. I am to hold two such violets in small plastic containers with soil as I say these words; then, after I am finished, the Standard Three class will all repeat the full verse.

For weeks the school practices, first in our hall, and then in the big municipal one with the high windows and the long velvet stage curtains. Miss Jeanette, the play's director, teaches me to say my words with intense wonder at the beauty of creation—the same excitement, she instructs me, as I feel on the first morning I wake up and it's school holidays. Through the rehearsals and run-throughs I get more and more enthusiastic about my lines: I love the lilting *f* sounds of the first chorus: *viooltjies, voorhuis.* Even the other fifth-grade boys get into the spirit of things.

The evening of the show arrives, and the adults of the village all gather to sit in the rows of theater seats. Grades one through four—what we call Grade One to Standard Two—do their gigs; finally it's time for our class to go on stage. We perform our first poem, about a greengrocer selling vegetables. Then I step forward with my violets, and it happens: the words of the poem, along with the adrenaline of the performance, fill me with an ecstatic cheer that goes beyond even my best recitals, and I all but sing for joy, my voice reaching upward for the cadences:

> *Violets in the entrance hall!*
> *Violets blue and red!*
> *Violets everywhere in the veld,*
> *And everything, oh, so beautiful!*

When I am finished reciting, the class catches my enthusiasm and belts out the rest of the poem with gusto, whistling to imitate the cicadas and crickets. The audience claps and howls. From the piano below the stage, Miss Jeanette turns and bows. And when the play is over, and I am standing with my parents beside the table of tea and cookies at the back, Peet, Kobus's father—a short, bearded man in khaki shirt and shorts—comes over to congratulate my parents.

"Amazing," he tells my father. "He really felt his way inside the language. I'm proud of him! Not bad for an Englishman." He rumples my hair. Then he pauses. "Actually," he adds, "we're having a Voortrekker awards ceremony in November. I'd love it, you know, if Glen could give his little Leipoldt recital. We're celebrating the sesquicentennial, too, and, well, it would be good for our kids to see an English boy getting carried away by that poetry."

I am half expecting Daddy to say no. But to my surprise both he and my mother say yes, oh, for sure, that would be wonderful—they are so proud of me. They didn't want me to *become* a Voortrekker, but they are happy for me to make a contribution. And I stand with them under the pale electric overhead lights, holding a marzipan biscuit and barely daring to believe what has just happened.

I build the day up in my mind. This is going to be the moment when I appear in my uniform just like the Verhoef boys, grown-up and confident. On this occasion I won't be different anymore. At last the day arrives, sunny and warm like most Kruger Park days. Late in the afternoon I ride over to the Van der Walts' house, where, in Kobus's room, he and his younger brother, Nico, help me dress in Kobus's long-sleeved khaki shirt—I am not allowed to wear a necktie or badges. Dusk is falling when the four of us arrive at the Kruger Gate entrance to our national park. On the far side of the Sabie River, cars and minibuses are parked on the sides of the road. On the grassy field below the giant granite head of the late Boer president, perhaps two or three hundred uniformed children are lining up in platoons in front of a makeshift stage fronted by two enormous flags of the defunct Boer republics, drooping across each to form a rough W. Burning torches surround the whole gathering, flaring upward, filling the air with wood smoke and giving the whole place a suitably romantic and mysterious aura.

I take my place next to Peet Van der Walt on the stage, carefully placing my two violets at the bottom of the chair. I look out across the hundreds of faces in front of me, trying to spot Kobus, his brother Nico, or either of the two Verhoef boys, but it is getting dark now and the light of the torches is shimmering and indistinct.

The meeting is called to order and then the proceedings begin. A suited preacher opens the gathering with a prayer for the youth of the country, and for understanding from the rest of the world for the plight of the Afrikaner defending his land. A regional commandant offers opening remarks about the guiding principles of the Voortrekkers: Afrikanerness, citizenship, and Christianity. So far, this is almost exactly like one of our school assemblies. I've heard it before. Why all the secrecy about something so ordinary?

The evening drags. After the opening speeches, innumerable awards and badges are handed out—for teamwork, for tent pitching, for rowing and bridge building and community service. Boys and girls traipse onto the stage. They shake the regional commandant's hand, pose for a photograph, and then stride off again. Bored, I look out behind me, to my left, to the statue of Paul Kruger, the thick white granite curls of hair streaking back from his forehead like snakes. What have I been so obsessed about? Is this the whole mysterious edifice of Afrikanerdom?

And then I hear the word "Leipoldt" and tune back in.

"To celebrate this 150th year of our great poet's life, our Skukuza branch has asked a guest—Glen Retief—to share with us a recital of one of the poet's great works."

Applause. Uncle Peet slaps me on the back and gives me a thumbs-up. This is it: I step forward to the microphone, holding the violets. I say the lines of the poem. But something is wrong. The flames of the torches distract me. The microphone distorts my voice and makes it tinny. I hear myself singing through those words about violets and beauty, but I feel nothing at all—no sense of it being the beginning of a holiday. When I return to my seat, people clap. It seems to me they do so politely—nothing like the hoots I got the first time. Peet Van der Walt looks at me, smiles, and nods—"Good job!"—but I do not feel that I performed adequately. I rushed, fumbled, got nervous.

But after dismissal, Kobus, Hannes, and both Nicos run up to me in their uniforms and neck scarves. "*Lekker*, hey! You remembered every word!" they shout, smiling and happy. Hannes Verhoef tackles me for fun, rugby-style. I fall to the ground and laugh—despite everything, I am one of them.

"Do you want to play a game with us?" asks Kobus.

As the grown-ups and senior Voortrekkers pack up the stage equipment and stack the chairs in piles along the sides, the five of us play Pass the Stink Bomb, where the aim is to chase someone else and touch them with the violets. For a while Danie and Jacques join us. The violets are quite a big hit; I have never owned anything that's been such a magnet. We charge each other with them, get mud on our fingers and threaten to smear it on each other's uniforms, pretend to be terrorists hiding the violets somewhere under the stage—unless the opposing guys, the security police, manage to find them, there'll be blood. At one moment I look at Uncle Peet to see if it's okay that we are running around like this among the stage poles and the rolled-up electrical wires, but he is deep in conversation with a cluster of grown-ups.

Johan and Jeanette Verhoef arrive to pick up their boys. So do Danie's parents and Jacques'; progressively the clearing empties. Now it is just Kobus, Nico, and me, charging around and giggling, ducking behind piles of plastic stage chairs and circling the burning torches. At some point I am in front of the remnants of the stage. I am now the stink bomb: I am holding the violets, one in each hand, and I am charging after Kobus, trying to brush him with them. He veers left in front of me, dashing behind the two crossed flags of the Boer republics. I charge straight at him, through the soft cloth of the flags. I see Kobus, preparing to duck under the stage skeleton; giggling, I hold out what I think are the violets, preparing to push their leaves and petals against the khaki of his shirt back.

"You!" It is the preacher in the black suit, who opened the ceremonies. He is standing twenty yards or so to the left of me, talking to Uncle Peet and the other grown-ups. His pale face is flushed.

Did I do something wrong? The preacher begins to stride towards me.

"Look," he says, pointing behind me, "what you've done."

Peet Van der Walt follows the preacher. I look at Uncle Peet, but his face is expressionless. Then I glance back at the flags. The flag of the Orange Free State has a semi-horizontal stripe of mud running across it. The Vierkleur, the flag of Paul Kruger's Transvaal Republic, with its three horizontal red, white, and blue panels and its vertical green one, is a worse mess: it is splattered all over with black dribbles. I realize the plastic casing in my right hand is empty. The violet must have fallen out, soil and all, as I ran through the flags.

A bottomless shame floods over me. My face and arms are hot. I sense I've done something even more unforgivable and outrageous than being a sissy. This is the nadir; I am going to be in trouble now—probably Mr. Louis will even hear about it at school, and he'll call me to his office after assembly.

"Young man," the preacher says, standing next to me now, huffing, "you should never run through flags like that. It shows disrespect for something sacred."

Peet Van der Walt is behind the preacher. He touches his shoulder. "He's English, Jannie. He's not really a Voortrekker. He's just a guest."

"That makes it even worse, Peet." The preacher does not take his eyes off me. "You," he says again. "You've slapped the Afrikaner in the face tonight. This is not the way we build positive relationships between peoples. This is not the way nations get along. Do you understand, son?"

"Jannie," says Uncle Peet again. "He didn't mean to."

I nod. "Sorry, *dominee,*" I say. I feel stupid and careless. I feel there's something I should know but don't—something I should be but am not. It's time to go home. I don't belong here. I glance over at Kobus, who was playing the game with me. He refuses to meet my eye.

"That's okay, son. People make mistakes. But I just wanted to make sure you understood." The preacher turns around and leaves.

"We should go, boys," Uncle Peet says. Kobus grabs Uncle Peet's green army duffel bag stuffed with supplies for the Skukuza platoon, and then we drive home in the dark, the headlights of the car illuminating the yellow elephant grass along the roadside. "That was an accident, Glen, with the flags," Uncle Peet repeats. "Don't feel bad, hey? It isn't nice when a flag gets damaged like that. But we'll be able to get new ones. Or maybe they'll be able to clean them. You didn't know." But his words fail to dispel the hot, throbbing rash of embarrassment.

Later that evening, when I am back home, climbing under my duvet cover with its big orange suns with plain brown dots at the center of them, I tell Mommy that I don't think I want to be a Voortrekker after all.

"I'd rather stay here on a Friday and watch *Jopie Adam,*" I tell her. *Jopie Adam* is a dubbed American TV series about a man who lives in a log cabin and makes friends with a grizzly bear. "I want to stay with you and Daddy. I don't want to go anywhere else, ever."

"That's good, Glen," Mommy says. She has showered for bed already and is wearing her blue dressing gown. "You don't have to join any group, darling. With Daddy and me you are fine the way you are." She folds the empty duvet cover around my neck and kisses me on the forehead; then she leaves. As I lie in the darkness, with the bedclothes pulled up to my chin and the moonlight coming in through the side window, I am aware of the softness of the linen—smooth as violet leaves or shirt cotton. I am conscious of its smell—fresh, clean, like shampoo. I revel in its vastness, its downy caress—like the flags brushing against me as I ran through them, except unmuddied, unsullied, mine to roll around in or toss off the bed in a crumpled heap.

The Killer's Nephew

It's an ordinary summer evening. I'm ten years old, in Standard Four—sixth grade—and I'm lying on the carpet in my parents' living room, watching *Buck Rogers in the 25th Century*. Mommy's in the bathroom, getting Lisa and David ready for bed. Daddy's behind me in his La-Z-Boy recliner, drinking the glass of milk that blunts his nightly heartburn.

"Why don't you invite one of the boys from your class to play here one afternoon, Glen?" he asks. I look back. He drains his milk glass, then leans forward and peers at me through rectangular, rimless spectacles. His plump face, with the mole that protrudes from his nose, is kindly, gentle, and inquisitive. This question is caring; still, even at age ten I sense a familiar trap in it—a vision of myself as less than, unacceptable: the one who flubs a rugby catch, who bores his classmates with his talk of hobbits and orcs rather than Kyalami racing. "You should have some friends your own age. A boy has to be able to relate to other kids. Playing with younger children is fine. Hannes and Nico are great, it's nice you're close to Lorna and Neil. But at some point you'll have to learn how to be pals with people like Kobus or Danie."

My heart sinks. This is the thing that most scares me about myself, the ache that ebbs and rises but never entirely goes away. "I don't like the boys at school, Daddy," I say now, "and they don't like me, either. I can't become friends with them. I've tried, but it hasn't worked."

Daddy sighs, but says nothing. I am expecting him to give me another speech about how when I'm a grown-up I'll need workplace social skills, how human life is cooperative rather than solitary, how you never see our biological cousins, the baboons, wandering around by themselves like elephant bulls. But instead he simply says softly: "I understand, One Cent Man." "One Cent Man" is his nickname for me—a derivative of "Glenny Penny." "I'll see what I can do to help you."

Daddy? Help me? How? He has about as much to do with the Skukuza Elementary School playground as the tourists do—the ones who stay in the neighboring rest camp, go looking for lions and rhinos, and never come near our village. But to my surprise, the next day he arrives with the news that Ben Coetzee, his office mate, has invited me to go over to their house today after lunch to play with Dirkie, his son.

Dirkie Coetzee? This Dirkie sits behind me in class and sometimes falls asleep when Mr. Flip explains area problems. At recess he hangs out with Bennie Joubert, a gifted fighter and athlete; he plays hooker in the first team rugby scrum and regularly gets out balls that lead to penalty kicks and tries. I think he's even a member of a gang, a *bende*: in the afternoons the Afrikaners split up into groups of kids who have collective fights down in the riverbed, beyond where we're technically allowed to play—slingshot battles, wrestling tournaments, even pellet gun shootouts. What would he want with the likes of me, a bookworm and a social eccentric? But my father will brook no disagreement: "Dirkie and

Uncle Ben are being very kind, Glen. This is what we do with invitations. We accept them, and we behave ourselves, and we try to be friendly and gracious, okay? Can I trust you on this?" And so that very afternoon after lunch—a white hot two o'clock, with the house shadows etched as black rectangles on the blinding emerald lawns—I knock at the Coetzees' porch screen door, without having any clear idea why I am doing so. A pulsing band of anxiety grips my rib cage.

Dirkie opens up. He is a short, diminutive boy with dark brown hair, pale skin, and a small belly. When he blinks he peers and frowns as if his eyes are struggling to focus. "It's you," he says, a plain statement of fact.

"Yes."

Isn't he meant to say hello or something? But now he holds the door open, and I step inside—the rules of social engagement require these actions of both of us. The house is very quiet—I notice a maid hovering somewhere in the background, a rustling green uniform. But apart from that it is just the rattan porch furniture, the fan, a clock ticking somewhere in the living room next door. What exactly do we say to each other now? How do human beings behave in situations of such intense, artificial awkwardness when thrust upon each other by powers greater than themselves?

"Do you want to look around?" Dirkie asks. I nod, and Dirkie points at the leather lounge furniture, the botany books lining the shelves, the rugby posters in his room, and the rose-covered wallpaper in his baby sister's room. I cannot think of any comments to make about it, so all I do is grin. Language seems to have become stringy, lumpy, and glutinous. I am a spare ornament in this house: another cabinet, like the one in the lounge with the family china. Why is Daddy doing this to me? *We try to be friendly and gracious, Glen.*

"Something to drink?" Dirkie asks then. Despite myself I'm

impressed by the smoothness of his miniature grown-up routine—perhaps he's even enjoying this? When I nod he says, "Orange juice, please, Josie," to his housekeeper, and in due course a tray arrives on the verandah with a jug of Clifton orange, glasses, and a plate of Bakers lemon creams. Eating the biscuits, we wordlessly watch each other chew, drink, and swallow. This too, can't help but impress me. The only one who's allowed to give the housekeeper orders in our house is Mommy.

"*Hinne,* man," Dirkie says, "but do you like comic books, hey? I have a whole collection in my room of Captain Marvel." I nod again. "Come and check this, then!" But in his room, sitting on his bed and glancing through the pictures of Billy Batson being struck by lightning and then turning into a red-suited Hercules, it quickly becomes obvious that I lack the slightest idea about the plot lines. I have never heard of Rocco de Wet, border fighter; I have only the vaguest idea of who's the better superhero to have around in a crisis, Spiderman or Batman.

"You don't *really* like comic books, do you?" asks Dirkie, and when I shake my head no, he nods: "I see." Then I set the comic books aside and glance up at Dirkie's posters of Naas Botha drop-kicking for the Blue Bulls against Western Province.

"Do you like rugby?"

But he already knows the answer to that one: when I am forced to play fly half in Physical Training class, I stand along the touch-line with my arms folded, running only when the teacher yells at me. This isn't going well. He's starting to fidget and look at his sports watch—one of the ones the athletics coach uses to time our sprints and runs. Then, at last, he asks, doggedly trying to establish a shared interest, determinedly trying to get some rise out of this shy dumbstruck kid sitting in his room (what has Uncle Ben, his father, told him?):

"Do you want to play soldiers, hey, Glen? I have a *lekker* set, I say, back in the yard."

"That sounds nice." Actually, it doesn't—Mommy and Daddy have never given me a plastic soldier in my life. Nor does Mommy approve of kids playing with toy guns and weaponry; she says it's ugly to pretend to kill and hurt (though this doesn't stop my siblings, my cousins, and me from having shootouts with imaginary revolvers). But now, with Dirkie, feigned enthusiasm seems to be what's needed: *When you visit someone you must act pleased.*

"Sure! That's *kief*!"

But Dirkie's soldier set is in fact much more than a regular one. It's a detailed diorama of a desert battle scene, something reminiscent of a museum display. I have never seen such a thing at a regular house—all bright paint and papier-mâché and miniature palm trees, laid out on the back lawn in the sunshine on a sheet of hardboard. It's almost as large as the surface of our dining room table. On it, brown plastic-looking sand dunes tower over dark rocky gulleys. Toy railway sidings edge a turquoise-painted sea. Sprinkled across all this are small green plastic soldiers, crouching, crawling, or standing with their rifles, miniature tanks, and propeller planes sized for nine- or ten-year-old boys' hands.

"*Lekker, né?*" Dirkie asks.

"Really *lekker*," I reply, and I mean it.

And now comes the stroke of luck or inspiration that changes everything between the two of us—lonely, bookish imagination constructing a bridge to everyday masculinity. Correctly or not— the details of this diorama will certainly eventually be lost to me— I now see in this world Dirkie has created with his father and friends, the outlines of familiar terrain, specifically the battle of El Alamein, about which my maternal grandfather, Pa, has frequently told me. Pa fought here under Auchinleck and Montgomery and considers this battle one of the most glorious of World War II. He has described the flies and heat, shown me pictures of Montgomery's tanks charging through clouds of dust, and sat me on his lap and pointed at maps. So now, in front of Dirkie's diorama, I recognize, or imagine I do, the Alexandria railroad along the Mediterranean, the lines of Allied and Axis minefields.

"This is so *kief*," I tell Dirkie. "Amazing. That's where my Pa fought." I point to the south of the battlefield, the rocky Qattara Depression.

"Really? Your grandfather fought in a place like this?" Dirkie's getting visibly excited. "Hey, do you want to play? You can be the English general—what was his name?"

"Monty."

"Right. I'll be the Nazi."

We play all afternoon. My discomfort dissipates. I explain to Dirkie that the German Panzer tanks had a gear drive that often failed when they got into mud. So we mire Rommel's tanks in the gully below the hills, where they can be picked off by roaming Spitfires. I inform him that the Focke-Wulf aircraft handles better than any of the Spitfires, but there are not enough of them at El Alamein to damage Montgomery's Sherman tanks. I mention the dummy armored cars that Montgomery amassed in the south of El Alamein, to fool Rommel into thinking he was going to attack from that direction, and we duly designate several kitchen match-boxes as fake tanks.

"*Yissis*," Dirkie says when we are done, "but that was *lekker*, hey! Do you want to come back on Saturday and play again?"

And I do. Play's elixir has dissolved the differences between us. To my surprise I really *like* Dirkie—he's friendly and smiles a lot and gives me lots of presents: regular refills of Clifton orange juice and Romany creams, a collection of comics to read. These I enjoy more than I expected: I discover that the Joker, Batman's nemesis, has a sadistic but funny sense of humor; I learn that Wolverine can speak different languages.

And now, over the following weeks, Dirkie and I develop a firm friendship—what will turn out to be the most important so-cial connection of my elementary school years. He shows me his

fighter jet playing cards and teaches me about war technology—
Lockheed Blackbirds, which can rip across the skies of our entire
country in less than an hour; nimble French Mirages, which our
own air force uses against the Soviet MIGS in southern Angola.
We conduct mock dog fights in my front garden—this is better
than playing alone at home. We share an interest in tennis: when
we hit a winner or save a cross-court smash, we fall to our knees
and shake our rackets at the sun, like Björn Borg. Dirkie explains
rugby strategy to mc. I begin to learn about the uses of knock-ons
and mauls; the value of Gary Owen kicks and of being able to spot
the gate to a ruck. I feel much better now in the mornings when
the other boys talk about Naas's drop kicks the previous night, or
Morné's strategizing, and I can confidently interject:

"*Yissis*, hey, but that kick from the halfway line was incredible!"

"He's learning something!" the others say, which warms me.

With surprising speed, I also start to become more integrated
into the village's youth culture. Apparently, sometimes it only
takes a single contact to break open a world, one additional thread
to change the texture of the social fabric. Now, I soon begin hanging out more often with all of Dirkie's friends, with Danie, Albert,
Bennie, and others. Dirkie informs me about classroom social intrigue: about the group pettings that take place at one of the standard five girls' houses; about the ongoing gang vendettas—the
time one *bende* burned another's hideout down and almost caused
a bush fire. He tells me about Jannie de Vos being captured,
smeared with honey, and tied down on an anthill as a form of torture: apparently he jumped up so vigorously from the bites on his
bum, he broke the cords holding him to the tree stump.

"You mustn't say anything to the grown-ups," Dirkie insists
when he reports this. "Those *ouks* would get a pack of blows if
their parents found out." An admonition that both thrills and comforts me: even at age ten I sense the implied inclusion in being entrusted with secrets.

We go camping together in the tourist resort. Somehow, by a grown-up alchemy that's mysterious to me, the fact of my being friends with Dirkie loosens parental strictures and permits me to venture unsupervised into the world of the Skukuza cafeteria, where Dirkie and I eat our way three times through the prix-fixe menu of buffalo soup and impala steaks; into the neon-lit camp ablution blocks, where we throw water bombs at each other and flick each other with towels; and into my small blue two-man tent where we lie in the darkness and tell each other ghost stories. Daddy and Uncle Ben, who are collaborating on a study of the impact of elephant populations on vegetation cover, ask Dirkie and me to join them on a research trip. Here, they let us map-read, navigate with a compass, and build campfires. We compete to see who can build the biggest one, and when we get back to school we regale the other kids with stories of bonfires that lick as high as the lowest branches of marula trees. What fun and laughter!

"You couldn't see the stars because of all the sparks," I tell Kobus and Danie.

"*Ja,* hey, we didn't even hear a hyena calling that night because the flames made all the animals think there was a bush fire."

Who's to say we're embellishing when there were two of us?

With Dirkie's help I even briefly join a bona fide Skukuza gang called the Hooligans. Led by Dirkie's old friend, Bennie, this grouping tries its best to terrorize the game reserve, stomping on ant and termite colonies; breaking stork and swallow nests; stoning kudus and bushbuck. Any of its members that get bullied or insulted can bring forth the gang's collective revenge. There have been boys with lunch boxes filled with impala dung. A rival who dared to call Bennie a coward got force-fed a chili pepper.

"Let that Neels try to mess with you," says Bennie now, referring to the boy who tried to start a fight with me the previous year.

"Let anyone call you a *rooinek* or a *soutpiel*—we'll feed his toes to the crocodiles." Next day I meet Neels's eye on the school playground. I look down at his bare feet. Neels's feet are tanned and shapely, with neatly raised arches, but it's easy to imagine them *sans* one or two dactyls—perhaps his two middle ones, making his feet look like ostrich claws.

In the Hooligans' gang house—a tree in the dry riverbed in the no-go wildlife zone, with leaves that hang down so low they form a natural barrier—Dirkie and I perform a public blood-brother ceremony. "Check this," Dirkie says as we sit behind the perfect green curtain of leaves, in the clean warm smell of the river sand. Out of his pocket he pulls his Swiss Army knife. He flips open a blade, nicks his wrist so red blood oozes out, sluggish and viscous, in irregular dollops. He does the same to my wrist, then rubs the wound together so our blood mixes.

"As good as real brothers," he says.

"Yes, real brothers." The other gang members cheer. Dirkie and I high-five, then embrace. And at this moment he actually does signify more to me than my real brother, who is just five years old and no fun to play with. He means more than my sister and cousins, with their dolls and their Swingball tournaments; in a sense, he is more important even than Mommy, Daddy, Uncle Ian, and Auntie Merle. Within a week or two I do something to annoy Bennie and I'm politely asked to leave the gang—perhaps I chicken out when dared to crawl behind the squash courts at night and smack a hippo on its bottom. But when this happens Dirkie quits too, to show solidarity with me. The two of us play marbles together on the sidelines, in the area of the perimeter fence. We share our sandwiches. I am not alone.

Rocco de Wet, Border Fighter, about an Afrikaans reconnaissance soldier on the Namibian-Angolan border, is the most popular comic among the Skukuza boys. He's much more widely read than *Trompie,* the popular Afrikaans adventure series; far more fashionable than *Superman,* the *Fantastic Four,* or *Spider-Woman.* At recess, the boys sit around in the shade of the hall and peer at Rocco stories—stapled black-and-white magazine issues. "Check how *kief* he is as a sharpshooter," they might say, noting how he picks off a bearded Cuban who's holding a nurse hostage in a tin-roofed house with a hammer and sickle flag in front of it. "*Yissis,* what an explosion!"—this, perhaps, when Rocco singlehandedly blows up a bridge ahead of a column of advancing Soviet tanks. And when, say, Rocco dons blackface to infiltrate a terrorist training camp and tricks a guard with his rudimentary Ovambo, we exclaim: "*Hirre,* but he's a jackal, hey! It's good he's on our side and not the *terris'*!"

The reasons for Rocco's popularity aren't hard to discern. No campy darkness here—no balustrades, clocktowers, and recessed setbacks that we see drawn all over the pages of *Batman.* Nor do kryptonite and x-ray vision seem really connected to our surroundings. *Rocco* resonates with us, talks our language, and inhabits our environment. The squat, straggly mopani trees and the parched yellow elephant grass of the borderlands where our hero fights terrorists appear much like the north of our game reserve, the area near Punda and Shingwedzi. The gray metal limpet mines are the same as those the military commanders bring us when they visit the school for *Paraatheid* ("Readiness") assemblies—the older boys in fact patrol the school grounds during recess and assembly with whistles hanging around their necks, looking out for precisely these magnetic steel loaves clinging to the bottom of the zinc classroom roof eaves. And, of course, the battle Rocco's fighting is the one our older brothers and cousins are involved in, as white conscripts on the border—the one we'll participate in too, when we turn eighteen or finish college. We, too, will outwit

Cuban apparatchiks—their swarthy Latin faces remind me of Greek and Portuguese convenience store owners behind their hot-chips counters in Nelspruit and White River. We, too, will be shooting black terrorists in khaki uniforms, who hold AK-47 rifles with long, curved magazines: to my surprise the captured ones never look the least bit villainous but rather seem like the Kruger Park's black assistant rangers—straight-backed, calm, authoritative.

Rocco de Wet is certainly Dirkie's favorite comic book hero, outshining all the others put together: the X-men, Captain Marvel, and Spider-Man; Superman and the Fantastic Four. He, like the other boys, praises the realism of the Rocco series, the fact that it's so true—none of those babyish fantasies.

"That's what *recces* are like," he says, when the two of us sit in his room and read about how Rocco de Wet never takes advantage of the beautiful Afrikaner girls who fall in love with him: he's a good-looking guy, Rocco, with a thick mustache, muscular body, and clean-cut, square-jawed Afrikaner features, but he always puts his army buddies and his country first.

"It wouldn't be fair," Rocco tells a slender, blond farmgirl whose family he's rescued.

"*Ja,* hey, that's true," Dirkie comments. "These *recces* don't have time to chase after girls."

Or we'll share some story of how Rocco told off a subordinate who was racist to one of the *recces'* ace Bushman trackers.

"*Ja,*" Dirkie will confirm again. "There's no *baas* or *kaffir* on the border, *né*? Not like here." Dirkie has explained to me the difference between a *recce* platoon and a normal South African Defence Force contingent, how the *recces,* because they are Permanent Force volunteers rather than conscripts, often get to work directly alongside soldiers of different racial backgrounds. "My Uncle Dirk says there's no brotherhood between the races like when you're fighting *terris* together."

This Uncle Dirk quite frequently comes up in our conversations. Uncle Dirk, whom I have never met, is a policeman who lives in Pretoria with Dirkie's aunt, Jeanette, and Dirkie's cousins, Dirkie Jr. and Kallas. It seems Uncle Dirk is something of a real-life Rocco. He works for the South African Police, but not as an ordinary detective. Rather, he's involved in tracking the men who come into our country to plow up power pylons and leave explosives in restaurants—a counterinsurgency expert; a kind of spy. When Dirkie tells me this I shiver down my spine, as if I'm one step away from James Bond. Dirkie says this Uncle Dirk can't tell any of them what he does from week to week working for the government. If news were to get out, the terrorists could use this information to plan massacres.

Uncle Dirk apparently gave Dirkie some of his *Rocco* comic collection. Whenever Uncle Dirk comes to visit from Pretoria, he brings the best presents: blue-and-white Ice Queen marbles; picture books about the nuclear arsenals of the Soviet Union and United States.

"Even Uncle Dirk says Rocco's true, hey," Dirkie informs me now. "He says you can tell the authors have done their homework, hey? He says they've probably been on the border themselves."

When he grows up, Dirkie wants to be a *recce,* like Rocco. He knows it's difficult—less than 1 percent of applicants get accepted. Also, like me, he isn't the best at the kinds of exercises needed to get into the unit: he never gets beyond fifteen rapid pushups with his back straight, for example, whereas forty are needed to qualify. I do even worse: after six or so my arms feel like they are about to collapse, and I simply give up and lie on the lawn.

But according to Dirkie, Uncle Dirk continues to encourage his nephew, saying that these things just take time and persistence. This is the advice that Dirkie gives me, too.

"We just have to keep practicing," he says. "You can do it, too,

Glen. Like Rocco." At what point does it become a shared assumption in our friendship that I, too, am going to apply to be an elite soldier—that the two of us will be buddies together and watch out for each other in the bush? I have never had any idea what I want to do in the future, other than become a missionary in Papua New Guinea or a sweet-shop owner. At least with becoming a *recce* I'd get to stay friends with Dirkie.

So the two of us whisper "Rocco!" as we practice leopard crawl next to the World War II diorama in his backyard.

"De Wet!" we yell when we nail a masked weaver in the yellow-barked fever tree with Dirkie's pellet gun—we pretend the birds, which have black heads and yellow bodies, are hooded guerilla fighters; we toss their bloodied bodies into the drainage pipes.

Mommy and Daddy are a bit baffled by the notion that I'm going to be a reconnaissance soldier, as well as by my sudden interest in Rocco comics and the military.

"Is Border Fighter really better than Superman, Glennie?" That's Daddy—when he was a boy he was a Superman fan; he even drove us kids all of the way to Nelspruit to see the movie debut when it first came out—Christopher Reeve with his hands clenched in front of him and his red cape fluttering in the breeze.

"*Ja,* Daddy. No one really likes Superman anymore. He's too . . . stupid." Daddy shrugs at me, a new kind of shrug that has much less of his pre-Dirkie worry in it—*Is Glen going to be* okay?— than frustrated incomprehension: *the youth of today.*

Mommy is much more emphatic.

"Listen, my darling," she says, "just because someone wants you to be friends with him, or even if Mommy or Daddy wants you to have a friend—none of this means you *have* to do anything, hey? You should just be yourself. It's the most important thing."

What is she talking about? Myself? Who is doing all of this if not me? Who is sitting up with Dirkie on the rugby field in the early mornings—twenty-five rapid sit-ups in a row; then

twenty-eight, thirty—another thirty to go before we meet the
recce requirement? Who is riding up and down the golf course
hill on his bike with Dirkie, Bennie, and Jacques, throwing clods
at the warthogs and imagining they're hand grenades that are
going to cause the animals' insides to splatter? Who is imagining
himself with uniforms and guns, plastic explosives and fists—
violence new, sexy, and natural on me, tight-fitting as a freshly
bought shirt?

"I hate this place!" Dirkie complains, picking his nose and flicking a snot ball outside our tent. "Nothing to do here. Bugger all.
Niks."

It's a humid evening and the two of us are overnighting in the
tourist camp, as we do now every other week—the illuminated
ablution blocks islands of white neon in the silent dark. We are
bored out of our eleven-year-old minds. Over the past year or so,
somehow the world has changed for us, along with our growing
bodies. Skukuza has come to seem confining, hemmed in like
one of those racetracks where the men drive round and round at
breakneck speeds without any room to burst out. Even Jaco, a
Standard Three we used to invite along on these camping trips,
has been abandoned as a companion. Danie and Jacques have long
ago graduated onto other activities. Here, in the campground,
at midnight on a Saturday, our camping lamp's bulb is out, so we
can't read or play cards. We have played I Spy and rock-paper-
scissors and think-of-a-number games until our heads feel ready
to pop. In our cotton duvet covers—it is much too hot for sleeping bags—we have kicked and play-wrestled and slapped imaginary malaria mosquitoes on each other, until now at last, blasé
and exhausted, we simply lie still, listening to the screech of the
night crickets.

"I wish my Uncle Dirk were here," Dirkie says at last. "He'd think of a game to play. I bet you Dirkie Jr. and Callas are doing something *lekker* tonight."

"What game would we play if we lived in Pretoria?" I ask him. This is something that has changed between Dirkie and me. Where once we took pride in our *recce*-like bush smarts—the way we'd hear the distant go-away bird crow its alarm and know a large animal was moving nearby; the way we could spot the difference between lion and leopard tracks—now we dream of life in Pretoria, what fun we'd have if we lived there, how many movies we'd see and video game arcades we'd frequent and cool things we'd shoplift from the rich stores in the shopping malls.

"*Yissis*," Dirkie replies. "*Yissis*." He pauses for dramatic effect. "If you and I lived in Pretoria . . ." He continues: "If you and I lived in Pretoria we could hang out at a mall and meet some chicks. We could get into a fight with a gang of larneys"—posh kids—"maybe we could even interrupt a crime." He seems quite cheered by this vision of badness, or is it Rocco de Wet style superhero interventions? In our passion for anything to puncture the boredom, are we forgetting the distinction?

A month or two ago, for example, the two of us were in the black people's shop to buy torch batteries—our whites-only store had run out of them. I asked Dirkie if we were allowed to do this. After all, if a black person wanted to buy something in our store, she had to have a note from a white person saying the shopping was being done for a white family.

But Dirkie laughed at me. "We're fucking white," he told me. And then, in the store itself—a twilit, mysterious place smelling of the things black people do, of dust and sweat and the cheap green bars of Sunlight soap they like to use—Dirkie pushed to the front of a long line of housekeepers, many of them balancing their intended purchases perfectly on their heads, like circus tightrope walkers.

"But what would your dad say if he knew?" I asked him

afterward. Dirkie's father is, like mine, somewhat liberal: for example, he does not permit Dirkie to say *kaffir* in front of him, although unlike mine, he does allow Dirkie to give orders to their maid.

"*Ag*," Dirkie replied. This Afrikaans exclamation of impatience is pronounced like a throat-clearing, as if Dirkie was about to spew my question out onto the side of the road. "You're always so worried about parents, hey? But my Uncle Dirk, he's right, he says a man has to make his own decisions rather than listen to what others tell him."

Since I couldn't think of a response to this, I let the disagreement go.

Now, in the camp, though, all of this talk of entertaining wickedness—fights and robberies and the like—only worsens the frustration of being here, under this starless overcast sky: the trilling of the bullfrogs is a mockery of our desire for a real rock concert.

"What are we going to do now, Dirkie?" How long ago was it I could keep myself busy for hours simply by telling myself stories?

Dirkie pauses: I cannot see him clearly in the darkness, but I imagine him frowning and pursing his lips.

"We can streak around the camp," he says at last. "That's what the privates do sometimes in the army, to get back at a sergeant-major who's being an arsehole. Listen!" I've come to know this voice of Dirkie's now, where it jumps up half an octave with excitement. It's the voice he's using when he's planning a raid on the gang house of a group of kids we don't like or when he's seen something interesting on television about, say, Mirage aerodynamics. "We can run naked to the VIP cottage, where all the generals and police chiefs stay! Uncle Dirk says those higher-ups are really disgusting, hey. We should moon them."

This wasn't actually what I had in mind. To me, this sounds like the kind of thing that could get me in serious trouble if news of it got back home—worse than pushing in front of black people in their own store. Once, when we were watching the Wimbledon tennis championships at my aunt and uncle's house, and a streaker ran onto the court, Mommy said: "That's totally selfish! If any of you did that, I'd spank your bottom." Daddy, for his part, is always reminding me that when Dirkie and I go camping near the tourists, we're being entrusted with his and Uncle Ben's work reputations.

So now, in the tent, I shake my head. "My parents would kill me, Dirkie. I've told you what my father says."

"*Ag*, Glen!" This time, Dirkie spits it like a sour marula. "Pa this. Ma that. When are you going to grow out of your nappies, hey?"

Silence lies heavy. Despite the familiarity of this line of attack, the old wound throbs again: in the end there is, quite possibly, something the matter with me. Mommy's boy! This is the first thing the Skukuza boys said to me when our family arrived in the village, and I refused to climb the perimeter fence to retrieve a ball lost in hand tennis. Sissy! Although it seems a long time ago since I stood on the edge of the girls' playground with a peanut butter and syrup sandwich, I haven't forgotten the sense of being cloaked by some mysterious existential ugliness.

As if he's reading my thoughts, Dirkie says now: "You're not much fun, Glen, when you insist on being good. If you're always obeying all the rules and doing what others tell you, you never grow up, I say."

What could be clearer? If I want to stay connected to people like Dirkie, I must do more grown-up, normal, rebellious things, like taking off my clothes. Is Dirkie right? I think of my father and Uncle Ian telling stories of their childhoods. They certainly did naughty things. Sometimes they talk about boarding school, which they attended after Standard Six—eighth grade—when South

Africans enter high school. Running away from the boys' hostel, up in their chilly highveld town and stealing peaches from a farmer who'd come out and shoot at them with his rifle. Even Mommy and Auntie Merle tubed in the Nels River, which ran by Mataffin farm, where they all grew up together. They could have got bilharzias from this—they did it, and enjoyed it, and today they relish telling the stories, even though if they saw *me* tubing in the Nels River they'd throw a small fit.

"Come on, Glen," Dirkie says. "Nobody will even see us. Don't be a scaredy-cat."

He leaps up, strips off his sleeping shorts, unzips the tent, and runs off through the starlit campground—a moving blob of ashen pallor, dancing through patches of ground thorns. Perhaps forty or fifty feet away, he turns around to face me, his front shielded in shadow. He leans forward and laughs; I see his cap of dark hair tip downward, a falling scythe, and I hear his giggles, bubbles of sound plopping in the darkness. He beckons at me. Is the moment erotic? At this instant all I'm aware of is anxiety: a dryness in my throat, my stomach fluttering. Later, though, I will be struck by this as a kind of physical consummation of a year and a half of baths together in the camp ablution blocks; towel-snapping contests; nights close together in our tent—the sustained physical proximity of boyhood friendship.

I strip down. Outside, the feeling of nakedness is surprisingly empowering: nothing is hidden anymore. The tourists are in their trailers and tents, asleep. What do they care about anything? Dirkie speeds away, downhill. The earth is sharp and warm on my feet. Before I know it we've skirted the block of huts in front of the tent area and have landed up at the edge of the tourist camp by the river, alongside one of the camp's luxury guesthouses usually reserved for VIPs. I know Adrian Vlok, the minister of police, has stayed there on occasion, as has State President P. W. Botha.

"Look," Dirkie says. He is standing against the perimeter fence, two hands raised and gripping the diamond-shaped chain links, his genitalia pressed through a third gap as he lets loose a stream of urine. He guffaws, shakes his head: "I'm giving the lions something to sniff."

Now for the first time in our friendship, I really am sexually attracted to Dirkie. I've never seen him with such macho swagger before, such self-aggrandizing confidence—legs wide and penis thrust outward. Why is my cock beginning to harden? I fold my hands over it and turn away from Dirkie, which leaves me facing the VIP cottage, with its long thatched eaves shading darkened windows.

Fortunately my penis wilts. But then Dirkie immediately notices the direction of my gaze. "Bastards!" he suddenly yells at the dark house. "Go shit yourselves! Your mother's puss!" He bends over and spreads his bum cheeks at the guest cottage: again that blade of hair flips forward and those giggles peal right out of him—pebbles falling into a wide, lazy river.

"Dirkie!" I punch him on the shoulder, and he straightens up. "Someone will come." Has he gone crazy? If he were a grown-up, I'd wonder if he'd been drinking.

Dirkie stops laughing and looks a little startled. "Nobody's around," he says. "Anyway, why you getting so nervous again? I thought this was going to be the night you stopped being stupid."

Stupid: all of the huts near us are still dark. Probably Dirkie is right. Probably this is what a soldier would do.

"What now, Dirkie?" I want to know. "There's nothing more going on here. See? There isn't even a car in the driveway. This place is empty."

I'm right: the parking spot beyond the cottage is vacant. Dirkie pauses for a second and tries to work it out.

"I have an idea," he says. "Come!" He begins to run.

We sprint across the rest camp, him ahead again, a pale shadow. We pass our small blue tent, next to the outside tap and the baboon-proof rubbish bin. We head further up, past the abandoned petrol station and the building materials warehouse. The petrol station, while empty, is illuminated, a bright bubble of white and blue. Following Dirkie's lead I make sure to sidle along the side of the road in the shadows. At last we end up at the entrance to the black workers' compound, right near the store where we came for the batteries. He's heaving and panting—sweating—and so am I. In front of us, two plain beige-painted brick pillars suspend a chained gate, behind which stand the rows of tiny, single-room brick houses in which the gardeners, housekeepers, and cooks live.

It is, of course, the weekend, so probably the place is half empty. Forbidden by law to bring their families with them into white South Africa, many of the black workers in Kruger head to the nearby Bantustans on weekends when they're free—for example, Sarah, our housekeeper, has two weekends off a month. Still, there will be sleepers here: waiters and cleaners off-shift. We pause and catch our breath: the air is fresh and cool on my body.

"See," he says, "nobody will come here. And the *kaffirs* will know better than to get us into trouble."

At first, I don't quite absorb his words: not standing naked in front of that gate. What has happened to my mother's admonitions? For that matter, what about Dirkie's dad? In some strange way I don't fully understand, these thoughts all now seem to have receded into another realm.

"Hey!" Dirkie calls into the night. "Little *kaffirs*! Come out!"

No response. Is it possible they could be sleeping through this? And why is Dirkie acting this way?

"We know you're hiding terrorists! This is Rocco de Wet, border fighter! You are surrounded by the *recces,* people! Come out immediately with your passbooks and prepare to line up alphabetically."

I think I'm beginning to get it. This is all a game, something that's going on in Dirkie's head. He isn't here at all, in Skukuza: he's somewhere beside some SWAPO-supporting village, trying to round up enemies. This is all still part of his being courageous, like Rocco. But there are real people inside that workers compound, not comic-book characters. In *Border Fighter,* Rocco would never do this to an Ovambo village that had done nothing wrong.

"Let's go home, Dirkie," I say. Despite myself, a hollow, guilty feeling is growing in me. "These people are sleeping. You aren't Rocco de Wet, hey? *Yissis!*"

But Dirkie's still not ready to give up. "Come on, man," he says. "Just get one of them to come out. When we see them, we'll moon them, then run away before they see who we are." He picks up a stone and hands it to me. "You try. It'll be fun."

I have come this far in proving myself—why not one small step further? I throw the pebble over the fence, so it lands on one of the roofs with a dull, rattling clatter. "The *tokoloshe!*" I yell out then, in an unexpected flash of inspiration. "It's coming to rape you!" The *tokoloshe* is the mythical goblin whom the black people fear so much they sleep with their beds raised on bricks—the practice provokes no end of amusement in the white community in general. I know my joke will be foolproof—a way to humor Dirkie while also providing myself with an exit strategy. I turn around and run back towards the tent before someone can emerge from the houses; a few seconds later, Dirkie follows me as I guessed he would, giggling helplessly. It worked. We didn't get caught. "The *tokoloshe,*" Dirkie exclaims, chuckling. "Good one, Glen. Those little *kaffirs* must have been wondering, hey." Back in our sleeping bags, the two of us chortle ourselves to sleep.

Next day Mommy, perhaps noticing something shifty in my manner—do I avoid eye contact with Sarah? Do I carry out a special penitential glass of water to Sinias, the gardener?—asks: "Is something wrong, Glen?"

But vigorously, definitively, I shake my head.

It's a Saturday night. We're at Dirkie's house, and Uncle Dirk and Auntie Karin, from Pretoria, are visiting Uncle Ben and Auntie Jeanette. This is, of course, the famous Uncle Dirk: the real-life Rocco. The house is a hubbub of movement and activity. On the woofer in the backyard, David Kramer belts out "The Royal Hotel"; from the grill, where Uncle Ben and Uncle Dirk sit nursing beers, rise the smells of woodsmoke, *boerewors* sausage, and steak. Inside, Auntie Karin hovers over Dirkie Jr. and Callas in the bathroom, while Dirkie and I, in the lounge, struggle to unpack his latest present from Uncle Dirk, a pair of walkie-talkies.

Why aren't the two of us more fascinated by the policeman uncle who's so near us? We have talked so often—for more than a year now—about Rocco, him, the whole world of counterterrorism. Why aren't the two of us bothering him, where he's talking in hushed tones to his brother in the backyard? *Uncle Dirk, is it true that the terris shoot themselves and their comrades rather than fall into our boys' hands? Is it true they torture you if they catch you?* But probably Uncle Ben or Auntie Jeanette has told us not to bother the men at the back. However much we may want to be more grown-up than we are—cool, knowledgeable teenagers—really we are still, at this moment, mere *laaities*, pipsqueaks—distracted by toys and trinkets.

And these walkie-talkies! They are not even a bit like the cheap plastic toy ones my parents once bought me. They're authentic, police-style portable radios, heavy and metallic. We shout and hoot with delight. Auntie Jeanette grabs Dirkie's shoulder and asks him what he needs to say.

"Thank you, Uncle Dirk!"

But Uncle Dirk's busy. The two of us waste no time trying the radios out. We pretend to be motorcycle cops on different Los Angeles highways. I'm Larry Wilcox, watching for speeders on the turnpike, right in the front yard by the sausage tree. He's Ponch Poncherello who has stepped inside a Dunkin' Donuts to take a break.

Uncle Dirk stays in the background. Much of that evening I signal Ponch with a Morse SOS when I spot a speeder or radio Hutch when a shootout starts in a diner. "Roger, Retief," crackles Dirkie's voice when I summon him.

We play on with those intercoms. We become astronauts on a moon base, game rangers radioing nature conservation headquarters, soldiers storming a guerilla safehouse. The barbecue passes in a blur. We stop at a table, grab meat, corn porridge, and tomato sauce. We eat in the kitchen, so the grown-ups can sit around outside and talk about adult things. Despite all I've heard about him before, Uncle Dirk must not matter to me all that much, for in time I will retain almost no recollection of him from this first part of the night—no matter how hard I try, after I have learned the truth, to parse up something specific.

At some point, though, Dirkie and I do return to his diorama.

"This is Montgomery, calling Rommel," I say into the walkie-talkie. "Are you ready to surrender yet?" I pin down a tent encampment: Dirkie is defeated, and in this moment the English prevail over the Germans.

Then I am alone, charging between Uncle Dirk's and Uncle Ben's chairs after an imaginary bank robber, pressing the talk button, and saying "Over and out," wind whooshing past my open car windows.

Uncle Dirk play-tackles me. Two arms grab my legs and I fall forward: *Aaaaahh!* Blurring stars and tree shadows. When I relive this moment eight years later, after learning the truth about Dirk Coetzee, this falling will seem to me like a kind of miniature death, but of course this is nonsense, a glib, after-the-fact psychological projection. Death, when it comes after bullet wounds, police detention, days spent hanging upside down from a metal ceiling hook with electric shocks being applied to the foot soles, cannot possibly be like this blissful slip earthwards on a cool summer night. Probably it's more of a terrified shrinking: blackness descending like a blanket.

At any rate what happens now is that Uncle Dirk stands up again, brushes grass and mud off his knees and elbows, and smiles at me. He is a handsome man, clean-cut, square-jawed, like his brother. He smells of beer and wood smoke.

"A nice friend for Dirkie," he says. "Hey, *laaitie?*" He takes his seat again. I am a bit taken aback by him, but he seems so nice, his eyes so warm and relaxed, if a little melancholy and removed. This is one thing I will recall about him, his surprisingly forlorn demeanor—slumped shoulders, dangling hands. There is something about him that reminds me of Derrick, the glum German TV detective.

"Uncle is a policeman," I remark. Uncle Dirk is significantly plumper than Rocco de Wet. Maybe Dirkie can be a terrorist fighter after all. "Uncle is a bit like Border Fighter, hey?"

He bursts into laughter. "That's just a comic, son," he says. "I'm not really like a border fighter at all."

He sounds just like Daddy, now. What does Uncle Dirk think is wrong with *Border Fighter*? "But Dirkie and I *like Border Fighter,* Uncle. We want to be border fighters when we grow up."

Uncle Dirk sighs. Now his eyes look tired. Why does he suddenly seem like Mommy and Daddy just before bed? "You and just about every other young boy in the country."

"Has Uncle ever caught a terrorist?"

Uncle Dirk looks at Uncle Ben. Now something unfathomable

passes between the brothers: some grown-up knowledge. I am starting to get uncomfortable. What can the secret be? Uncle Dirk ignores my question. Instead he draws me closer, takes the walkie-talkie from me. Uncle Ben stands up to get something from in-doors.

"Here, let me show you, hey—you're doing your radio all wrong." Uncle Dirk seems to cheer at the change of topic: he smiles; his eyes seem lighter; suddenly I like him again—he's as kind and friendly as Uncle Ben.

He cups his whole brown hand around the back of the walkie-talkie, its weight resting in his palm, with his right index finger against the talk button.

"See, you never say 'Over and out.' 'Over' means you are wait-ing for a reply." He holds up the microphone and presses the talk button. "Coetzee senior."

"Go ahead, Uncle Dirk. Over."

He leans back. "Your partner spotted a Code Seven behind us here. Requesting backup. Over."

"Backup coming, Uncle Dirk. Over."

"Roger that. Out."

He hands the walkie-talkie back to me. The instrument is still warm from his hand. So this is what authenticity looks and sounds like: *Roger that. Out.* "Perhaps you'll become a cop, too, one day," he says, and winks. "Just remember: *Out.*" And now I run off, de-lighted: I have learned something. And Uncle Dirk actually thinks I can be a policeman.

Dirkie's in the front yard.

"Your uncle is *kief,*" I say. I jump up and down, panting. "He's better than Buck Rogers. He's better than Starsky." I show Dirkie how to hold the walkie-talkie correctly. I tell him the two of us can probably share a cop car one day and shoot the bad guys.

"Uncle Dirk *is lekker,* hey?" replies Dirkie. We play and play. Above us the moon shines like an ingot. In the lambent softness of all that moonlight, in that quicksilver, fragrant, lukewarm stillness, everything still seems so right in my world: the boundaries between good and evil clearly demarcated.

A Man of Extraordinary Taste

Of our four grandparents there is no doubt he is the outlier. In a way, of course, they are all bizarre, these gray-haired, leathery-skinned people who arrive to visit us every month or so in their rickety cars: Pa and Gogo, my maternal grandparents, in their coughing Mazda; Yaya and Grandpa in Yaya's blue Mini barely larger than a shower cubicle. On the citrus estate near Nelspruit, an hour and a half from the game reserve, where all four of them live a mere hundred yards from each other off leafy poinciana-lined streets, they preside jointly over hushed, camphor-scented realms of exotic antiquity. Crowfoot floral armchairs adorn their living rooms. World War II–era wireless sets, with large brass knobs you have to turn to get the radio station, serve as LP stands: *Bing Crosby, The Sound of Music, The Snow Goose.*

Yet even in that otherworldly dominion Grandpa Retief seems different. To begin with, he is an actor. In this landscape of acacia thorns, railway sidings, and eucalyptus and orange plantations I do not meet painters, musicians, and politicians; I only read about them in history books. Cashier-bookkeepers, like Gogo, game ranger–researchers like Daddy and Uncle Ian, railway foremen, yes—like Pa, who organizes the unloading and storage of the supplies that arrive by train from Durban. But actors, no.

Grandpa Retief isn't a *professional* actor—those are the women and men he talks about, like Meryl Streep: "They can shape-shift like chameleons—*chameleons*, do you hear me?" He works as maintenance supervisor for the citrus estate. But this is not what he talks about. Instead, into the barbecue conversations at Merle and Ian's, sitting around the fire in plastic chairs with the maid bringing out the carrot salad—into these tableaux he will drop romantic and foreign-sounding names of plays being put on by the amateur repertory company he cofounded: *Lear, Hedda Gabler.* He will talk about banana entrances and script breakdowns and overhead rigging.

"The Moor is of a free and open nature that thinks men honest that but seem to be so," he proclaims without warning, in the middle of a conversation about how surprised everyone is at a local game ranger's selling collected ivory to poachers. What does he mean? We children play horses around the grown-ups' chairs— little seven-year-old Lisa, with her blond pig tails and missing front teeth, holding up a stick for the rest of us to jump over. Mommy and Auntie Merle chat away about neighbors and relatives, the too-frequent visits of Uncle So-and-so to Auntie Whatnot, whose pilot husband is regularly out of town. Then Grandpa says, blinking, non sequitur, his wizened face, with the pointed mole growing out the left side of his chin, betraying no awareness of his own peculiarity: "Madness in great ones must not unwatched go."

"Cultured." This is the word for strange, half-crazy people like him—at least this is what Gogo tells Lisa and me, when the three of us lie curled up under her eiderdown on early mornings, reading Enid Blyton adventure mysteries. "Well-read" means you read good books—not spy stories, detective thrillers, or the Mills and Boon romances Gogo keeps on her bedside, but the black leatherbound Great Books collection on Grandpa Retief's bookshelf: *Franken-stein, Lolita, Justine.* "Cultivated" means being insufferably fussy with your food, the way he is—rice with butter and salt rather than brown gravy; sending back postcards from places like Lake Kariba and Swakopmund; holding a filterless Pall Mall in your right hand, the way Grandpa Retief does, with the brown, bony fingers sticking up like a porcupine's spine, and closing your eyes as you inhale: "Ah, but some pleasures are worth the lung cancer."

I think Mommy does not particularly like this culturedness. Mommy, who dropped out of nursing school to marry Daddy, is always complaining about how much he smokes—one or two packs a day, the cigarettes stacking up as squashed *stompies* in Mommy's hippo-shaped ashtrays. Mommy worries about the smoke we children breathe in when we're around him.

"I've seen lung cancer," she says, "and it's nothing pretty. Wait till he ends up in intensive care."

But he laughs off her hints about quitting. The reek of tobacco on him is so potent, a sour, acrid cloak, that my cousins, siblings, and I pinch our noses shut and make our voices all high-pitched and nasal—"Stinky Grandpa!"—when the grown-ups are out of earshot. And one day Lisa and Lorna chase the rest of us around Merle and Ian's backyard with one of Grandpa's unwashed shirts.

Then there is something with him and money.

"Enjoying life is *great*," says Auntie Merle as she, Uncle Ian, Daddy, and Mommy sit around in their lounge. To accentuate her point she lifts up her gin and tonic. "But you don't spend your wife's inheritance on toys and fancy holidays." His wife—that would be Yaya, who has a share in a family farm in the Free State. We kids are always pressuring Mommy and Daddy to go there, so we can water real cornfields and milk a dairy cow. What does Auntie Merle mean—can farms be spent? When we ask, however, the grown-ups shake their heads no, such questions are not for children. Grandpa Retief's mystique grows.

He buys a yacht and moors it at Lake Da Gama, an artificial reservoir in the blue-gum plantations on the outskirts of the game reserve. He invites us to drive out for a day on the water. He dresses up for the occasion in a skipper's uniform. There he is, all in white, standing on the foredeck of the gleaming boat as we arrive, nautical cap with gold trimming perched on his head, cigarette dangling, as always, from his mouth, a tumbler of Coca-Cola in his right hand. He salutes me, then Lisa, then David.

"Mates, ahoy!" he proclaims, happy and expansive. He is in his element, somehow; now he is acting in real life—he's Captain Hook or Sinbad the sailor. Theatricality makes him a boy, and we children play with him.

"Luffing to starboard, young mariners!" he calls from the tiller, as we race through blue water, sails flapping overhead, the trees on the shoreline all bright green, nothing remotely like our own parched tawny-brown game reserve. By now the three of us have learned: whenever the yacht turns starboard, or right, the taut overhead canvas triangle swings in the opposite direction, a rigid wooden boom sweeping across the deck of the yacht, forcing us to duck, giggling and screaming. And then Grandpa lets me, the oldest, have my own turn at the helm.

"Luffing to port, ahoy!" I yell. The boat a free-flying extension of my body.

It's lunchtime. Back at the marina, Grandpa lays out a feast for us on the picnic tables: glass bowls of anchovies; small rectangles of toast; goat's milk cheese from the Western Cape; pears and oranges.

The others do not especially appreciate this lunch. Mommy says, "You shouldn't have, Dad. This is too much." Daddy says very little, standing off to the side with his food. Lisa makes a face when she tastes the toast and anchovies. "Sis!" she says, and runs to the sink to spit it out. Mommy frowns at her—"That's rude, Lees, my love"—but Grandpa just chuckles. "It's an acquired taste."

But I love it. The anchovies in particular are extraordinary: an explosion of salty fish flavor on my tongue and palate, like tinned sardines, except more so—the piquancy of several fish packed into a pale sliver of flesh the size of a monkey's tongue. With the crunchiness of the white toast and the smoothness of the real Mataffin farm butter, it's exquisite.

"Mmm," I say.

"My, my." He reaches over and prepares me another slice. "Looks like we have a gourmet in the family." He rumples my hair, winks, and smiles at me. His blue eyes sparkle. "Aristotle said you can tell character by desire, in other words, by taste." To my mother: "Dee, I would have to say by those standards Glennie's a paragon."

I don't understand what he's saying. But his pleasure in me is clear. Later, I ask Mommy what "gourmet" and "paragon" mean. She explains that they convey outstanding merit and judgment, qualities that make a person stand out from ordinary humanity. How long have I suspected I am not quite like other people—that there is something strange in me that makes me somehow alien to, say, the other boys on the playground, Dirkie Coetzee and the Hooligans gang notwithstanding? Somewhere I sense I'm different even from Daddy, with his endless jokes and teasing and his boring computer magazines; perhaps even Mommy with her Anne Murray Christmas carols we children like to laugh at. Now I have actual concepts for this discongruity, specific vowels and consonants I hold inside myself, exotic and delicious: paragon, gourmet—like soft, expanding loaves.

But I am not his favorite. This much I sense: he does not after all pay much attention to me. When Mommy and Daddy leave Lisa,

David, and me at their house, it is Yaya, kindly and sweet-smelling, who teaches us to trim rosebushes, who colors in with us and plays hymns at the piano while the three of us sing along: "What a friend we have in Jesus!" He, Grandpa Retief, vanishes into the living room, closing the door. We hear him shuffling among his records; then something sad and sonorous comes on: *Don Giovanni!* Smoke tendrils curl under the door and upward; when we ask Yaya if we can knock on the door and bother him, she says: "Would you want him to forget his lines in front of a hundred people?" Apparently Strauss and Mozart help him concentrate.

I try to get him to notice me. When I get my part in the school play, where I recite the C. Louis Leipold poem about violets to the hallfull of cheering Afrikaans families, I run up to him at Auntie Merle and Uncle Ian's and perform it. But he just shrugs.

"I've never been much for the Afrikaner poets," he says. He gives me a Wilson's peppermint. "You did it well, though, Glennie." Of the grown-ups he asks: "Have the Afrikaners really had their Wordsworth?" Funny: he is originally an Afrikaner himself. But now he is more English than anyone: he is even a deacon in the Anglican church in Nelspruit, where according to Lorna he wears a white frock and helps hand out communion.

If there is any one of us grandchildren he likes more than the others, I am beginning to realize it's Lisa: shy, skinny-legged Lisa, who likes to carry David around the village on her back the way the black women do with their babies. Lisa, now nine years old, two years younger than I am, has been changing. She has two pretty, white front teeth, making her face look like the rest of ours, whereas before her smile exposed a wide, red gap. She has replaced her two blond pigtails with a single ponytail, which bounces up and down when she and Lorna skip rope. Her body, too, is developing. She is still slender and flat-chested, but she is getting taller and stronger: now, she sometimes beats me at arm wrestling. In the mornings when she, Mommy, and I go out running with the school coach, Albert Linsky, she now trails behind my left shoulder until the very final stretch, when I have to use my long legs to draw out ahead of her.

As the year goes by, she becomes something of a local track star. At the Inter-Primary Athletics Championship, she wins the 1500-meter race by at least a lap: a whole ocean of parents stand to cheer and support her, and Miss Jeanette, dressed in green and gold, our school colors, leads a chant: "What have you got? LI-SA!" She wins the Lowveld Championships, too, soaring away from the big town primary school girls. By contrast, I come dead last in my race, half a lap behind the other boys. And then, at the Eastern Transvaal Regional Championships in Waterval-Boven, she actually comes within a few seconds of breaking the Under-Ten South African Middle Distance record, set five years ago by rising world champion Zola Budd.

"Budd minus one, Budd minus two, Budd minus three," says the announcer over the loudspeaker as she flutters down the home stretch, with her bright golden ponytail bobbing. "Ladies and gentlemen—a round of applause for Lisa Retief!" The whole stadium claps for her. These are people from Witbank, near Johannesburg, and Phalaborwa, near the north of the park. They are jumping up and down and hurrahing for one little girl, my sister Lisa. I'm proud and jealous at the same time.

Grandpa Retief, though, is visibly pleased with these developments.

"A healthy mind in a healthy body," he says, dishing up an extra portion of Yaya's chicken pie for Lisa. "Wonderful to see!"

When Daddy and Albert Linsky take Lisa to the Skukuza sports fields to run laps on the grass track, he comes along to hold the stopwatch and compares Zola's published middle distance records to Lisa's. "Definite potential," he says, smoking his cigarette. "You never know."

On another family occasion, when the grown-ups are sitting

around on his verandah, Grandpa gets into an argument with Mommy, Daddy, Gogo, and Pa about what kind of training Lisa should be receiving. All Skukuza kids leave home at age twelve or so, to attend boarding school; but he thinks she should leave earlier than that for an expensive private Johannesburg academy.

"No offence to Albert," he says, "but someone with her talent—she could make her mark on sporting history."

We children are in the dining room, playing a game at the piano—probably it is the usual routine, where I pretend to be the teacher and give them scales to play, and then mark their mistakes on little handwritten rubrics. My ears prick up when I hear this statement. Sporting history? Lisa?

"Sorry, Dad." That's Mommy's voice, now, irritated. "All the Olympic Gold Medals in the world don't matter if you lose your childhood. Look at that poor Budd girl, day after day, being pushed by her father."

The conversation goes back and forth like this, Mommy, Gogo, and Pa on one side, Grandpa Retief on the other. Daddy and Yaya keep quiet, even though I know Daddy feels the way Mommy does: they have talked it over before with Merle and Ian. I hear all of this in the background, but keep focused, too, on Lisa's musical performance; I nod my head to the beat the way our neighbor Auntie Elise does, when she teaches Lisa and me piano. This discussion doesn't really matter. Although I wouldn't have the precise words to articulate it, I've already figured out that Grandpa Retief is, in some indefinable way, unimportant. Among the grown-ups his peculiarity makes him ephemeral—as irrelevant as those old songs he listens to.

"You played that sonata really well, Lisa," I tell her when she finishes. I hear Grandpa Retief's chair scrape on the verandah.

"Hmm!" he says. "Here in the Lowveld, mediocrity is our true religion."

He comes through to the dining room, pats Lisa on the head,

and then leans forward and kisses her just above her ponytail, his arm resting on her shoulder blade. The gesture is brief and straightforward; still, there is something about it qualitatively different from the behavior of the other adult males—something physically tender and intimate. I look at him, mildly surprised. He smiles.

"Grandpa thinks Lisa's special."

He leaves to do something—unstop a toilet, fix a broken lean-to. The Mataffin village residents, I will later learn, regularly remark to my parents and aunt and uncle about how nice and helpful he is, how willing to drive a sick child to the hospital or feed a horse. There is nothing creepy or disturbing about him. At his theatrical performances people ask for autographs. He is solicited to serve on boards, participate in labor associations, drop by for bridge. It's unlikely I say anything to Mommy, Daddy, or Lisa that day—what words would I use to define the peculiarity of Grandpa's statement, which is only, after all, an extension of his eccentricity? If I do remark on it, I retain no recollection.

But the two of them get closer. As time goes by it becomes more noticeable: Lisa is invited to sit on his lap at family gatherings. There she is, blond, pale, and small, perched on his gray cotton trousers and playing with his blue plastic cigarette lighter. *Click, click, click.* She struggles to raise a spark, but then he shows her: "Slow down, Lees." And she holds the flame for his cigarette.

"Come and play with us, Lisa!" we cry out. But no, Grandpa tells her she should stay with him, and she nods: she is having fun here; she is like a little grown-up. When I ask if I, too, can try the lighter, he replies: "Grandpa only has one lighter, and there are five of you."

Mommy tells Daddy she doesn't like how he's teaching Lisa to smoke. "All that touching and fiddling—nicotine on her fingertips—I've even seen her put them in her mouth."

But Daddy disagrees. "I think it's pretty harmless."

Then there are their trips. At Mataffin, when Yaya runs out of tomatoes or cooking oil, it is Grandpa Retief who offers to run to the store.

"Want to come along, Lisa?" he calls, and then the two of them are pulling out of the driveway in his white Chevrolet, to return later with plastic Pick 'n Pay bags full of vegetables.

"Can I come along too?" This is a point of contention with me; I have always loved supermarkets, those warehouses of delight unknown in the wilderness, with their arrays of sweet breakfast cereals and refrigerated trays of cold meats. But Mommy and Daddy say Pick 'n Pay is hectic enough without lugging three kids along, and Grandpa Retief says no, I should stay and help Yaya with her cooking.

An unremarkable Saturday morning, for example. Mommy and Daddy are away doing errands; the sun shines overhead; turtle doves murmur in the trees; David, Lisa, and I help Yaya plant nasturtiums. Grandpa Retief materializes behind us, smelling of stale tobacco, jingling his car keys: "Want to help me feed the Snaddons' horses, Lees?" The two of them disappear for perhaps half an hour.

From our childish point of view, however, the most egregious aspect of this favoritism is the caddying. Once a month or so, when Grandpa and Yaya come to visit Merle and Ian, Uncle Ian and Grandpa play golf together. Lorna is usually Uncle Ian's caddy. Neil likes to play golf himself, so Uncle Ian gets annoyed when Neil wants to hit his father's puts. For his part, Grandpa Retief insists on Lisa. Officially she gets ten rand for this work, just like Lorna, but when all the thank-you gifts are included it's much more than that: Venda first-edition stamp collections, which Grandpa says will one day be enormously valuable—the two of them stand at the display case in the post office, him leaning over her and pointing: "See the quality of the inks and the paper?" Extra guava rolls: she drives me mad with envy, standing under Lorna and Neil's backyard mahogany tree, nibbling and sucking at the sugared fruit. One time, as a special tip for an extra-long day, he even gives her imported Toblerone. Lisa gives me just a taste. The flavor is sheer heaven, a smooth, cocoa-buttery sweetness that causes my jowls to tighten.

I run to Mommy. "Why can't David and I be golf caddies?"

I can tell that something in Mommy agrees with me. I sense she has problems with Grandpa Retief: there is that blankness that descends on her face sometimes when I ask her questions about him, as well as the fact that she usually sits away from him at barbecues. Now, however, she tries to mollify me by saying she'll ask Daddy if I can wash the car one of these days when the gardener doesn't come.

"Life isn't fair, Glennie," she says. "A nice person doesn't complain about other people's luck, though. So run along!"

Run along, she says, motherly, logical. And that is what I do.

A brilliant afternoon, an afternoon with something of the quality of a camera flash about it, the blazing whiteness, the bleached lifelessness. Those farmhouses, so pale and luminous: thatched lime-plastered English cottages with hedges and rose gardens, re-created in the tropics. The smell of roses and jasmine. Oranges: a hint, or so it will later seem to me, of the balmy Mediterranean, of breezy Naples, where he got stationed after the war—he would always talk to us about the Neapolitan opera, glass bowls of multicolored *gelato* during intermission. Could any South African habitat have been more perfect for this Humbert Humbert dandy?

A bright, white afternoon, then. This time, everyone is gone. Mommy and Daddy have taken David somewhere—to a Nelspruit doctor, maybe; Mommy thinks Dr. Ferreira, the general practitioner in the game reserve, is good only for small things like colds, rashes, and sinus infections. Yaya has driven off in the blue Mini on errands. Lisa and I run around, bored, in his back garden. We peer inside the shed, between the dark slats of treated wood that smell sweet and vaguely burned, and note the plastic jugs of petrol and paraffin, metal forks, spades, pruning shears, and sacks of fertilizer. When we get tired of listing all the items we can see, we play Chicken in the hedge that runs along the back of his house. This game involves standing on the main, palm-lined Mataffin road where we are not allowed because of the traffic, and then ducking back through the pedestrian gap when a car comes along. When we tire of this diversion, we dig in the compost heap behind the washing line, where we find rotting lettuce leaves, fermenting Bartlett pears, and smelly avocados.

"Avocado!" Lisa yells at me. I hate them. Just the sight of one makes me nauseous; now, I run from her as she chases me with it, giggling and laughing. Then it's my turn to pursue her with a glutinous lettuce leaf: "Slimy Lisa!"

At some point she is gone. Has she left because of my teasing? Did she just run inside to bother Grandpa? All I know is I have been playing by myself near the garden shed. Washing hangs on the line, limp, inert. The sun, bright, unblinking, glints off the bonnet of Grandpa's white Chevrolet in the driveway.

I try the kitchen door, and it's locked. The front door, by the verandah—that's locked, too; I pull and pull at it, bangety-clap, but no go. Even the living room windows are bolted with the curtains drawn.

Strange. Where are they? Grown-ups aren't in the habit of vanishing. When I expect Mommy to be in the kitchen preparing supper, there she is—if she is going to the store or Auntie Merle's, she tells us. I know I am not in real danger, with Mommy and Daddy coming back soon, but still, my mouth is dry and my hands and legs tingle.

"Grandpa! Lisa!" I yell. I bang on the side windows, the ones that open out from the living room, but there is no answer—the place is silent as a storeroom.

I decide to check out nearby places. Opposite the house is the pool enclosure. Usually this is one of the biggest treats of visiting any of the grandparents, during the nine or ten months of the year when swimming is pleasant and refreshing. This bright facility is hemmed in by hedges and surrounded by emerald lawns: the pool is both nicer and closer to home than the municipal one in Skukuza, with its crowds of families and swimming lessons filling up the place three or four afternoons a week. As teenagers Mommy and Daddy lay around here with their friends and listened to the Top 40 on shortwave from the Portuguese colony of Lorenzo Marques. "Let's meet at the pool!"—for as long as I can remember, this mantra has conjured up belly flops and suntan lotion. But today the complex is empty, the blue water surreally still, the wooden bleachers and plastic garden chairs unoccupied.

Gogo and Pa's house just down the road is locked up, too.

"*Hau*, no, the *baas* and *miesies,* they are in town," says Gogo's maid, Esther, who is just leaving for the day: she is a beaming black woman who dresses all in white, with a towering *doek,* or wrap, on her head. "They will be back in a little while." *Everyone* seems to be leaving. What if a terrorist attack happened in Nelspruit and they all died together, leaving just me? I can check the stables and the dairy, across the railway tracks and down the hill, for Grandpa and Lisa, or I can ask Esther to let me into Gogo's lounge where I can read Pa's war encyclopedias and wait for everyone to return, but then Mommy and Daddy will come back and won't know where to find me. So instead I head back to Yaya and Grandpa's. And sure enough, just as I get there, the yellow and white minibus rumbles by, Mommy and David wave at me, and then, to my astonishment, the verandah door opens and *he* is standing there with Lisa. She holds his hand.

"Hello, hello!" he smiles at me and at Mommy and Daddy, disembarking. He raises his free hand, index finger raised, in a wave. I run up.

"Where were you?" I ask them. "The door was locked."

"What do you mean, Glennie?" asks Grandpa. "We were inside, in the lounge. I was teaching Lisa how to play Scrabble."

How is this possible? I banged on those windows.

"But I knocked and shouted. And all the doors were locked."

"No they weren't, Glen!" He chuckles, rumples my hair. Daddy arrives now, takes Lisa and me by the hand. I glance at Lisa, eyebrows raised, but she looks away. "These doors can be difficult to open, you know!" Grandpa closes it behind him and then presses it forward so the wooden edge catches against the doorframe. He indicates that I should open it, and sure enough, it's really stuck. Could I have been mistaken?

And that is the end of it, for that day. The five of us drive home. Lisa sleeps in the back, Mommy in the passenger seat. Daddy, when I tell him about the door and the window-knocking, says: "You did the right thing, coming back to Grandpa's." And it all seems light and trivial: absent-minded Glennie, who fails woodwork and metalwork, not being able to shout loud enough to attract their attention, and getting flummoxed by a door.

It is a decade or more before I hear from my mother the rest of this story, the events that unfold when I am away, first at boarding school, then at university. "Glen, we have something we need to tell you," my mother will say on this occasion. A bright morning; the two of us sitting on a swing bench behind their house, a suburban two-story home where they moved after my father left the National Parks Board. We are holding mugs of *rooibos* tea. In front of us, their new backyard swimming pool—shimmering, oblong, turquoise, beneath a towering banana tree from which erupt shiny green, elongated leaves. I am twenty-three years old at this point. Lisa, at the time, is very distant—a computer science student a thousand miles away in Cape Town. On the rare occasions we see each other, we talk about classes and about the weather. Since the two of us chased each other around Grandpa Retief's compost heap, life has severed something in our childish bond—among other things we both attend boarding school from the eighth to the twelfth grade, where the boys and girls are kept separate from each other behind locks and burglar bars.

"The one thing Lees made me promise when she was a kid was to never tell you or David," Mommy says that day on the swing bench. "Now, Dad and I have decided you have a right. But you can't tell Licks-bicks, okay? I just wouldn't be able to face her, Glen, my love. Promise?"

And I nod. *Sure, Mommy.* Do I think, even for a moment, about the implications of this vow? That sibling solidarity is about to be perverted. That I, too, am about to be drawn into secrecy, the invisible shadowy figure of Grandpa Retief at last opening that meshed verandah door for me.

Of course I do not. The childish impulse to listen to a mother, to give her what she wants, remains strong, and besides, of course, I am curious. With Lisa so far away, keeping something from her does not seem so bad. The first frank words we three siblings will say to each other about all this come perhaps eight years after this mother-son conversation, when I am already in my early thirties, living abroad, and Lisa has confronted my parents with her residual pain and anger. Over email David and I will express support for her; on a visit I make back to South Africa, the three of us will sit in coffee shops and restaurants and exchange anecdotes:

"You really noticed as a child something strange was going on with all those shopping trips? Why didn't our parents?"

"Remember, Lees, I've got hindsight."

A gulf between us, though: *you shared a secret with the grown-ups.*

Still, this is the story I learn from Mommy on the swing bench overlooking the swimming pool—a tale that will later be elaborated and expanded in conversations with Mommy, Daddy, Lisa, David, Merle, and Ian.

It begins when I'm twelve or thirteen. I've already left the house to attend boarding school an hour and a half away in Nelspruit, which is what all rural white kids do in South Africa— there are not enough of us to support a school within driving distance. It's a weekday evening. Lisa is ten. It is perhaps two years or so after the guava roll, the cigarette lighter, and Grandpa Retief's hand on her eight-year-old shoulder—a year after the locked verandah door. Lisa has a poster of George Michael over her bed—she likes Wham, Culture Club, and Paul Young. She's cut her hair short. Sometimes, nowadays, the teacher at school yells at her for chewing gum.

Mommy enters Lisa's bedroom to tuck her in and kiss her good night. This is normal. Mommy is here every night, smelling of perfume and shampoo; she always does exactly the same thing—a kiss on Lisa's forehead: *Good night, Licks-bicks, my love, sleep tight, hey, my little girl?* Now, though, as she folds the soft cream-colored eiderdown under the mattress edges, Lisa suddenly says, without warning: "Grandpa's been doing funny things with me, Mommy. I don't like it."

Later, Mommy will describe this to me as the second her world first becomes hollow. "There I was, Glen," she tells me. "That beautiful house, in Skukuza." A stream bank running in front of it, with verdant ficus and sausage trees, hummingbirds and flycatchers feeding from the hibiscus bushes. Three beautiful children. Kind, loving parents. A gentle, affectionate husband.

"Above all, I had my faith in God." She trusts him—the Good Shepherd, he will take care of all of us.

Now. This. These words. Her chest tightens. "What funny things, Lisa? What are you telling Mommy?" And Lisa tells her: little games. Let Grandpa kiss you on the mouth. Let Grandpa lie naked on top of you. Locked house and bedroom doors: *If you tell anyone, Lees, you'll get into really big trouble.*

A spike turns in Mommy's heart. Her little girl, so thin and small with her freckles, pigtails, and white cheeks—how? Looking at Lisa, Mommy's anguish is overwhelming: *Oh no. Not sweet Licky.* At the thought of her father-in-law she recoils, morally sickened: *How evil and disgusting.* And there in the middle of all those other feelings, she again experiences that sense of scooped-outness. It is as if her life has become as empty as a poinciana husk. Poincianas, which South Africans call flamboyant trees, line the gravel roads of the staff village, where she and Daddy grew up—where we kids ran and played on visits to the grandparents. We'd use the long, elongated brown pods, lying everywhere on the ground, as musketeer swords and Jedi light sabers; we'd make them wizards' wands, use them as antennas to call E.T. Once Yaya showed us how to paint them with oils: turquoise blue, with ochre circles. But now it is Mommy's existence that feels like this—pretty and sturdy on the outside, with nothing within.

"It's okay, Lisa, my love," she manages to get out. "You haven't done anything wrong. It's Grandpa that's been bad. Mommy loves you." Then it is all too much for her. She kisses her daughter good night, closes the door, and goes into the kitchen.

Just the sight of Daddy, sitting there at the breakfast nook with a mug of Milo, is enough to start her crying. This man she adores—his own father. It takes several minutes for her to even choke the words out. He hugs her. When she finally comes up with coherent phrases, he goes pale, sits dazed and confused, gripping the kitchen table. What does he feel at that moment? He is a man faced by a betrayal almost mythic in its scope, except that there are no cultural fables giving voice to this reverse-Oedipalism, this old man's lust for granddaughters. The old stories all prefer men to women, fathers to sons.

Something must be done. This is Daddy's personality: he does not like to feel agony; he likes to fix and improve. Faced with a rupture in the universe, he will try to sew back together what he can. So now he calls his sisters. At this moment I think of him in his animal behaviorist and computer scientist mode. He is used to observing a pride of lions stalking a zebra, plugging numbers into a database, and then reaching conclusions. But in this father of extraordinary tastes he has met a predator too complex for research hypotheses. Analyses are impotent. So Daddy needs advice, consultation, the wisdom of other interested parties.

They meet, three siblings around Merle and Ian's dining room table on a Saturday morning. Mommy stays home to look after Lisa and David. At the time this feels protective and motherly to her, this refusal to let out of sight her little girl who has been so hurt. She observes Lisa and David watching cartoons on the TV, dashing in and out of the sprayers, baking mud cakes next to the maid's quarters. This little blond girl looks so happy and normal, so strong and resilient. Dare Mommy hope that, after all, the poinciana pod is solid? She must still believe in the essential trustworthiness of other people, to take care of her and her children's interests—no longer the old tobacco-scented grandfather, perhaps, but still two sisters-in-law and a husband, sitting around a mahogany dining room table. Above all, Daddy. She trusts Daddy, the clever, grown-up one. Only later will it occur to her that by missing a family meeting to decide what to do with a relative who has abused her daughter, she is unable to protect her daughter at a critical moment.

On the other side of town, in the dining room, Merle makes tea. Lois asks for wine: the family alcoholic, she often drinks from early morning till close to midnight, slurring her words and stumbling around in front of her own children. This looming conversation about sexual abuse is about to test the limits of her emotional stamina, to take her out, back, to the throbbing wound that always makes her reach for her vintage Pinotage and Cabernet: her, a little girl. Him, with her in the orange orchards. *Just a quick touch for Daddy, Lo. Good girl—here's a toffee.*

"It's too early for that," Merle tells her now, and it is. The three of them begin to talk.

When Lois admits that she, too, was abused as a child—"I don't remember very clearly, Pete, but I'm pretty sure of it"—he is filled, or so he will later tell me, with an inchoate rage. "Why didn't you say anything?" he wants to ask her. A raised eyebrow; a frown when the granddaughter-grandfather pair vanished off to buy cream soda—anything like this could have saved his daughter from the potential suffering that now seems so evident to him in his sister: the puffy eyes, the way she often blinks at a direct question. A woman gutted out by her father's tastes.

But Daddy does not express these feelings. He has, in ways he cannot even precisely define, been emotionally damaged, too. Bullying, manipulation, put-downs—he's mentioned before in passing how his father gave him used golf clubs on his twenty-first birthday, while Grandpa Retief bought himself a gleaming new silver set. This subtle childhood battering, these quiet attacks on selfhood, have taught him self-denial. Intellectualization has become his Chenin Blanc. For his hurt he builds a cage of logic.

"Let's think clearly," I imagine him saying, at this, the meeting that will turn out to be the most critical of his adult life. A flow chart. A Venn diagram. On family road trips, when I sit in the passenger seat and ask him about what he thinks of the reports of detainee torture we heard on the BBC, he always says, "Let's look at this logically, from different angles." His colleagues, fascinated by what he can make a silicon chip do for them, have stuck up on his office door a picture of a hyena with its head stuck in a tin, and the caption *Blikbrein,* tin brain—later, in a rebellious young adult stage, I will think of the character from *The Wizard of Oz.*

Now, around the dining room table, Auntie Merle says: "Mom

would be devastated, Pete. You know that." Yaya, whom they regard as something of a living saint, who never gossips, swears, or
criticizes. More than that, the one who saved them from Grandpa
Retief's coldness—the one to whom they owe everything as
children—this Yaya would feel as if her world was blown apart.

Lois: "She doesn't deserve that."

Merle: "Not at all."

This, too, makes a kind of sense, I suppose, if you abstract it out
from the abomination: Yaya has, after all, done nothing wrong.
She cannot be blamed for leaving one Saturday morning after another to buy hibiscus and nasturtium seeds.

Merle, again, or maybe it's Lois; the two of them seem inter-
changeable as I imagine this scene, two sober-faced Fates finger-
ing the white crocheted tablecloth of our family destiny. "What's
to *gain,* Pete, by blowing this into the open? Imagine Lisa's expo-
sure!"

"I don't see the point!"

What indeed are the benefits? Clarity, truth, justice—but these
are, like taste, in the eye of the beholder. The heart's truth, which
may be unpalatable but has always required homage: Oedipus's
eyes, bloody, on the Thebes cobblestones. A child's heart—Lisa's
heart, and later mine when I hear about this—needs, if not blood
offerings and raised knives, at least a visible, visceral honoring of
the depth of the violation that has occurred. Shouted outrage:
*Come near my daughter again and I'll fucking kill you, you vile
monster.*

But this is not Daddy. None of this is logical or scientific. In these
siblings' world, in 1980s white South African culture, there is no
public discussion of sexuality. Mommy and Daddy kiss in front of
us, but they lock their bedroom door on Sunday afternoons when
they take their "naps." When a male baboon chases a female one
with his penis sticking out pink as an impala lily blossom, Mommy

tells us not to stare. And beyond all this, of course, secrecy and avoidance are the primal cultural instincts. A Kruger Park ranger sees, through binoculars, soldiers throwing a black man's body into a crocodile-infested lake and he knows not to make a formal report. A few weeks after the meeting of the siblings, Mommy and Daddy will travel to Pretoria to consult a psychiatrist, and she will say, with the full weight of intellectual authority: *Listen, I've seen some of these court cases, where the parents go public. So traumatic for the kid, with all the lawyers' questions. The pedophile gets off anyway. So my advice is to just keep things stable.*

So now, around the dining room table, these three siblings make a decision that's logical, which is to say they choose to hush, to dissemble, to put an abused child's needs below those of a grown woman, to become actors in this, their father's final play, his unacknowledged directorial masterpiece. They decide to give him a warning, so that from now on he will forgo girls and stick to Strauss and Pall Malls. They will keep things as normal for Lisa and Yaya as possible. They will maintain a façade of family happiness—Christmas presents and dinners; drinks and golf and walks around Mataffin village, swatting at midges while the hills turn rose-golden in the sunset—while their hearts pulse with an unnamable grief.

Daddy drives into town to see Grandpa Retief. For privacy's sake the two of them meet in his church, in a pew in front of the altar, sunlight falling in through the stained-glass windows, dust, birdsong outside, the Book of Common Prayer and the pictures of the saints. Daddy says, "I know about Lisa, Dad, and I want you to know that if I ever see you around a young girl again, I'm going straight to the police."

He, Grandpa Retief, drops his head, but says nothing. They do not say much more to each other; they have never done all that much talking.

Family gatherings continue. At perhaps a dozen of them over the next two years, I imagine Grandpa Retief sitting, cross-legged on a plastic lawn chair, sipping a Coca-Cola with ice.

"Picasso—the greatest genius of the twentieth century. Einstein's breakthroughs were intellectual. But Picasso's were intuitive."

Yaya making the egg sandwiches. The grown-ups drinking their beer and wine. Lisa playing with the younger kids, huddling at the edge of the gathering next to Mommy, then at last leaving to join me in boarding school. What is all this like for her? Later, she will describe an all-encompassing emptiness, a profound sense of abandonment and betrayal, as if puppets are now claiming to love her. Daddy, I imagine in the middle of all this, suppressing his heart's clamor, keeping things bland and cerebral, as per the psychiatrist's instructions:

"But Dad, Einstein had much more practical impact!"

Two years or so after my parents find out about the abuse, a brain tumor begins in Grandpa Retief's cerebellum: a secretive clump of cells, multiplying and expanding, speeding out through the parietal and sensory cortexes before arriving, finally, in the frontal lobes, his anchors of aesthetic and moral discernment. In a matter of weeks he is lying in the bed in intensive care. He struggles for words, has lost much of his capacity for language, is incapable now, at the end, of articulating the difference between a Beethoven symphony and a Schumann sonata, but manages through his bewilderment to explain to Yaya that he needs to see Daddy.

Daddy thinks it over, then drives to the Nelspruit hospital. After all, a father only dies once. Now is not the moment to deny him opportunities to apologize. But in fact Grandpa Retief perishes when Daddy joins the crowd by his bedside—a brief cough into a respiration machine, a drone on the vital signs monitor, no time for final apologies. At our grandfather's funeral—which both my mother and sister decline to attend—people describe him, as they always do, as the kindest and most helpful of men, who could whistle a Vaughan Williams movement as well as put up drywall. The reception provides, among other delights—this is what I remember most clearly about the event—anchovies in olive oil and tiny chocolate cupcakes with slivers of imported chocolate on top.

It takes another decade for the last pod shreds to crumble: my sister decides she wants nothing to do with this family of chronic thespians; she sets off as separate from the rest of us as she was behind his bolted windows. Phone calls, by me, my parents, and sometimes even by David, the person in the family to whom she remains closest, will be unreturned. Emails will go unanswered. On one trip home from the United States, where I'm then living, she says she's too busy to see me, even though I only get back every two or three years and opportunities to spend time together aren't exactly plentiful. She explicitly forbids contact with my parents; even years later, when she has a child and permits occasional grandson visitation privileges, the daughter-parent relationship remains chilly. If somewhere in the world some swimming pool enclosure exists where we could find each other, could lie on our towels and put on sunscreen and laugh as if Grandpa Retief had never wreaked his havoc, this place remains empty, the lifeguard's chair abandoned, the lawn a solid green uncluttered by towels and deck chairs.

The Jack Bank

I do not anticipate anything like John and his jack bank. Jumping in the municipal swimming pool with my primary school uniform on at the end of Standard Five, seventh grade, as per Skukuza village tradition; saying good-bye to Dirkie, Danie, and the other guys; trying on my new school uniforms in the Nelspruit clothes shops; choosing courses for the first time in my life, accountancy over woodwork, German over Latin; practicing folding hospital bed corners and polishing shoes and tying windsor knots in my new navy blue tie—doing all of this, I cannot imagine I am about to experience my life's defining trauma. Still ignorant of my grandfather, I haven't registered the grown-up capacity for sealing secrets; still unaware of Dirk Coetzee's crimes, I continue to view the world as us versus them, good people like those around me versus villains who shatter eyeballs in restaurants and blow shrapnel into unsuspecting pedestrians. Above all, every night before I go to bed, Mommy and Daddy still come into my room, hug me, and tell me that they love me, and this is still how I think the world is meant to be: safe and happy, protected by inscrutable but comforting forces much larger than me.

Then, on a fine January summer day in the early 1980s, my parents drive me through tribal shantytowns, pristine eucalyptus plantations, and banana tree–covered hills to a farming town about an hour and a half from home. They drop me off at a complex of red-brick buildings surrounded by a tall wire fence, where they help me unpack my clothes, all with neat name tags sewn on by my grandmother. The room is filled with about forty or so other boys my age, none of whom I know— the Skukuza Primary School boys are all at the Afrikaans schools. My parents shake hands with the head of the hostel, the bald assistant principal whom the students call "Dome" on account of his prominent, bulbous head, and with our two dormitory prefects, John and Neville—both seventeen-year-old matrics, or twelfth graders. One thing I do know—it has been explained to me ad nauseum by my father and uncle—is that it is these two who will be entrusted with the responsibility of maintaining discipline.

"Whatever you do, don't antagonize them," my father has warned me. He knows because he and Uncle Ian also went to boarding school in the 1960s, where he was caned by senior boys and subjected to hazing, including one time when the matrics tied him to a rugby post in his pajamas in freezing temperatures. "They can make your life hell. But if you obey the rules and keep your sense of humor, you'll be okay." Uncle Ian agrees, saying initiation and skivvying help Standard Sixes bond and develop character. He too says the key to surviving Standard Six is being able to laugh and crack jokes.

Today, however, in the dormitory, it does not take me long to get into trouble. At 5:30 p.m., shower time for the boys' hostel, John and Neville yell for us to undress, get our toiletry bags, and come downstairs in our towels. There, in a stark and unpainted bathroom, with sheer, rough cinder-block walls still smelling of cement dust and builders' glue, and hot white steam billowing through the joint, filling lungs, alcoves, and toilet stalls, John yells out: "STANDARD SIX! TOWELS OFF!"

Towels? Why would he want us to get rid of our towels? I don't get it; I am too young to get it—my little blond head, perched on my thin neck, cannot wrestle meaning out of this. I look around me and see that several of the other boys have let their towels slip and are grinning at the rest of us, in that bashful way twelve-year-old boys have, as if to say, *Hey,* oukie, *isn't this weird?*

"I SAID OFF!" John shouts.

We take off our towels. A few of the shyer boys fold their hands over their private parts—quiet, reverent, protective gestures reminiscent of supplicants' doubling their hands—but most of us stand there, clumsy, open, and awkward.

"Hands on your heads!" John says then. "And jump up and down! HIGH!"

We do this, bouncing up and down, little jack-in-the-boxes. Our genitals flap in front of us like birds' wings. Is this a joke? If it isn't funny, why are we all laughing at ourselves, grinning and guffawing as John shouts "HIGHER!" and joining Neville in free-spirited merriment when a plump kid slips and falls on his back? Neville guffaws something about an "initiation prank." A boy standing near looks at me and comments, "*Yissis,* hey, I heard about these prefect tricks, but—" John yells, "STOP LAUGHING! NO TALKING!" and then we are quiet.

John and Neville soap themselves, slowly, thoroughly. This, I will later learn, is standard practice for boarding school: although there are forty juniors who need to get showered within the next fifteen or so minutes, the seniors take their time as a matter of principle. We continue to jump, our genitalia slapping and the occasional soft, muffled giggles behind us—it is really impossible to do oddball calisthenics like this without at least chortling.

Then, at some point—I will retain nothing of the prior chain of thoughts or images—I notice John's cock is hard. It's standing out in front of him at a forty-five-degree angle, bright pink from the shower water, on the one hand rather grotesque and otherworldly, like a crimson bromeliad, and on the other vaguely erotic. I have never seen a mature male hard-on before. This is like a revelation of my own future. My penis becomes tumescent.

I meet John's eyes. He has been looking directly at me. The expression on his face—knowing, wise to me—causes an icy terror to pool around my kidneys. What does he see?

"Come here," he says.

I stop springing and step toward him. John says something about how Standard Six can now stop leaping and watch what happens. My fellow twelve-year-olds stop jumping. A pregnant stillness ripples through the room.

"What's your name, *oukie*?" His use here of the friendly form of address should probably reassure me, but for some reason it doesn't—I sense already in him an easy marriage of cruelty and affection. Instead, nausea now grips my throat. I look at the other boys, some of them staring, wide-eyed, others looking down and scrawling patterns with their toes on the humid concrete floor. They seem unreachable.

"Glen Retief, sir."

John puts his finger under his penis and lifts it.

"Do you want this?"

What is the right answer?

"No, sir," I reply. Then, hesitating—perhaps I am insulting him—what exactly does he mean by *want?* "Well, maybe, sir. I mean, I don't know."

Neville laughs again, turns off his shower, and leaves. A few of my classmates snicker.

"Retief, didn't anyone teach you it was rude to stare?" John asks. I do not reply. "Especially at a guy's dick, like a *moffie*. That's not *lekker*. That's not what we do, here."

I nod. "Yes, sir. Sorry, sir." Is there a joke I can crack, like Daddy told me to do? But the ice has spread from my sides all the way around my midriff and into my stomach; it has fanned out to my hands. I am too scared to quip. If I tried it, it would only make things worse.

John points toward an alcove to our right where, beneath a row of several white enamel basins, a cricket bat stands in the corner. "Bring it."

"Bend over."

He hits me four times on the buttocks: four cracks so loud they echo off the windows and walls. They are the sound of ice breaking on some far Antarctic plain. They are cracks of lightning. Initially, I don't feel the blows—the shock is so severe that I just straighten up, stunned. Then my backside is being pressed onto a red-hot meat grille. There is nothing between me and pain; it snuffs me out. When I come to, I am standing over the white enamel basin, running cold water and holding my buttocks with my wet hands.

"You took those jacks well, Retief," John says. "That's good." He smiles. *Jacks.* That is the word for what he just gave me. I don't yet know that it's a word I'll be hearing a lot at boarding school. "Four's a lot. I hope you've learned to respect your seniors." The transformation is almost magical: he is soft now, in his wrapped white towel, tender, boyish, all tension spent; he swings his cricket bat loosely—a child playing with his toy. "No hard feelings, hey, *laaitie*?"

I shake my head. And at age twelve, I mean it—there is no indignation or umbrage. Just confusion. Emptiness. Terror. A longing for my mother—warm protective arms and the fresh, shampooed heat of her sun-dried hair. Worming around somewhere deep inside my brain, however: something new. A beam in a freshly built house, slipping an inch or two in response to four thundering tremors. Cracks appearing in mental walls; a chisel chipping into an untried foundation block. Years later, life will provide me with words for these and later feelings of inadequacy. Stockholm syndrome. Battered victims' disease. Internalized homophobia. The ineluctable sense, as I watch John acting so masculine and nonchalant, talking to one of the other Standard Sixes about cricket scores, that there is something wrong with *me* for having warranted this punishment.

No, in the years ahead there will never be any shortage of labels. But at core, these academic designations will always remain, for me, rather bloodless. They will dance around my mind, flimsy moth shadows; from time to time they will make cameo appearances in my conceptual framework—handy epithets with which to classify and organize the experience. But they will never embody it. For that I must dig deeper into my recollections, into the sight and smell and taste of them, the imagery, texture, and moods of John, his voice, his cricket bat, and, at the end of it all, of course, the jack bank.

It happens both quickly and subtly, our defeat and terrorization: delicate as a first winter chill, sliding down from the crisp, tawny highveld plains into those subtropical valleys; unexpected as icy, crystallized spiders' webs. At what moment, exactly, does it occur? On what precise sweltering afternoon—in the whirring racket of the overhead ceiling fans, as we stand around among those metal lockers clutching our running shoes and chewing Dentyne spearmint gum and listening to F. R. David songs on our Sony Walkmans—do we lose ourselves?

Is it right at the beginning, on that first night, after I bend over for John in the showers? Surely not; surely, from this resonant summer evening filled with the din of crickets and tree frogs, I still remember a whole host of outrage, defiance, and spontaneous friendship, kids running up to me on the way back from supper and asking, *"Jislaaik*, how's your bum," and then saying, "That really wasn't too *kuif,* him hitting you like that just for looking at him?" And later, when we get back to the dormitory, John, Neville, and Greg, a third prefect who has walked down with them, grab five Standard Sixes and cane them for walking past an empty Coke bottle without picking it up—they make the juniors bend over beds, clutching the front metal rims with pale, skinny fingers. Surely here I remember an older boy, more physically developed than the rest of us, telling John, "But sir, this is unfair. *We* didn't leave that bottle on the stairway!"

"DON'T YOU FRICKING ARGUE WITH ME, YOUNG!" John explodes when he hears this. He puffs and heaves. His hands tremble. "I FRICKING WARNED YOU THAT IT WAS ALL OF YOUR RESPONSIBILITY TO KEEP THIS PLACE CLEAN!" He is running some kind of internal marathon against himself; his eyes are hard, his pupils narrow and focused. He smells of sweat, mixed with the pungent, acidic odor of Clearasil; at this moment he simply terrifies me, seems monstrous, inhuman, enormous.

"Fuck you, boy," says Greg to Young, and shoves him down on the bed. He holds the boy's head and shoulders still while John swings the cricket bat six times onto his arse so hard the blows clap like pistol shots. When he is done, Young remains lying still on the bed, quiet, a corpse, until struggling up, spiderlike, all arms, legs, and elbows.

"Fricking wastes of white skin," John says now, looking at all of us. I don't know it yet, but this is another one of his standard turns of phrase. At Youth Preparedness lessons John will stand next to the school commandant, who'll lecture us to ready ourselves for lifelong struggle against racist terrorists like Nelson Mandela. Back in the dormitory he'll call meetings to repeat what the commandant said, and say, "That's why you shouldn't behave like *kaffirs,* guys—if you're lucky enough to be born white, you shouldn't waste it." Now, though, he shrugs and grins. His eyes light up. He bends back and stretches out both arms, a cat arching its back. He seems nice, now, so relaxed and warm, and yet he isn't—my heart skips in my chest. Is it then that some obsequious survive-at-all-costs evolutionary response arises in the firing of my synapses and a part of me vanishes?

Or what about this moment, from the end of the first week of school? In that week we have been assigned skivvy masters: seventeen-year-old matrics for whom we must play black South Africans, making their beds in the morning, polishing their shoes, and taking their clothes to the laundry room, where Swazi and Shangani maids will launder, iron, and fold them. Also that week we have endured hazing rituals and pranks: an evening concert in the school hall, where we each had to step on stage and put on a standup comic routine; a day when we had to walk around the hostel carrying signs around our necks saying, "I'm a worm." We have been jacked several times a week on average, on our buttocks with the cricket bat and on our fingertips with a hardboard square—"finger jacks."

Perhaps after a full week of this I have had enough. Perhaps within me some childhood notion of entitlement still flickers— some idea that this is all wrong and unreasonable, and that I have the right to be treated the way my parents and teachers have always treated me. At any rate, that Thursday morning, there is a clash between the instructions I receive from Mrs. Eliot, my maths teacher, to stay at home on Thursday night and study hard for an important placement test, and those I get from John, to attend an orientation dance at the school hall. "Only poofters stay at home during a *skoffel,* Retief," John says to me when I share my dilemma with him.

I am indignant. Didn't the assistant principal himself, this very morning after breakfast, say that the dance was voluntary? Since when does John make every rule and policy? Righteous outrage bubbles up in me; it befuddles and intoxicates me, and before I can really think about what I am doing I cross the grassy courtyard, turn left at the entrance to the main hostel, and knock at the front door of Mr. Cartwright, the teacher on duty.

The door opens. "Yes?" says Cartwright, blinking at me from under thick reddish-gray eyebrows. I notice that he is a short, slender man; among the students he has a reputation for being tough—people say that in the Rhodesian bush war he hunted the most wanted terrorist assassins in the Chimanimani Mountains.

Now, however, he shows no sign of harshness as he listens to my predicament. I have always been a good student, I explain to him. My parents told me before I left that I had to keep up my marks if I wanted to go to university, and what am *I* supposed to do if Mrs. Eliot schedules her test on Friday?

"Don't worry, my friend," Mr. Cartwright says. He rumples my hair and smiles. "You're obviously a good kid. I'll have a word with John. I'm sure this is all just a misunderstanding." His voice is so warm, gentle, and reassuring, his touch so kind and affectionate, that my eyes mist over and I turn away from him so he won't see how much of a sissy I am.

An hour or so after lights out that evening, though, I wake from queasy, unsettled sleep to find that somebody has pulled my sheets from the bed. I reach down to pull them up again. Then I see him: John standing next to me, in a parallelogram of moonlight, holding a pillow slip filled with something bulky and uneven. He laughs. He seems so crazed and unearthly; his sneering face and broad toothy grin have something nightmarish and hyena-like about them. Am I still dreaming?

"You little snitch," John says. He begins to beat me, bam, bam, on my naked back. Strangely, despite the force of the wallops, none of them really sting. I think: why is he beating me with this instead of the cricket bat? This is not a real hiding. Again it is a bit dreamlike. John laughs again.

"Ha, ha, you are so funny, Retief. You thought you could go over my head to Cartwright. *Yissis!* Ha!" Some of the Standard Sixes in the surrounding beds are lifting up their heads. Then he stops, and I realize my back is wet. It's blood. I jump up to stop it getting onto the white sheets.

"Go back to sleep!" John shouts to a neighbor who is sitting up and staring at me, transfixed. He wallops the boy on the legs with the pillow slip, but something goes wrong and about half the contents fly and clatter out: athletics spikes, their hard steel barbs sticking out, bright metal thorn clusters.

"Pick them up!" he yells at the Standard Six.

Later, I sit in the downstairs bathroom trying to stanch the blood with rolled-up bits of toilet paper, the way my father does with shaving cuts. John appears in the doorway, the sweat on his pale naked chest glistening in the light falling in through the windows, his white pajama pants wan and luminous in the darkness.

"Sorry if I got carried away, Retief," he says. He enters the bathroom. "It's just—snitching is the worst thing anyone can do in boarding school. Everybody will hate you for it. You know that, don't you?" I nod, and right then, sitting in front of him on that wooden bench in the shadows, with the sound of the water trickling into the septic tanks, it seems to me that I do know it. I have always recognized this; I don't have any idea why I forgot it and did something so stupid as to talk to Cartwright. Why do I yield so easily to his worldview? Of course, part of me now wants to run back to Cartwright—report this added violation; insist on John's being kicked out of the school, even though I recognize the extreme danger of this course of action. This part of me simply hates John and wants him punished. But there is another part of me, as well. A loose brick in my soul. A termite-ridden crossbeam.

The laughter of the Skukuza kids; Dirkie Coetzee: Ag, *Glen, come on!* Does every twelve-year-old have such a crack in their being? I am again weird, strange, lacking.

"I agree with Cartwright, though, Retief—you're not bad. I like you, hey. You're *lekker.*" He hugs me around the shoulders. Some of the bits of bloody toilet paper fall off. "You're going to be okay," John continues. "I was just like you, once." And although these words may at first have a strange ring to them—*Like me? Going to be okay?*—still they must mean something to my young brain, because when James, my best friend in the upstairs dormitory, asks me, "What the hell happened, hey?" and Jacques checks out my scratches, "*Yissis,* but he's crazy!"—when they say this I shrug:

"He got the *moer in* about my tattletaling to Cartwright about the *skoffel* dance. I probably shouldn't have done it."

Is my surrender an accumulation—a piling-up of small incidents of deliberate blindness, like the time I walk past John's room en route to chess club? A clump of Standard Sixes stand at John's room entrance that day, looking in and smiling. Curious, I slow down and lean my head just enough to catch a glimpse. A twelve-year-old naked boy stands in front of John holding back his foreskin, while John brings closer the stripped forked end of a copper electrical wire hooked up to an old crank telephone. I do not hesitate. I stroll forward purposely as if I have seen nothing; I block out the yelp of pain and the laughter that then applauds it—giggles that reach me on the downstairs pathway heading for the main campus classrooms. I have blocked out other stories, much like this one: about the guy in the bed next to me who had his hand taped to his penis and then had to knock on every door in the matric passage; about the kid who was handed a pillow slip lined with Vaseline and Tabasco sauce and told to demonstrate the sexual act. Is this the essence of self-defeat, its sickly core: when you refuse to look at reality because it has become too embarrassing and painful?

Or perhaps I am still on the wrong track here. Perhaps the key to my consent to being part of that great cycle of apartheid violence—the apparatus whereby white boys are bullied when they are young so that later they will know how to beat blacks into continued submission—does not lie in John. Perhaps it lies with my companions, those other skinny, freckled twelve-year-olds kept away from even phoning or writing to our parents by weekend athletics meetings, curfews, and impossibly long lines of seniors at the downstairs call box. For those ten weeks, we are kept in semi-isolation: it is not just John and Neville but the whole matric cohort, which beats us as a group with fists, sneakers, and cricket bats, and threatens us with dire consequences if any of us run to our parents or teachers. This whole experience is meant to unite us. "Work together, Standard Six!" John or Neville will yell when some guys get told to do push-ups in the shower room; they want us to lift the bottom guy's hips so he can straighten his arms. But sometime during those ten weeks, in fact the opposite of solidarity develops. We stop trusting each other. We become vicious and feral; start proclaiming, half in jest and half in seriousness—"Him!"—when John asks who is making noise or giggling in the shadows. Is this the crux of psychological submission, when the captives abandon each other's well-being?

One evening, towards the end of John's tenure as our dormitory prefect, an announcement comes just after lights-out: "Special bog meeting in the matric passage!" There, as we stand in our boxer shorts and pajamas in the "bogs," or bathrooms, Greg, John's friend from the matric passage who, like him, seems to take special pleasure in administering beatings, explains to us that someone has been complaining to their parents about the prefects. They have a suspect. Once a rat, always a rat—this much is clear. He looks right at me.

"Not me," I blurt out, quickly—too quickly. Terror clutches my

Adam's apple. "I think—I might have heard something on the phone."

André, a short, skinny, blond, slightly effeminate boy, is something of a pal. The two of us sit on his bed sometimes in the afternoons and talk about history, which we both enjoy. He tells me about the French Revolution, how people's eyes kept on blinking after the guillotine; I tell André about my fourth-grade teacher who told us the Soviets had satellites beaming down brain waves. As far as I can tell, André is also the only Standard Six who gets up at 5:30 a.m. to raise his parents out of bed. Just today, John was making fun of him for this, asking him if he'd share any care packages with his prefects if he received them—he said yes, of course, he wouldn't be selfish. Now, in these matric toilets, my lie is brilliant and inspired. André is the ideal suspect, all the more so, probably, because the two of us are known to be reasonably friendly. The matrics, a wild-dog pack, rip off his striped white pajama bottoms so his tiny genitalia are exposed to the light. They tie his hands behind his back with rope and blindfold him with a handkerchief. They bring a desk into the bathroom, position it below the lintel of the shower entrance, and lift him up onto it. He shivers with fear, but makes no sound.

"LAUGH!" bellows one of the matrics. We do as he says, a forced and artificial ha-ha-ha until we get into the spirit of things and begin to giggle at our own amusement. We are still laughing when the matrics bring a white sheet and tie a noose around André's neck. They string this noose to the lintel, kick out the desk and then catch him rugby-style, both arms outstretched. We roar with gusto—what a hilarious trick—and even more so when we realize André has peed on himself.

Later, with André, I feign benevolence—I did not of course mean *him* when I mentioned the phone; I meant a Standard Eight who was talking to his parents about how rough our hazing was. But André easily sees through this.

"*Ja*, Retief, hey, whatever."

We no longer chat about spies or assassinations. For the rest of my boarding school career he is a kid who drifts around the outside of my world, someone I like but no longer feel I have much in common with—I wave to him when we pass on the walkways and he gestures back, a smile, a nod, *Howzit, man, how are you?* But it is nothing more than politeness.

I miss Mommy and Daddy. This is the ground bass to those ten or so weeks with John, the grief lying beneath the terror that forms the surface melody. I long for my parents, siblings, and cousins—I miss them and the whole world I have left behind, klipspringers on *kopjes* and rose-golden sunrises. At the same time these two people disappear from my life, John arrives. Here he is, so many nights before lights-out, sitting on the edge of my bed in that dormitory with the polished gray floor tiles and the sounds of boys getting undressed, the clatter of shoes and the scrape of toiletry bags in metal lockers.

"What's news, Retief?" John asks. "How's athletics? Maths?" He's an older brother or pal—concerned, interested in me. "I like this guy," he'll say, again, to Jacques, or Martin, or James. He'll talk about band: "God, those American Negroes, hey, they can make a trumpet seem *alive*." Cricket: "*Yissis,* but bowling's better than batting." It would be an exaggeration to say that this relaxed, homestyle chitchat—the affectionate hand patting the bedcovers above my thigh, the questions about English class and geography— makes me *like* him. There is still a horror-octopus running its tentacles and suction cups over my stomach, nights when I lie under the blue-and-white-checkered counterpane after he's gone and dream of hounds circling a baobab—and I wake up in the sultry darkness to hear the neighborhood dogs barking.

But as time goes by, a kind of strange comfort does develop

between us. Among the many lessons I learn is that if I volunteer for suffering—if I step forward, bravely, to take the punch or belting or torment—if I do this, I will prompt from him love and compassion.

"Standard Six!" Say we're in the showers again, as per our evening routine. John and Neville are, as usual, standing and soaping themselves, letting the water run over themselves in long, warm, foaming sheets. Neville: ginger-haired, lithe, defined. He has the muscled body of a senior on the rugby team. All the senior girls apparently have crushes on him. Now, showering, he smiles a lot at us and laughs; his penis nests inside his bush of wet hair. But as a prefect, he does very little yelling and disciplining: he only sporadically interacts with us; mostly he is out with his girlfriend or playing rugby. It is John who towers over us—John, with his own matric friends who come over to his cubicle to talk. Even though he is not as physically attractive as Neville—skinny chest, with the rib cage pushing out against his skin; all those tiny slick hairs on his body—it is John who continues to draw my discreet flickering glances when we're naked like this. He has never again beaten me for looking at him.

"Standard Six!" he asks now. "Who wants to volunteer for the punch test?"

Make no mistake: my instinct is still to shrink into the background, the way I did at the beginning of boarding school. But as time has gone by, I've learned this is an error. He's watching me. If I try to be inconspicuous or distracted, later he'll find some reason to stumble around in my direction: "Why didn't you take a punch, hey, Retief?" His eyes on my cupboard, which is always supposed to be neat—a cookie crumb below the door rim is cause for at least two jacks; a mud stripe on the floor, three or four. Better to get it over with: "I'll try, sir!"

The good thing is that it's never more than one—my shoulder

lined up to the frame of the shower doorway, John's fist-blow from behind so forceful it leaves purple-indigo blossoms both on the back where it lands, and in the front where the bone is slammed up against concrete.

But then, the nighttime afterdiscussion: "I'm proud of this guy, hey, chaps. Did you see how he just stood there? Didn't even close his eyes! *Lekker,* man!" The bruises, for communal examination: "Nice, man! Works of bloody art!"

By contrast, in this new life of mine, Mommy and Daddy are all but absent. What happened to them, on that day they rumbled out of the dormitory parking lot in their white and yellow Kombi and turned right and uphill? Although, of course, at this moment I would never string these words together into a coherent thought—would never think, *They might as well have died*—later, as a young adult, there will be days I'll feel as though they might as well have driven off a bridge.

It is not, needless to say, that Mommy and Daddy have *literally* vanished. Intellectually, as I trudge along those concrete walkways shaded by their corrugated iron roofs, I know they are still there, in that little village with the golf course and the low-water bridge, and this awareness comforts me. Just one week, two, or three, until the first weekend without an athletics meeting for which I'm required to stay and cheer, and I'll be safe and loved again. I will be eating Mommy's maltabella porridge, with the creamy milk, and I'll be making my own toast with marmalade. I will be riding my bicycle down the red brick road to Daddy's Nature Conservation office to say hello.

While I am here at boarding school, though, it's hard to get a grip on these two parallel realities. John's soft hand on my shoulder before he instructs me to purse my fingertips together for jacks: "It won't be so bad, Retief." John's patting my back just before, say, the test he once devised for me where he made me lie under a pile of blankets, without water, on an afternoon when the temperature was a hundred degrees Fahrenheit. (Like the athletics spikes, this torture was nothing as bad as it sounded. The blankets warded off the waves of soupy air coming through the windows, and inside my gray, wooly cocoon I felt snug.)

In the early mornings, just before classes start, I make a habit of trekking, book bag slung over my shoulder, to the east classroom building, the one overlooking both the farm where my grandparents live, and the countryside to the northeast, out in the direction of the game park. There, on the top floor, I hang on the metal railing. I observe the line of tiny toy palm trees next to my grandparents' houses and try to pick out their precise whitewashed thatched cottages: maybe if I look hard enough I can spot Gogo, strolling down to the bookkeeping office. I look into the sunrise, towards Lion's Head Mountain, a hunched granite hillock on the edges of the Kruger Park. I imagine that if I close my eyes and listen to the breeze, I might pick up a snatch of Mommy calling good-bye to Lisa and David as they leave on their bikes for school, or a whiff of the fever tree grove around the Dutch Reformed church—sweet sticky sap, mixed with the acidic odor of bird guano. But it is too far.

Phoning Mommy or Daddy is difficult. The downstairs pay phone has no privacy and is in any case always busy with matrics and Standard Nines, who get preference over juniors. The only practical way to do it is to walk to my Auntie Lois's office, near the school, in the printing press of a small community newspaper she co-owns with my Uncle Karl. This, in itself, involves an elaborate subterfuge: at the front gates a prefect will be standing in his blue blazer with its red-and-white braid.

"I'm buying chips and cokes for Alister MacLean," I'll have to say—or I'll have to name another matric, one who's unlikely to walk by and debunk my story. Once out, a quick run to Auntie Lois's office on the second floor of the strip mall, with the piles of phone books and newspapers and the alcoholic wafts of glue and printing ink. I have fifteen minutes, half an hour at most before the gate prefect will start wondering. Holding that beige plastic receiver and dialing our home number, listening to Mommy's voice all broken up and crackly from the shared rural telephone lines—often, another conversation will pop up in the middle of ours, some Afrikaner auntie making arrangements for baby-sitting or afternoon tea—doing all this, I am a reservoir pressing up against a dam wall, soup pulsing against the lid of a pressure cooker. I want to yield. I want to be all over the walls and ceiling. But something in me prevents it.

"Hi, my love," Mommy says. "Is everything alright?"

Is it John who stands in my way? *If you rat on me again, Retief, I'm going to* moer *you.*

Or something else? A vague, incomprehensible shame—something unspeakably humiliating—something emphatically *not-Mommy*—about shower erections and cock-shock machines and the way John once snapped a boy's dick and balls into a padlock and then pretended to throw the key out of the dormitory window.

"I'm just homesick, Mommy." I say. "I don't like it here. The prefects are nasty."

"Oh, but that's normal, Glen, my love. Remember what Daddy said, and Pa. You just have to get through the first few months, my darling, and then it gets much better."

A free weekend arrives. Of the whole time catching the bus back to Skukuza from the sidewalk outside the hostel; collapsing in front of the TV and reading books in my room again, in blissful privacy; and eating all the food I've been missing—canned pears with evaporated milk, and *koeksusters* from the church sale, and as much *rooibos* and buttermilk rusks as I like—from all this, I'll retain only a single substantive recollection.

Mommy steps into my room, where I'm lying on my bed, in the Saturday afternoon sunshine, reading a novel. How comfortable this bed is beneath my back! A few yards outside my window, a young impala drinks from the mouth of a hose pipe that's been left on by the gardener.

"Glen, my love," Mommy says. She sits next to me, and lays her hand on my legs, much as John has started to do in the evenings. "Darling, what's going on at school? You have to talk to Daddy and me. I can see something's wrong, and if you don't tell us, we can't decide what we need to do."

What I think is: *What can* you *do, Mommy?*

What I feel is: *Oh no. Not* that. *I just want to enjoy this weekend—want to forget that that other place even exists.*

"I don't know, Mommy," I say—or something along these lines. "The prefects steal our money. They hit us for *everything.* I told you, Mommy—I just don't like John. He's *horrible."* None of the specific details that are necessary to convey the full truth of the situation.

The weekend finishes, as it always will during my years of boarding school, much too soon. On the bus back home early on Monday morning—the bus that's accompanied by a convoy of armored cars with rifle-wielding soldiers, against the possibility of stones or firebombs thrown by revolutionaries living in the black tribal areas—with dread I count the minutes until I'm back in my whites-only school dormitory. *Two and a half hours left.* At Hazyview the armored cars turn around. *An hour. Fifteen minutes.* Then, back through the gates and into the wire-enclosed school complex, where violence and danger are assumed to be innocuous.

When the truth ruptures out of me—or part of the truth, enough to combust in my world and make a concrete difference in the universe—it happens more or less at random, a slip of the tongue.

There is no precipitating incident. Or if there is, let's say I lose my recollection of it: what will remain, years later, is just a sprawl of random film clippings, a fist in my stomach when I come back from the store with Marlboros instead of Pall Malls, for John's friend, Greg. Kinder moments, too, of course: my skivvymaster, whose name will eventually be lost to me, shaking his head at my anecdotes of John.

"That guy's got something seriously wrong with him," he said. "I'm really sorry."

Just this, though. It's perhaps nine weeks or so into the school year. An early morning, the blue-gray light only just beginning to gather outside; my bladder is full. Why exactly do I wake? Usually I sleep as soundly as a suitcase until the electric bell saws open the dawn. But this morning I go down to the toilet. I pee into the bowl. And then, bleary-eyed, I see in the entrance foyer of the dormitory the phone booth standing unoccupied, a pod of orange plastic enclosing the blue metal box.

I reverse the call charges. This, probably, is the first tip-off to Mommy and Daddy: it is five o'clock in the morning, I have no qualms about waking them, and then this—the calm, matter-of-fact voice of the operator asking them if they'll accept a collect call.

"Glen!" Daddy's voice sounds raspy. "What's the matter?"

Even now, even in this whispered conversation conducted in terror of hearing footfalls above, the scraping of a door—even now I don't say anything about athletics spikes, copper wire electrodes, or shower jacks. Perhaps I feel partly responsible—I did, after all, stare at John in the showers. Perhaps I sense that talk of adolescent sex play is terrain on which, given my sense of difference from other boys, I have more to lose than win. At any rate, what I focus on now is simply complaints about the jacks and punishments—"always so many of them, Daddy, and they hit us so hard." I hear Daddy whisper something to Mommy about it being "time to do something, Deeling." I lash back:

"Please don't talk to the teachers. It'll make it worse. John will *kill* me."

Is it roundabouts now, during my regretful change of heart, that I hang up abruptly because of a noise upstairs—thus inadvertently communicating to them the extent of my horror? But when I slink back to bed, through the rows of sleepers, John and Neville lie, sprawled-out. Forty boys breathe peacefully. Overhead the ceiling fans whirl on.

And for a day or two nothing out of the ordinary happens. My parents don't tell me about their trip into school to speak to the principal, Mr. Grey, and Dome, his assistant. Their goal, I will later learn, is to protect me if I'm confronted with being a tattletale—to allow me to sincerely deny being the one whose parents brought down John. So I'm genuinely unaware of the bright weekday morning, ten o'clock sharp, with the four of them—Mommy, Daddy, Grey, and Dome—sitting around in the office with the big teak desk and the sports trophies. Here, apparently, Dome says something about how a difficult adjustment to boarding school is perfectly normal. Mommy will fume about how I have visibly lost weight and my grades have slid. Grey remarks about high school being tougher than primary school; Daddy replies, cowboy-style, John Wayne in his khaki Parks Board uniform, "Mr. Grey, you're going to live to eat those words." The turning point comes when my father threatens to sue the school if they don't move John out of the Standard Six dormitory.

"My sister and brother-in-law own a newspaper," he tells them. "One more illegal cricket bat laid on my son, and I hope you're ready for a public scandal." The two school administrators look at each other, then nod.

"Thank you for bringing this matter to our attention."

But for the forty of us Standard Sixes, the first sign that the world's about to shift comes when Dome asks the matrics to stay behind in the dining hall after lunch. We juniors are not allowed to stick around and eavesdrop—a prefect is stationed outside to patrol the area and shoo all of us away. But even down in that dormitory, as we laugh and toss collar shirts into laundry bags and leather shoes onto metal cupboard floors, indistinguishable fragments of Dome's booming voice thunder down to the dormitory across the lawns and flower beds—a distant rainstorm. And then later that afternoon, as we run between our clubs and appointments, the gossip begins to spread.

"Did you hear, hey? Neville got called into Dome's office. I wonder if he's in trouble?"

"*Yissis*! They say John's been with Grey all afternoon!"

Shower time is strange, with John absent. There are no games, jokes, punching tests, or exercises. Even Neville gets out after five minutes—he won't be drawn on our questions about Dome and the meetings; he says John will tell us. So we have enough time to shower slowly, without wriggling like eels. And then during study hall, for the first time we're supervised by a teacher, Mr. Van der Merwe. So there are no finger jacks, nor does anyone have to stab a geometry compass at high speed between his own spread fingers. What's going on? This is like a different boarding school.

After study hall, we walk back from the dining room with our satchels slung over our shoulders—and then, as we enter the front doors of the dormitory, there's John waiting for us: a forlorn figure in a white T-shirt and black boxer shorts sitting at the edge of a blue-and-white-checkered bed.

"Meeting, Standard Six," he says softly, as we file in.

Something's wrong. He has never been quite like this: so loose, flaccid, and exhausted. He looks down at the floor and does not meet our eyes. His long arms dangle. What has happened to him? He looks grief-stricken, like someone who's lost a parent or a girlfriend. My stomach tightens—this cannot possibly be good. Every time before this when he's been upset about something, it's always led to some catastrophe

"I have some bad news for you," John says to us now. He sighs. Do I imagine it, or do I hear a note of wounded bravado creep into his voice—a vague rage that begins to condense in his syllables and harden his vowels, consonants, and phonemes? My heart speeds some more. Later, years later, I will wonder how he got to be such an angry teenager. Was there a father in the background of his childhood, lashing him with the army belt and leaving far too many glasses full of whiskey bitters and ice on the end tables?

"Sorry to say," John continues now, "but some people have apparently been complaining to their parents about the way Neville and I have been treating you." Does he glance at me, for an instant, when he says the words "some people"? I feel a prick of guilt and fear: *Surely not. I asked them not to.*

A murmur of outrage begins to rise up among us Standard Sixes. For ten weeks now, we have been subjected to John and the matrics' worldview: we are trying to prove ourselves as a group. We are tough; we can handle punishment. Sissies, *dooses,* poofters, and rats—these are our problem, not the Johns of this world. It is crybabies who make the matrics disrespect us, make them think we don't have it in ourselves to survive.

"What the fuck," says one boy.

"Bloody snitches," says another.

Are they putting on masks? Or have John's ideas by now so thoroughly permeated their consciousnesses that they have adopted them as their own?

"That's not the way Dome sees it," John says. So he *did* get into trouble with Dome. "Dome says—he thinks—" John's voice acquires a throttled quality, and he looks down at the floor. Then he seems to pull himself together. "Dome thinks I've been a bully and a really bad prefect. He told Neville and me we're not to lay a hand on any of you for any reason. He says if he hears of anything like this again, I'll have to take the prefect braid off my blazer and move back into a normal room in the matric passage."

Is he lying? In the moment the thought does not cross my mind. Later, though, replaying all this, I won't be able to stop myself wondering: has he already been told he's being transferred to a senior passage, where if he tries to bully his charges he'll have to fend for himself in a fistfight?

"What's going to happen, sir?" This is Anton—one of the bigger boys. I like Anton, as does John. He has the frank, open face of a sugar farmer's son. When his family delivers farm produce, he throws impromptu parties on his bed; we are all invited to gobble down bananas and bite into wedges of orange.

"Oh, detentions," replies John. "Dome's orders. A full afternoon with me for minor offences, instead of finger jacks. Three afternoons for big things, instead of a normal hiding." Is he telling the truth now? Or has he been planning all this manipulation ahead of time?

Either way, stunned outrage builds among us. A restless, confused fury, first at the unfamiliar, presented to us like this so brutally, and second at the draconian harshness of this idea—so many detentions? We will be spending our lives in the dormitory, confined to our beds. Even for someone like me, who hates jacks even more than the average boy, this is awful. The walls seem to press down on me.

"That's unfair," says one boy. "Dome's fricking—nuts!"

"I hate this," says another. "It's much worse than jacks, I say."

"Still," John says, sighing, "that's the way it's got to be. Unless—" He pauses and frowns. Is this where a new thought crosses his mind? Or has he hatched this ahead of time? "Unless, Standard Six, you really feel strongly about this."

Feel strongly? Hell, yes, we feel strongly! What does he think, that we want to spend hours looking at the ceiling?

"Sir, jacks are much better!"

"We should have jacks!"

For my part I don't say anything. For all those evenings on my bed, chatting with John, I still don't enjoy being beaten. Sure, there's a part of John in me: for a long time I've wanted to be stronger, manlier. But, now, at this moment, still more potent than John, there's Daddy: *He's a bully, Glen, and you shouldn't feel you have to listen to him.*

"Well," John says. He stops and ponders here, weighs up options. "I wonder . . . come to think of it, Dome couldn't really object if you *chose* to be jacked, could he?"

He is still deadpan, nonchalant. Happy, even; he is starting to smile; he is getting some of the old boyish spark back in him, the wild anarchic springiness. Part of me notices he still doesn't look at me, and I'm relieved.

"No, he couldn't," someone says.

"It'd be our choice," says another.

"Yes, that's what I think we should do," says John. "How about if you do something wrong, you choose between jacks or detention. If you choose jacks, you'll have to sign something, though—a release, in case Dome blows a gasket. No way Dome can argue if you sign a fricking *waiver,* hey?"

Waiver: as if this scrawny seventeen-year-old cricketer has already stepped into the world of high finance and donned a suit.

"Would you like that?"

"Yes!" we roar.

"Screw Dome!"

"Actually," John says then. "How about—" He pauses, raises his eyebrows, looks out the back window towards the zinc roofing over the walkway. How long does he wait? "How about if I just give you your jacks ahead of time? We could keep a record of them—a kind of jack bank. You could make deposits into an account. When you do something wrong, we could deduct from that." Apparently as an afterthought, he adds: "I could even pay you interest, just to reward you for your bravery. Two jacks tonight, and you get three jacks deposited in the bank. Four, and you get six of the best, valid from me or Neville."

More chatter and discussion. Opinions seem to be divided on this one. This, it must be said, goes a good step or two beyond jacks instead of detentions; this goes into the realm of hypothesis and possibility, of probable and improbable outcomes. Some of the boys, however, immediately regard it as a good deal.

"It's almost guaranteed we'll do something wrong," says one. "Look how often we get jacks already, man! I'll have used up my deposits by the weekend."

Others of us are not so sure.

"Who says?" I point out. "You might never do anything wrong."

Still John doesn't look at me. What I'm saying is of course cowardly and sissyish. John must see right through me: I am reasoning out of fear rather than rational self-interest. I am being my father's and mother's son. But John still doesn't react. He doesn't lose his temper at me, tell me I've learned nothing from him— he is as nonchalant as I've ever seen him. Later I'll wonder at the source of this marvelous serenity, so soon after his talk with the headmaster.

John has a notebook handy—a soft-covered accountancy one, with a dense grid of blue lines and a red margin. Bookkeeping is one of his six matriculation subjects; while we deliberate in the dormitory, he sits at his desk ruling lines across the page to create accounts for each of us. All he intersperses in our conversation is the occasional reminder: "Remember, Standard Six. This is completely voluntary. I don't want anyone putting pressure on anyone else. Just like a normal bank—nobody *has* to make money on their investments."

At last Rodney, a boy a year or so older than us, volunteers to take four jacks. John shows him where to sign in the brown notebook, in the column that says "Freely Chosen." There are three more columns in the book: one neatly labeled "Jacks"; the other "Interest Accrued"; and the third, offset to the right, "Running Total."

Rodney bends over in front of all of us, in his checkered boxers in which he sleeps. In the time that we have been ruminating about the jack bank, most of us have changed into our night clothes. John whacks him four times, hard, with the cricket bat. Rodney's face contorts with the pain, as our faces usually do when we get beaten, but then when the hiding is done, he stands up, rubs his buttocks, and laughs.

"Six of the best, with interest!" he whoops, high-fiving two of his friends. John laughs, too. "Pretty *kuif*," he says. "Good job." Such is the power, it seems, of consent.

Next a boy named Sven volunteers for four. Then Graham does the same. Then Anton, the blond farmer—he gets a total credit of nine in the jack bank. John goes into his room and gets one of his medals. He drapes it around Anton's neck and raises Anton's fist.

"Check this *ou!*" John says. "He's stunning, hey! He's ready for anything Dome could give him—even Grey. I say, even if the *terris* got hold of him on the border and tried to pull out all his fingernails I think he'd beat them."

There is, of course, no greater compliment in our world than being able to overcome terrorists. So now a competition ensues to equal Anton's achievement. Rodney makes a second four-jack deposit, to make his total twelve, so he can get the medal. Ten o'clock rolls around, and the lights get turned out. In the dark, though, more boys, caught up in the excitement, ask to make deposits. People jump up and down. They giggle and laugh. I, on the other hand, get into bed. I look at some of my friends—at James, the redhead from Graskop; Nick, the brainy blond who sleeps in the section ahead of me. They, like me, aren't lining up—for some of us, at least, this still seems crazy, stupid, and ridiculous.

As I doze off, snatches of conversation mingle with the crash of the cricket bat—trees splitting in a summer berg wind; cumulo-nimbus clouds rumbling on smudged horizons.

At some point Neville returns. Through my groggy half-sleep I hear both the prefects' voices raised in argument. Neville says "Dome" several times, and "prefect badge"; John replies with "joke," "fun," and "voluntary." Neville must have left again, because silence descends. I fall back to sleep; do I hear the usual stray dogs bark-ing? Do I dream of thunderstorms causing klipspringers to dart into their rock hollows? Then, suddenly I'm awake again. John is right next to me, jacking my neighbor, Jacques, with whom I some-times share chips and talk running and tennis. Whack! The cricket bat lands on Jacques's blue pajamas with thin black stripes. Jacques moans, straightens up. *Yissis!* John laughs at him. *Come on, Jacques!* He jacks Jacques again. And again. And then some more: eight times. How many blows does Jacques take in total? At the very end he lets out a choking sound, like an animal being stran-gled, and he falls down on his bed. The boys applaud.

"Three cheers for the champion!" John says. I look over at Jacques. Even he is getting up again. He seems fine, nods at me as if to say so. Then John spots me. "Do you want to deposit any-thing, Retief?"

"Come on," says Martin, a boy who sits with me sometimes at recess. "Don't be a sissy. They're not as bad as real jacks."

"Yes, Retief," says Anton. "You should do it, too. It's not so bad."

They seem to be picking on the holdouts. Across from me, someone's pestering James, too, to volunteer for at least two, the minimum to qualify for an interest payment. Nick's being left alone—he's fast asleep. But on the other side of the row of lockers, I can hear several other boys trying to persuade someone—André, perhaps?—to take as many as he can.

"Who's all put jacks in?" I mumble.

John stands next to my bed and leans both his foot and the

cricket bat against it. He does not answer my question. Did he hear it? Someone else—Jacques, maybe—says something like "everyone," but I'm focused on John, who seems lost in thought. At last he says, with a hint of sadness: "*Ja*, Retief, hey. You and I—we've come a long way."

The tiredness seems to have descended on him again. He rests a hand on my shoulder. What is he sad about? It is as if something has drained out of him. "You're not the same person you were when you came in here. I like you. I've told you many times. Even when you've been a sissy and an idiot, I liked you, man. But I look at you, Retief, and I think, that *oukie* really doesn't like me."

Now my heart stops. *He knows.* How he found out, I have no idea. But he's figured out about the phone call to Daddy.

I begin to protest, "No, sir, what are you talking about," but John shakes his head for me to keep quiet. "No need." Then he says: "Come on, Retief. Are you sure you don't want to make a deposit? Just because I like you, I'll give one to one as an interest rate."

Jacques offers up a howl of protest from the neighboring bed: "One to one! That's unfair!" But John hushes him with a finger on the lips. Now the dormitory quietens. A muted drama is unfolding. John really wants to hammer me tonight. They can sense this. I can, too. But John seems calm—not at all vengeful or aggravated. He gently sits down at the foot of my bed, places a hand on my feet. Have the last ten weeks been building to this?

"Only if you like, man," he says.

Part of me really doesn't want him to thrash me. I just want to curl up in the tightness of the sheets and fall asleep again; I want John to leave me alone. Yet something wild and magnetic is also drawing me toward him, something crazy, primitive, and self-destructive. *Show him that you're worthy.*

"Three for two," John says then. "Four jacks, and you'll have ten in the bank—only two less than your friend Jacques here."

"Retief!" yells Jacques. "You're such an idiot! Why wouldn't you do it?"

"Retief!" echo the others. "Don't be a *doos!*"

But still I resist. It's a standoff: perhaps one minute, perhaps a minute and a half, me with the blanket up under my chin and my eyes focused vacantly on John's white T-shirt as I quietly shake my head, John asking me if I am sure about this, me saying yes. Are these my last moments of childhood? Of mere brushing against the world's jack banks—rather than being wrapped up in them? The others keep shouting for me to do it. Martin asks, "Why *not*?" But at last John squeezes my shoulder and gets up.

"It's okay, Retief." He sighs. "We're both all right, you know. We're going to be just fine."

He turns around, apparently finished with me, but now his words—something about the concepts of *all right* and *fine*—have unlocked a casket of desperation in me. I still don't have language for this despair, this hopelessness. It will be years before I look up the word "homosexual" in the encyclopedia, let alone link it to the idea of "nothing wrong"; more time still before I wrestle with apartheid, authoritarianism, patriarchy, and cycles of violence. It will be even longer still before I try to piece together the complex flux of emotional currents in this interaction: the seventeen-year-old boy, perhaps gay or bisexual, filled with both love and hatred for the twelve-year-old who so reminds him of himself; the desire to bash out of me the sexual traits that fill him with disgust. All I know now, in this dormitory, is that some mysterious umbilical cord links me to John, and that this somehow makes it blindingly imperative that, right now, I win his approval.

The boys all cheer. "*Lekker*, Retief!" they shout, when I throw off the bedclothes and stand up. Rodney hands John the exercise book, opened to the page with my account.

"How many, Retief?" Rodney asks me.

I pause and think. "Six," I am about to say, thinking that this will get me the medal, plus enough jacks stored up to keep me safe for several weeks; but then I remember what six jacks feel like, and my cowardice gets the better of me. "Four."

"Four," John repeats. He points at my bed. I bend over the mattress with my hands clutching at the far metal rim. John pulls down my boxer shorts.

"Since you're getting so much credit, this hiding should be *kaalgat,* don't you think, guys?" he asks the others, and they nod.

One. Two. Three. Four. As always, the hiding is excruciating. My pelvic bone, just above my groin, is knocked up against the bed rim so severely it leaves crushed-leaf bruises beneath my stomach. I gulp down my tears. Then I pull up my pants and shake John's hand. John writes down a total of ten jacks in the bank. "Good job," he says, and rubs my hair one more time. "I'm proud of you." And self-esteem rises in my throat, as sudden and unbidden as grief.

Next afternoon after lunch, he and all of his possessions are gone. We reenter the dormitory and see Patrick, the affable head boy of the school, busy moving his clothes, books, and tennis rackets into the room.

"*Ja,* John's been moved," Neville confirms, when we ask him. "He was a crazy bugger, I say. Me and Patrick, we are your prefects now—no more of those funny perverts' games. Just work and play and normal stuff."

"But what about the jack bank?"

This is, of course, the critical question. We have thrashings written down in blue ballpoint ink, with signatures. We have a contract.

But Neville and Patrick laugh at us.

"You fucking idiots," Neville says. "Nobody else here cares about the jack bank. And we aren't allowed to jack you anymore, anyway. From now on it's just detentions."

"He should be kicked out of the school," Patrick adds. This is the first time I've ever heard anyone say this so directly. Neville's nodding as Patrick says this: why, if he agrees with this view, didn't he say something when John was here? "And as for you boffins—" Here Patrick looks at me, the kid with a reputation for bookishness. "You should all be sent to a special school for dummies."

We are twelve and thirteen years old and have just lost our hard-earned life savings. At first we are furious and outraged: Hirre, *man, but John really pulled a blind one on us!* At our age, however, losses, whether financial or otherwise, do not weigh as heavily on us as they do on grown-ups. We grumble and complain, but then as the weeks go by and we no longer see John—transferred to another passage, he steers clear of the Standard Six dormitory—we gradually forget about our deposits in the jack bank.

Beatings continue to be a part of boarding school life. While Neville and Patrick don't administer them, the other matrics do: if one fails at a skivvying task or simply looks at a matric in the wrong way in their passageway, one can be knocked about. The usual code applies here, namely that the dangers of ratting far outweigh any advantage from reporting older boys' misconduct.

Within a week or two of John's transfer, the teachers stop supervising evening study halls. Presumably it is not part of their paid contracts. Soon it is back to clouting parsed fingertips for infractions, to assigning jokes and pranks with sit-ups and absurd body contortions.

The following year, when the forty or so of us move into the Standard Seven passageway, our next two prefects jack and punish almost as much as John did. Put immature adolescents in charge of younger boys' discipline, and the results will tend to be Abu Ghraib, the Milgram and Stanford experiments, *Lord of the Flies.* As the years go by, we move from being victims to perpetrators. It becomes our job to control the incoming Standard Sixes, and of course we do so using the ingrained tools—we jack, strip, and humiliate. As in a Hindu parable of reincarnated foolishness, this is what's meant to continue to happen to us: bullied and then bullying, all the way through high school, military basic training, and then the whites-only conscript force, where, armed with tanks and rifles, our job will be to control forty million black South Africans. This is the treasury of cruelty that has opened its doors to me, at twelve going on thirteen, in this redbrick school in that jacaranda-lined valley town: the opportunity to buy into a reservoir of evil and violence, whose annual returns seem steady and lucrative, or to look elsewhere, for as-yet-unknown dividends and profits.

Best Friends

James, my best friend—what an enigma he is! A week or two ago, the two of us got permission from Dome, the assistant headmaster, to go shopping in town together. We cooked up some excuse. Probably we played the game reserve and timber farm cards:

"Oh, sir," I would have said. "There're no barbers in Skukuza. I need a haircut—it's the rules. Look, my hair is almost over my ears. Can I go into town?"

My Auntie Lois, the one who co-owns the community newspaper in the nearby strip mall, is fortunately also manipulable. I think she still feels sorry for me, from the days of John and his jack bank. She always says things like, "Wow, but you really had a rough beginning to your Standard Six year, Glen." Now, since John moved out, things have become much easier in the dormitory—the matrics are not supposed to enter there, and Patrick, John's replacement, never beats us. But on the day James and I went to town, Auntie Lois gave me forty rand. Forty! On top of our regular pocket money, and even after the haircuts, it was enough to buy milkshakes in the Wimpy Bar opposite the shopping center . . . to loiter in the Pick 'n Pay and drink the Juicy Lucy daily specials: freshly squeezed papaya and passion fruit . . . to buy Peppermint Crisps and Smarties and Cadbury's Aeros.

Was it on the way back home, on the walk across the stream and past the neat suburban houses, uphill to the school, that James noticed the sign advertising *Aida*?

AIDA ON SHOW, it said, in embossed blue-and-white lettering, on a rectangular metal placard on someone's front lawn.

And a block later, another sign: AIDA. Then a third: AIDA.

"What's *Aida*?" I asked James. The name seemed vaguely familiar: perhaps a song on Mommy's favorite record, a collection of opera's greatest arias sung by the likes of Mimi Coertse, Mario Lanza, and Nana Mouskouri. Or perhaps I'd overhead Grandpa Retief talk about it one day at a family gathering.

"*Aida*!" he replied. "That's a Verdi opera. It's stunning! It's one of the greatest pieces of music ever. We should see it!"

This is one of many things I like about James: from his Scottish mother, who grew up around art museums and symphony halls, he knows about things I find exotic: impressionist painters and classic Ming vases and playful limericks.

"Let's find out where it is!"

We ask around in the strip mall, but Auntie Lois is surprised: "Nothing like that ever comes to this little town unless Grandpa organizes it." In the end it's the Greek supermarket owner who smiles and breaks the news to us.

"Oh no, you are talking about those signs? That's for Aida Properties—it's the name of a company that buys and sells people's houses."

But even disappointment, when shared, even foolishness and ignorance, when laughed over in our dormitory beds, seem easy to endure when halved and divvied up between the two of us.

In fact we met at Standard Six orientation, right at the beginning of our boarding school careers, on that first weekend in the dormitory, after my hiding in the shower and my beating with the pillow slip filled with athletics spikes. John was still our prefect. Orientation spanned both Saturday and Sunday and included not just boarders but also teachers and day scholars, so it was a relatively calm environment, with orderly workshops, discussions, and activities. The event took place at a luxurious Christian camp about twenty minutes from town—a couple of dormitories with miniature golf alongside, a swimming pool with an artificial waterfall, and a fenced-off trampoline. Green, spiky aloes lined the hills behind the camp buildings and filled the air with a fragrance reminiscent of both lilies and onions.

Saturday morning consisted of social introduction games and lectures about the school rules. Then, that Saturday afternoon, for some reason I ended up eating lunch by myself at a picnic table under a flamboyant tree—a tuna sandwich, an apple, and me, solitary, silent, spooled up in myself. Hazy green leaves surrounded me. Suddenly, he came to sit with me—gangly, ginger-haired, and freckled, an urchin from a Dickens or Enid Blyton novel, utterly out of place in that parched, tawny landscape dotted with umbrella thorns.

I remember that he sat down at the picnic table, then blushed a shade of vivid coral so intense and all-encompassing—it went beyond his face and neck to his arms and hands—that it was a marvel to behold. He reached into his brown paper bag for his sandwich. Then, almost as an afterthought, he put out his hand and, without looking at me, said: "Hi. I'm James. Can I sit with you?"

Of course I'd seen him before. He'd been sleeping in the dormitory, a few beds down from me. We'd stood in line at the dining hall and fought for spaces under the communal showerheads. Yet I'd never especially noticed him. There was something so silent and self-effacing about him that his presence barely registered.

"Glen," I said, shaking his hand. "Where are you from?"

"Graskop," he said, referring to a town about an hour away. And that was how it started. Him, noticing something in me that attracted him. Was it just my palpable solitude? Did it have something to do with John himself, with the violence that had already been going on for a week or so—kindred spirits sensing a need for each other? At any rate, we struck up a conversation about teachers and classes, favorite sports and authors. He told me about his Scottish mother and his older sister—his father had died when he was two years old; the three of them live alone on that timber farm in the hills. I regaled him with anecdotes of the game park.

The rest of the weekend we sat together in lectures, joined activity teams to work out how to solve puzzles, and then, when it was all over, shared a seat on the bus back to the dorm. At school, John nominated us to carry duffel bags of equipment to the storage room next to the headmaster's office, and we both grunted under our breaths—two put-upon teenagers. That evening at cleaning time we teamed up to elbow our way under one of the showerheads.

As those weeks went by, we gained a reputation for being best friends. In the evenings before lights-out, we sat on each other's beds and exchanged Agatha Christie mysteries—I had never heard of her work before, but now I adored her sense of exotic grandeur and her gloriously convoluted plot lines. In the mornings, before we left for school, we traded music cassettes for our Walkmans: I was a Hotline fan, whereas James was obsessed with Pink Floyd, whose album, *The Wall,* got banned when rioting black schoolchildren began singing its lyrics. And then in the afternoons, before John and his friends got bored and began their pranks, James took me to the music room in the school hall behind the stage, that special room which he had a key to because he was a piano student. There, behind black silk curtains, high above the tennis courts and the dusty path that leads from the parking lot to the rugby field, we sat, talked, read, told each other jokes, and played tunes on the piano—sometimes I sang along in whispers, so as not to reveal my presence to outside listeners.

Once John knocked on the outside door, the one that opens from the back hallway onto the fire escape stairs. I will never forget what James did: he simply continued to play and pretended not to hear anything—an act of deliciously grand defiance. *Ratatat!* "Open up, now, or you'll be in trouble!" John bellowed. But he had no way of getting to us, or of seeing who was inside the room. In the end he had to simply give up; that evening, when he asked the Standard Sixes who'd been inside the music room that day, someone—Anton, perhaps, or Jacques—saved us by proclaiming:

"Sir, it's mostly day scholars who use that room."

Another time—a Friday morning—I had the chance to reciprocate when John, wearing his prefect blazer and gray pleated trousers, got himself worked up about the fact that James had forgotten to fold down the back of his shirt collar.

"Don't you know there are a million *kaffir* kids out there who dress better than you do?" John wanted to know. "Do you expect to get a job one day over them? Hey, Stroud?"

All the while this was happening, James's face, neck, and arms got redder and redder. He stared down at the ground, unresponsive. Unfortunately this quietness just seemed to get John more agitated: his hands darted around like sparrow pairs, his voice rose, and I noticed beads of sweat sliding down the back of his neck. By now the two of us both knew him. This could have only one outcome. Standing at attention beside my own bed, watching the morning sunlight flood in through the side windows and hearing a lawn mower start up somewhere below me, something about the idea of James being clobbered suddenly became unbearable.

I would rather have taken the strokes myself in all their bone-crushing intensity than watch James pinch his face shut and petrified.

"Excuse me, sir?" This was, of course, suicide; interruptions were never permitted during one of John's prefect lectures. Heads to the right and left of me, frozen in the "eyes front" position, turned and looked.

"What is it, Retief?"

"I'm sorry, sir, but I had a question I forgot to ask you this morning about Mrs. Eliot. She was saying to me yesterday—there are some math problems, sir, she said we should ask a senior about, and I was wondering if you, sir—could you recommend a Standard Nine or matric who might be able to help me with them?"

I thought: my ruse is so transparent. I thought: he is going to see right through it; now he is somehow going to use the fact of James's and my alliance against us. But, miraculously, on that morning, he appeared to miss the obvious: "Inspection isn't the moment for questions, Retief. You can polish my shoes this afternoon and sweep the dormitory room floor." Then he saw the clock: time for breakfast.

"Wake up, Stroud!" he commanded, folding down James's collar for him. "You're going through life asleep!" He slapped James across the ear—barely worse than a mosquito bite. And although James did not remark, either that morning at recess or later that afternoon when I joined him in the music room, on the risk I took for his sake, I knew that we had both, somewhere in our consciousnesses, registered that I would put myself on the line for his well-being.

Now the two of us spend reams of time together. Apart from the afternoons in the music room, which continues to be a refuge, we both join the chess club and the school operetta. In the latter we are in a scene together, where we toss a plastic beach ball at each other on a Parisian street. Behind us the two romantic leads, a male and female matric, look wistfully in our direction and sing about the innocence of childhood, about how one day when they are older they, too, want to have kids.

But on the actual opening night of the operetta—with the hall full of parents and grandparents, including Mommy, Daddy, Grandpa Retief, and Yaya, and all the teachers in the balcony—I throw the ball at James a little too hard, and he misses it. It bounces against a dark Parisian night sky. It flies right into the audience, where it bounces around three or four times until some kindly spectator throws it back at us; it smacks into the candlelit window of a brasserie before we regain control of it. The entire audience is laughing so hard that the lead actors have to improvise, talking about the happiness of Montmartre on a night like this that causes so many Parisians to laugh—the chortling in the hall crescendos louder and louder at each comment they make.

Later, Mommy and Daddy just smile about the mishap. "You were the star of that show without even meaning to be," Daddy says.

More surprisingly, at the hostel, too, that Monday, the two of us have become minor celebrities.

"Tweedledee and Tweedledum!" remarks Patrick. "The two of you should become a comedy team!" A gang of matric boys rag us that they'll give us a hundred rand to play volleyball on the lawn below their passageway, and if we break a window by accident, they'll throw in a bonus.

What has happened? We shrug off the invitations and the teasing.

"Ag, no," I say. "No, that's all right. No, thanks."

But the truth is, something fundamental has shifted. As with Dirkie Coetzee in primary school, two people seem to be better than one at breaking open a social world and defusing a conflict.

James and I even have the same religion—we are among the few boarders to get picked up by the local parish priest, Father Anthony, on Wednesday nights, and taken to an empty classroom where we study the catechism. We should be best friends naturally, or even adoptive brothers or honorary cousins, but I don't quite see it yet; not now, in the months after John leaves. That Standard Six year marches along toward December under Neville and Patrick's supervision. After weeks of training, I make it onto the cross-country team. As my marks improve, I'm transferred to higher classes. School becomes fun, easier, and as the weeks and months go by I am no longer so sure I really need and want James.

What is the matter with me? Why do I still so happily disappear into his music room some weeks—the metronome ticking on the piano top; the smell of dust and mothballs; wood composite wall shelves leaning downward on their metal brackets—when other weeks I reject him?

"Not today," I say, shaking my head.

He is—how should I put this?—graceless. Clumsy, certainly: when he tries to hit a tennis ball in Physical Training class he reminds me of young giraffes. What in the beginning I found charming now strikes me as bland and stupid: why does he always blush when he's teased about wanking?

"Tug on that," says Martin, pointing to some loose wiring on the ceiling of the balcony above us. "I hear you're a good wire puller, hey, Stroud!" Wire puller—ha ha!—masturbator! We all guffaw.

James never talks about girls; nor does he play any kind of sports. Worst of all, none of the other boys seem to like him. Apart from me he is friendless, or at least those friends he does have are worse than none: for example, there is Tony, an astonishingly effeminate kid who has latched onto James and me at break.

I have tried to get rid of this Tony, who lisps and giggles far more than seems decent and whom I'm embarrassed to be associated with: I fear if I'm seen with him it will confirm the worst things others have said about me. When Tony joins us I go pointedly silent and set and reset the timer on my wristwatch; when James invites him to join us in the music room in the afternoons, I sniff and walk off. Tony annoys me with the loudness of his chatter and the way his hands move as if he is swatting an invisible cloud of insects. His whoops remind me of baboon calls; his rapid-blinking eyes of a television test signal. He has a habit of hugging James and refusing to let go, as a kind of practical joke; when he does this, I clap him on the back of the head. None of the prefects like Tony: when John was still with us, Tony got beaten every day; but even Neville and Patrick get irritated with him and send him on more than his fair share of trips to the convenience store. When I've pressed James on how he feels about Tony, James has admitted he doesn't really care for him; given this, James's willingness to tolerate him seems a kind of character flaw.

There are other boys, now, whom I think I may like better than James. There is another friend—clever, tall Nick. In maths class we compete to see who gets the better score on tests, and in English we read each other our essay feedback. There is Stephen, admittedly a day student, and also in my maths class: he says his mother, a teacher at the school and a spiritualist, has summoned up ghosts into his living room. Jacques, my neighbor in the dormitory, is an old standby: although he likes cricket and rugby far more than I do, he does enjoy playing Pac-Man on a handheld console.

And then there is Paul, easily the handsomest of the Standard Six boys, with his Portuguese-looking olive skin and his nut brown eyes and seal dark hair. Wild, laughing Paul, who, when John was finally transferred out of the Standard Six dormitory, blew up a picture of John's face, drew a target on it, and organized a dart competition where the goal was to nail John between the eyes. "Jack bank robbery!" Paul yelled. Interestingly, Paul hated John, but John always seemed to like him.

After just a few months in this place, Paul already has a girl-friend, Stacy, in Standard Seven, a year ahead of us. At break he sits with her outside the school hall. Although she is somewhat on the plump side, and frumpy, she lies flat on her back on the dusty walkway down to the gym so that she can rest her head in Paul's lap. Paul, I think to myself, is more the type of person I'd like to be seen with. What's more, he actually seems to like me: one recent weekend when we had to stay in the hostel, he organized a domino game with Jacques and Nick and invited me to join in. Paul makes my heart speed up. When I sit at his bed and talk to him about Wimbledon tennis or Springbok rugby, I find my hands frequently brushing against him, feeling his biceps when he tenses them and inviting him to wrestling matches that end with him pressing my arms down hard beneath his knees.

Paul is pleased to have me join Nick, Stacy, and him in the corridor by the school hall during midmorning recess, while James sits on the opposite side of the school grounds with Tony. The four of us talk about how we can't wait to be in the army; we kibitz about whether Margaret Thatcher has male hormones in her body and wonder whether Reagan's Star Wars lasers can really stop Soviet missiles. On the day the conversation gets around to the new kind of dancing that Michael Jackson is doing in *Thriller*, Paul says, "*Yissis*, those moves look spastic, hey, but I'd dig to be able to do them. They say you tell what an *ouk*'s like in bed by the way he dances."

We guffaw and hoot. I lean over and slap Paul on the chest: we are all virgins. As Christians we plan to stay this way until we get married. Paul and Nick are in fact members of a popular born-again evangelical group that meets at the same time as the Catholic catechism. Paul has spoken in tongues; Nick has been slain in the Spirit.

They have completed questionnaires about what the Bible predicts for fornicators—the pit of fire in the book of Revelation—and have looked at pictures of AIDS victims, with ugly welts all over their arms and legs and ribs sticking out like refugees. In Catholic catechism the approach is more subtle. "The holy sacrament of marriage will mean much more to you if you keep yourselves pure until then," says Father Anthony.

Still, all this talk with Paul and Nick remains a world away from the kinds of things James and I chat about. Here, with Paul, Nick, and Stacy, there is no helpless, silly, giggling about renaming Hercule Poirot as Hercule Parrot. Here, there are no strange conjectures about girls' bodies: on one of the rare occasions James and I actually talk about sex, he tells me he'd heard it was very difficult, on one's wedding night, to figure out which of three orifices down there—one for peeing, one for babies, and one for poohing—was the correct one.

"Oh no," said Paul, when I told him about that one. "You don't have to worry, *ouk*. It'll be instinct."

Instinct: is it this that tells me to keep a certain distance from James, to take it easy with our intimacy? With Paul and Nick, I feel grown up, even normal. Here, it seems possible that I might one day, like them, ask a girl out to the movies. With James in our backstage hideout, I feel as if I am somehow erasing myself from the world, entering into a dream of twilight, dust, mimeographed sheet music, and piano sounds; locking out light, energy, and freedom.

It seems to me James understands all this. So I am genuinely surprised when, at the end of our Standard Six year, he casually mentions to me, as we both stand in line together at the dining hall, that we might want to apply together for one of the double rooms in the Standard Seven passage.

"Better a double room than one of those five-bed ones," he says to me. He is, of course, right. Those five-beds are awful, crowded and uncomfortable. In our hostel, being assigned to a room like this is in itself a sign of social failure, of not fitting in. And yet—how much more satisfying and appropriate it would be to room with someone else! Someone sexier than James, more popular.

The next morning, I ask Nick and Paul about their plans for next year, and Paul announces: "*Ja,* Nick and I have applied for a room together." It turns out that even all of our shared acquaintances, Sven, Clinton, Jacques, and Anton, have requested rooms in pairs and are not available for sharing. So, sulkily, I agree to James's suggestion.

But this is, in fact, the event that cements our friendship. Now, the two of us are welded together socially: in the mornings before breakfast, we remind each other what day it is on the schedule so we can pack the right notes and textbooks. We talk about everything for hours: about C. S. Lewis's Christian apologetics; about the riots that begin to break out that year in the Johannesburg townships. Perhaps because of our parents, we are more liberal than the other students: we do not blame just the black kids for throwing petrol bombs; we also consider our government responsible with its racist policies.

On the occasions that Paul and Nick come to visit, now they are by definition visiting us together. *GlenandJames,* they say to each other when they don't realize I'm there. Will GlenandJames have any biscuits this week? Have GlenandJames finished their homework?

At nights, when James has to write an essay or complete a chemistry worksheet long after he thinks I've fallen asleep, he jams his shoes under his desk feet to stop them clattering, so as not to disturb me.

He stacks his books carefully on the shelf. He tosses his clothes in the laundry bag before he leaves for the shower. I try to reciprocate, although I am not as neat as he is.

He shares with me his mother's home-baked shortbread. One

weekend he takes me to his timber farm to meet the rest of the family, the first time anyone in that hostel has invited me directly into his home. This farm has eucalyptus plantations and gravel firebreaks. From the verandah I can see the misty blue-green Drakensberg Mountains, repeating into apparent infinity, like a mantra. His mother serves me real cream and coffee in Victorian china that she inherited from long-dead Scottish ancestors. She takes me hiking to canyon views that make me hold my breath and think of the start of the world.

At the end of the year, when it is time to again request roommates, the two of us continue to board together—a pattern that will continue until we graduate. By then the two of us will have spent four years living together, in such close proximity that we can hear each other's pinch-farts after a baked-salmon supper and enumerate the birthmarks on each other's chest and legs. We will have shared tenderness and comforting touches on the shoulder when a teacher yells at one of us in class. We will have laughed together at Pink Floyd's gloomy, exaggerated anguish and at Jonathan Swift's modest proposals. In short, we will have discovered one of life's most sustaining pleasures, that of companionship of sensibility: a delight that can exceed so many others.

At the beginning of my tenth-grade year, Standard Eight, I reciprocate James's hospitality and invite him home to the game park to spend a weekend there with my family. They instantly adore him. David, now a ten-year-old fifth-grader, asks James to read him *Lord of the Rings*. The two of us form a relay team. James gets Sam and Frodo out of the Shire and past the cloaked Nazgûl that appear at the roadside inn; I read to David about Rivendell, about elves, waterfalls, and magical prophecies. David, once the infant crybaby whom I couldn't be bothered to play with, is becoming a sensitive, creative boy—much like Yaya, he is always reaching for a sketchbook, setting up a watercolor easel, farming silkworms in shoeboxes, or pestering Daddy to build a backyard pen for wild rabbits. By the maid's room, behind the washing line, he has grown a vegetable patch. He loads his pumpkins, corn, and watermelons in a wheelbarrow and ferries them around to the neighbors, who reward him with five- and ten-rand notes; there are jokes about David founding a supermarket chain.

James is singularly impressed with him. "He's amazingly bright for his age," he says. "He's the kind of kid who's going to do something special in the world." And David seems to respond to this admiration. According to Mommy, he's been having some social problems at primary school: an older kid named Stoffel persuaded some of my old childhood playmates, Hannes and Nico, to shun David whenever he was around. Now, David's eyes light up whenever James comes into the room. For the two of us, David plays back his favorite television shows—*Magnum, P.I.; Cagney and Lacey*—and shows us a handheld spelling computer Daddy bought him that speaks out difficult words like "exaggeration" and "dystopia" in an American accent.

Lisa, too, attends our boarding school—although on account of the strict segregation between girls and boys James and I see little of her. As an act of teenage rebellion she has dyed the tips of her blond hair black. "It looks so silly," Mommy confides to James and me, but I quite like the punk rocker effect, which goes well with her new Sex Pistols T-shirt. This is, of course, still long before I hear about Grandpa Retief and the trips to the horse stables. In Mommy and Daddy's lounge, with the hi-fi set and the fluffy yellow couches and the painting of the wildebeest kicking up dust under Mount Kilimanjaro, she plays James and me hard-core alternative rock of the kind her friends at the hostel like: Morissey and the Smiths; the Doors. It's a completely different sound from the innocuous, campy music James and I enjoy—Culture Club and the Pet Shop Boys.

"But there's no tune in any of these songs," I say.

Lisa shakes her head in despair. I am older than she is but so uncool. She has figured out the darkness in the world: for example, she despises Roman Catholicism. "All that nonsense— popes, men in dresses." She tells James and me about inadvertently summoning up a demon in her roommate's clothes cupboard. The sound of heavy breathing kept her awake for weeks. "I could feel the evil there. I could feel the coldness creep around the back of my neck." She shakes her head now; her black tips flick in the bright sunlight. She smells sour-stale, tobacco-soaked. She has been sneaking into the bushes at school to smoke cigarettes.

I do not think anything of all this. To me, Lees is just Lees, my sister: the two of us have told each other sensational stories since the days of pretending to see snakes in tambotie trees. As kids we stuffed elephant grass into river reeds and tried to smoke them. But something about Lisa's demeanor disturbs James: "She's angry about something."

One Sunday, my family has lunch with his on the Graskop timber farm, and James's sister and mother confirm this impression.

"Lisa doesn't seem to be all that comfortable in your family, Glen." What exactly do I do with information like this? I wave hello at Lisa when we pass in the hallways. I make a few ham-handed efforts to join her and her friends at break. But among her new crowd, these sly, rebellious, clever thirteen- and fourteen-year-old girls who lie on the concrete walkways by the English classrooms, chewing gum and talking about the size of Rob Lowe's bulge—here, I recoil as if from an unexpected mirror image.

"Lucky bitch," says one of her friends when they read in *You* or *Huisgenoot* about some Hollywood groupie who supposedly seduced her idol. They shriek with laughter—*bitch*—but I think, *disgusting*. Better, by far, to return to my own crowd, to James and

Stephen, sitting on the concrete embankment below the library. There, we talk about computer games. We talk about the *Guinness Book of Records*. Eventually, I hear about Lisa getting into trouble and Mommy and Daddy being called into the headmaster's office. One weekend she apparently snuck out of the hostel, and got picked up by the police for painting abusive graffiti on the walls of a neighboring high school.

"Oh, I wouldn't worry too much about it," says Mr. Stewart, the science teacher and running coach, one evening when Mommy and Daddy are at the school for a cross-country run. Even with her new smoking and drinking habits, Lisa can still outpace me at this sport. "It's all normal mischief, you know? Teenagers testing the boundaries, listening to their hormones. Honestly, I get more worried when I see the opposite happening. When a kid seems goody-two-shoes. Or when friends are joined too much at the hip."

Mr. Stewart looks at me as he says this. We are all of us standing at the little house next to the cricket field—me, Lisa, Mommy, Daddy, and then James, who is coming home with us again for the weekend. It's evening, shortly after sunset. They must be putting on some kind of barbecue for the athletes; perhaps there is also a night game—the white floodlights are switched on; blue plastic cups and polystyrene plates are stacked on the fold-up tables. I can smell meat—*boerewors* sausage, probably. Daddy drinks a Castle lager. I look at him, but he seems not to have registered the second part of Mr. Stewart's statement; he's still looking at Lisa and frowning, worried.

I glance over at James, who is carving out some sort of pattern in the dirt with the front rim of his blue rubber sandals. Finally, I look at Mommy. She has heard the whole of Mr. Stewart's statement and isn't happy about it.

"Kids develop differently!" she tells the running coach, half playful, half scolding. "My own father, Pa, didn't even have a girlfriend until he was twenty-eight! I don't think it's good for children to try things before they're ready for them." Now, she, too, looks at Lisa, but some breach I don't understand has opened between them. Lisa ignores her statement, which could hardly be more pointed. Instead she looks in my direction and asks, "Can we go now? It's getting late." James nods to this; Mommy says something about night accidents. We toss our bags into the minibus. On the way back to Skukuza, James and Daddy talk for a long time about Kruger Park geology.

Eventually, of course, the other boys in our grade begin to wonder about James and me. By now we are already towering Standard Nines. I have become copresident of the organizing committee for the matric farewell dance, while he's the school photographer. Where once the other boys just wisecracked about the fact that neither of us showed any interest in going out with girls, now they laugh with each other when they talk about us being best friends. When I join Nick and Paul for break, in the rain gutter below the main classroom building, with the winter crows cawing overhead and the glare of the sunlight off the windows, Nick asks me what kinds of girls I like, then looks at Paul and winks.

"I like nice girls," I say. "Christian ones." It is what Paul and Nick say they enjoy, too, but from me it's somehow unconvincing.

One Monday morning I report back on a weekend with James, where we slept on top of an escarpment mountaintop and woke in the morning to find our campsite a grassy green island surrounded by a wide white ocean of glowing mist.

"It was so beautiful!" I tell Paul and Nick. "Amazing. I tell you, it was like Genesis."

Paul sighs. He is single again, now; Stacy has graduated and taken up with some army guy. Paul looks at me and catches my eyes: "Sounds kind of romantic, actually. But if that's Genesis, then you guys must have been Adam and . . . !" His and Nick's eyes meet and crinkle with a wordless humor.

"Why are you joking?" I ask. But Paul won't be drawn. He just shrugs. "I meant exactly what I was saying, that it sounded like a nice place for a girl and boy."

The truth, although they act as if they don't believe me, is that I have no idea what they mean. James and I, latter-day Victorians, have never so much as hugged each other or kissed each other's sleeping head. When we see each other after a weekend when we've both been home to our families, we do nothing more than say *"Howzit,"* unpack our suitcases, and organize our pens and pencils. Sharing a bed at his mother's house, we sleep head to toe, as she instructs. Even meditating together in the early mornings as preparation for our respective Catholic confirmations, we lie in just our boxer shorts with our palms, stomachs, and faces pointed toward the ceiling, without so much as a glance at each other.

Although I do fantasize about boys, really I don't believe I can be gay or bisexual; that is a label that adheres to other people, to prancing Hillbrow hairdressers and glamorous Cape Town drag queens. If anything, I think I am just going through a stage caused by the fact that I have not yet been lucky enough to find a girl. Sex, at this point in my life, is something divorced from intimacy and tenderness. Sex is John's penis sticking out like a tree orchid, the steam billowing through the downstairs bathroom. Masturbation fantasy is a padlock snapping over a penis; it is Sven, naked, punching a younger boy one day in the showers and causing him to double up. In short, sexuality is something dark and secret, imbued with shame and violence—something connected to the jack bank, rather than the morning James and I slept together on the hill, huddled close in our separate sleeping bags.

No, I cannot understand in the slightest why people laugh at James and me. Not just laugh: nowadays, in the shower, some of our macho neighbors have started to horse around with us. *Whack!* goes

Tom's hand on James's buttocks, as he stands facing the wall and rinsing off the front of his body. James ignores this, even though the smack is hard enough to leave a big red palm print on his backside. Even when Will, Tom's roommate, sticks an index finger under James's balls and lifts them up before releasing them, James refuses to acknowledge that anything untoward is happening. I, on the other hand, do not react nearly so calmly. On the evening that Victor, a usually nice, polite Standard Nine, blows kisses first at James and then at me as the two of us stand drying by the basins, I ask, "Are you crazy?" And on the day the downstairs showers aren't working, and Dean, a tall Standard Eight known for being a drug addict, actually stands in the doorway of our room, grabs the front of his khaki shorts, and asks us if we want to let him join our special fan club, I let fly at Dean with my fists and feet and knees, wanting to break his long nose, slam his skull into the floor, and send a rib stabbing into his liver. How dare he? Our relationship is from Ecclesiastes, from a catechism verse: "Faithful friends are beyond price." Dean is smearing this treasure with his nastiness.

And, really, it couldn't be true, could it, that James and I are in any way like two married people? We who, at night, play 3D noughts-and-crosses until our eyes water? We who study each other's art work—me poring over his composite photographs, asking him how he managed to place his pictures of the lions' heads so perfectly onto the snapshot of the sandstone rocks, him asking me about line breaks in poems?

On a cool winter's afternoon my fellow cross-country runners and I stretch out our hamstrings on the upper rugby field. Suddenly we notice smoke billowing out of the school hall. Instantly, I sense James is in trouble: he still practices most afternoons in the music room. I get up and run to the fire escape by the tennis courts, where a small crowd has gathered. "Stroud!" they are yelling; somehow they have figured out it is him inside the room, playing the piece he has been practicing for the last week or two—by an otherworldly coincidence it is Vangelis's theme music for *Chariots of Fire.*

"James!" I yell, running halfway up the steps. James comes to the window, peers out wide-eyed, with that dazzled, skittish, impala-calf look I know so well. "Get out!" we all yell. "Fire!" I add, pointing in the direction of the hall. Up here the smoke is overwhelming. I cough and choke. A wall of heat presses against me. James disappears. There is a sickening, heart-stopping minute as nothing happens at all. Where is he? Should I go in for him?

"Get off there, Retief!" I hear Dome bellow from below. Then the emergency exit door opens, and James is safe, standing next to me. Something opens in me—some doorway to safety, love, and connection—and now I actually do move to hug him out of sheer relief. The unaccustomed physical affection makes him shrink away.

"You could have died," I say, and he nods, then runs down the stairs to the headmaster, who is still yelling for us. Back down among the crowd, I have to summon all my willpower not to break into tears; I do not have any idea why my sense of near desolation is so intense, as if I have come close to losing a reason for living.

It's our matric year; our last one. Somehow I have been elected a school prefect, like John before me. In a secret ballot, I have mustered the confidence of the student body as a whole that I will enforce the school rules fairly: my blue blazer is now trimmed with red and white stripes. I am aware that I only won this contest narrowly. A favorite teacher of mine has broken the school rules to confide in me that my election was close, and that several of the teachers, when discussing the results, were opposed to my appointment, saying I wouldn't be authoritative enough. But democracy won out, and so now James and I live in the Standard Seven passage, surrounded by thirteen-year-olds. Paul and I are coprefects of this hallway—James is too shy, and Paul's roommate is a Taiwanese student who barely speaks English and has been awarded honorary white status only because his dad works on a big state project. Paul and the Chinese guy are near the door of the passageway; James and I are at the far end. Paul and I walk up and down the passageway after lights-out, looking for illegal cigarettes, *dagga* joints, and drinking; we check to make sure all the boys are home when they are supposed to be and that the place is quiet. I don't mind it: the young guys in the passageway are for the most part polite and compliant.

Yet it seems to me, as the year goes by, that I develop a problem. A few doors down from James and me is a room with three rambunctious boys. Their room smells of tobacco smoke, sour and acrid. Admittedly, the school prohibition on tobacco is erratically enforced—some of the other prefects go so far as to send younger boys to the convenience store for Camels and Marlboros, the way John and his friends once did with us. And admittedly, I'm hypocritical: when my fellow prefects smoke and drink in front of me, I'm hardly bothered. But juniors are different. Perhaps I've inherited my mother's phobia of tobacco. At any rate, I stop in this room and screw up my nose in distaste at the rancidness of the curtains and upholstery.

"What's going on here? This room smells like a pigsty."

The three young boys dislike me—this doesn't require much divination on my part. Their leader, Waldo, is short, thin, and dark-haired, with a vaguely dissolute and perverse air. He is on the effeminate side, like James's old friend, Tony. On the way back from the showers he prances around in his towel, wiggles his buttocks, and bends down to blow kisses like Madonna in *Like a Virgin*. His mop of brunette hair has a fringe that sticks up like George Michael's: when he gets an erection, for a lark he carries his bath towel on his penis, as if it's a door hook.

I am always searching the three of them for brandy and cigarettes, even for shopping bags that might prove they went to town without signing out. It is becoming a bit like one of those addictive "Spot the Rabbit" cereal box puzzles: every futile shaking out of a fluffy pillow or patting of a blue-and-white counterpane only intensifies my desire to find solid proof for what I sense is there. Waldo doesn't even bother to hide his disgust with me. When I tell him to open his cupboard, he rolls his eyes, tears his lock open, and kicks the door ajar. When I shout at the three of them—"Quiet, Standard Seven!"—after lights-out they flat-out ignore me, and Paul has to come down from his end to threaten them with jacks or detentions.

"You have to jack them," Paul tells me. This is his take on the situation: the problem is that I never administer corporal punishment. For his part, Paul doesn't jack often: he saves his beatings for serious offences, like blatant insubordination. But when he does administer beatings, they are tough ones: he has a bookshelf in his room with a ledge he keeps empty, so the errant boy's head can be pushed down into it.

I have tried everything else with Waldo: I have sent him to the teacher on duty; I have forced him to miss weekend television nights in the common room, all for nothing: he is as sullen as ever. Now, one night, he oversteps a boundary. What exactly does he do to tip the scales? The detail is lost to me. Almost certainly, the offence is a sneering one, a *windgat* one, to use Paul's word. *Windgat:* an anus that farts all the time. Waldo is the perfect illustration, all puffed-up cockiness and sneering condescension.

So let's say I send him to Mr. Van der Merwe for making a noise one evening. Five minutes later he's back: probably he's persuaded Porky—Mr. Van der Merwe's nickname on account of his bright red face—that he did nothing wrong; I, the prefect, have it in for him. Let's say he pulls a prank. He looks me straight in the eye and then rubs his nose with his extended middle finger, so what he's really doing, even though as usual he'd deny it if directly confronted, is pulling me a zap sign, flicking me the bird. I've had enough: I'm sick to death of him.

"Six of the best," I say. "In Paul's room."

It's Paul's cricket bat, I use, of course: I don't possess such a thing. Waldo's head is stuck in the bookshelf; he wears white pajamas. Later, what I recall most vividly about the moment is the enormous, surprising pleasure. Violence is glorious. I crash the cricket bat forward with every ounce of my strength: Waldo's head knocks forward against the wood. He gasps; he struggles to breathe. On about the fourth blow he begins to whimper and cry softly. I do not care: in fact this satisfies me. He deserves this, the little prick—now he will respect me—the triumph in my muscles and sinews is sensual, physical.

What is it that makes me realize I've become John? Perhaps it is Waldo's helpless, kicked-donkey look, the way he leaves without making eye contact. Perhaps the dribbles I see on his chin: he has been unable to keep his mouth closed. Or maybe Paul's comment, a reality check:

"*Yissis,* hey, but you have only two settings. Either you let them walk over you or you *donner* them until they can hardly walk at all."

By coincidence that night I suffer from a stomach bug that keeps me on the toilet, with nausea and cramps. I crouch over the toilet bowl, but nothing comes up from my insides. I sit and sit, but the turds won't exit. The next day, James is angrier with me than I've ever seen before.

"What do you think you're doing?" he wants to know. "You're becoming a thug, an arsehole. *Yissis!*" I don't have much to say to this, except to remind James that Waldo has been making my life difficult for weeks.

I don't jack again, or least if I do I retain no recollection of it. The way I remember it, beating Waldo is, for all its cruelty and abusiveness, a highly effective disciplinary strategy. Now when I yell out at night quiet settles on the passageway and the fans of yellow light protruding from the juniors' rooms onto the orange hallway tiles flip closed and into darkness, one at a time.

It's the end of twelfth grade—what we call Standard Ten—and the matric farewell is coming up. This dance represents high school's social and emotional climax. After this will come university, military service, and then the job of building lives for ourselves: I am already talking about possibly moving abroad to avoid the coming racial bloodbath; he talks about returning to the farm, buying a house somewhere in these hills he loves so much and starting a family. For months, now, we have both been trying to find dates to accompany us to the dance. I have asked Fiona, a mousey, bespectacled girl in my Afrikaans class; she has rejected me outright. I have also asked Adele, a single epileptic girl who is good at hockey. She has said no thanks; she thinks I am a nice person and all, but really, you should spend your matric farewell with someone who means a lot to you, someone you've spent lots of time with and feel close to. Then, less than a week before the dance, James comes into our room, his blue eyes all lit up, a bashful smile on his lips.

"You're going to the matric farewell with Cheryl," he announces, referring to a red-haired girl in his art class. "And Joyce and I will be keeping each other company."

Joyce is another girl from his art class. Neither of these women, it must be admitted, is a hot catch for the matric farewell: they are fairly nondescript. Still, they are dates, *female* dates, and James has found them for both of us—nothing less than a miracle, or so it seems to me, for this ginger-haired boy with his erstwhile social anxieties and his no-longer-so-severe facial acne.

The torrid November night arrives. The four of us do, indeed, head to the matric farewell—James and me dressed, absurdly, like the other boys, in black tuxedos; Cheryl and Joyce are both in white, Afrikaner-style frilly frocks. But at the party itself, James scores an even more impressive coup: midway through, he gets invited first to hang out, and then dance, with yet another art student named Candice. Diva-like, Candice stands on her toes, in her cascading red dress and stilettos, on the dance floor, and kisses him, lightly, on the cheek. As the band swings into its bolero—the theme for the dance is Moorish nights, and the school hall, now repaired from the fire, is decorated with shining crescent moons, painted minarets, and palm trees silhouetted against a starry sky— the two of them twirl and pirouette, chuckle and sway, and clink their plastic punch glasses under the chandelier.

James and Candice, dancing together? Candice is the dark, voluptuous painter who throws parties with wine in her hostel room on the weekends, and has been suspended for skinny-dipping with several other girls and a couple of members of the rugby team. Candice pronounces her words with an aristocratic accent, like Princess Diana; smokes expensive, long, mint-flavored cigarettes with double filters; has announced in history class she has become an anarchist because she is inspired by the sexual views of Emma Goldman. How has James, with his beetroot blushes, distasteful freckles, and agitated hands, suddenly gained enough social clout to be specially pulled aside, at the matric farewell, by the school's most glamorous female?

"Oh, Candice and I have become good friends in art class," he says, nonchalant, when I ask him. "We chat a lot. She modeled for me once, for a photo shoot. We both like Marilyn Monroe. She's tired of hanging out with rugger buggers and athletes."

Photo shoots. Film star cults. What else don't I know anymore about James? Later, Cheryl and I stand outside the building, in the parking lot. She smokes a Pall Mall cigarette; at this moment, like James himself, she seems to have been transformed overnight into a free, sophisticated adult. "You really like him, don't you," Cheryl asks me. "Candice, Joyce, and I have grown to really adore him, too, over this year. He's such a talented painter—no one here has any idea."

I feel as if a whole dimension of James's life has been lost to me, a realm involving all of the elements of an appealing adulthood. Is this the way I should be living? "You and he are amazingly well suited," Cheryl continues, bending over to stub out her cigarette against a tree trunk. She is, in her own way, beautiful. Her hair, more auburn than red in the neon outside light, shows off the light flush of her skin. Her perfume reminds me vaguely of hibiscus. I wonder: am I supposed to kiss her? But then she says, "It's really wonderful that the two of you are so close." And she begins to head back to the dance.

Later that evening, at an afterparty at a farm near the Swaziland border, James and I get drunk together. Candice is there, too, along with Cheryl. It is the first time James has done this. I have drunk heavily on tournament weekends away with the cross-country team, but James has spent almost all of his life hidden away in his bedroom or in a darkroom or a music studio. For him, this tremulous, confused exhilaration is a brandnew sensation, and he cannot stop tittering and looking up at the stars, remarking on how strange they look—quivering, like looking at sugar crystals through jelly. Around us, perhaps a dozen or so boys and girls are in various stages of making out in the open, under a large canvas pavilion, on spread-out sleeping bags or crumpled tarpaulins. The air stinks of tequila mixed with vomit.

"*Yissis*," James says to us, staring at the petting and rolling bodies. "*Yissis*. I can't believe this."

I am also taken aback by the spectacle of drunken eros. Near me, a blond guy on the swim team pulls down a girl's shorts and pushes his hand between her legs; she moans in protest.

"*Yissis*," James says, "but this is a bit disgusting, hey." He frowns and looks away.

"People here are so trashy," Candice says, leaving to pour herself a tequila sunrise.

She doesn't come back. Perhaps she has run into an old boyfriend in the kitchen. Perhaps she is kissing him; perhaps she is chatting to a girlfriend while drinking brandy and Coke. Minutes later Cheryl, too, heads over to talk to a clump of my other friends: Paul is there with Tom and Will. James and I stand alone under a tree, perhaps fifty yards or so away from the others. Here, in addition to the liquor odor, the whole place reeks of vegetation: of mud, vine creeper, and coral tree bark. Perhaps it is the drink that motivates me, but something makes me put out my arm and hold him around the shoulder. I am stunned by how unsteady he is. My touching him is enough to make him almost fall over. I prop him up, and it occurs to me that the two of us have, for the best part of the last five years, been supporting each other like this.

James looks at me, then guffaws nervously.

"I really—*like* you, James," I say. The term that comes to mind is "love," but that cannot be right. Men do not love each other. "I'm—I'll miss you next year. Part of me—well, I think I'd like to come back here after varsity and the army, and maybe move into the shed at the back of your parents' farm, be family with you, sort of." I try to parse my thoughts, say exactly what I mean. "Family doesn't have to be—you know. It would just be nice to keep living close together, be a part of each other's lives." I am picturing the two of us, under a tree like this one, on the day we met. Without thinking about it, I lean forward and kiss James on the side of his neck, below his ear. The gesture isn't sexual—just light and affectionate.

James says nothing, but he does step away from me, so that I let go of his shoulder. A cricket chirps in the undergrowth. For some reason my heart thumps.

"I think," James ventures, choosing every word now slowly and deliberately, "that we should just be friends."

Just friends. Why does this adverb bother me so much? As if what the two of us have is less than the swimmer pressing down on the strange girl.

"I mean, I'm that way and everything, sure," James states, "but I'm just not into you, physically."

I do not register the full implications of this statement—the meaning, so obvious in hindsight, of "that way," the insistence that adult family is naturally and automatically linked to sexual attraction. Instead, I now simply shrug off his words.

"No, no," I say. "Me neither. Not at all."

A mental picture of a tin-roofed farmhouse somewhere, with James and me reading each other poems in front of a log fire, evaporates into the night sky.

"It's okay, James," I say, squeezing his arm, and I mean it—I really do not need him; I am ready to find my own way out from the life we have built together.

"I know," he says. "It's really fine, isn't it?"

The Castle

What was Frau Kunecke, the German teacher, thinking when she told my ninth-grade class we didn't have any castles in South Africa?

"Go to Bavaria!" she exhorted us, her Teutonic cheeks all flushed; her blond, shiny hair and skinny Barbie doll body giving her (although what did fourteen-year-olds in a Calvinist police state yet know of such things?) the aspect of a Playboy bunny, a millionaire's plaything to be fed escargot tidbits on a roof terrace.

"You should see the castles of the Black Forest! *Mein Gott,* but you have nothing old here."

She was wrong, of course: I could have explained to her even at age fifteen about the painted Bushman caves stretching back to the dawn of humanity.

But she was also wrong about castles. What she didn't know or care to mention was that citadels can come in many different types. And in all of them we can hide, safe, muffled, and fortified: invisible.

———

Fact is, I'm trying to get *away* from things like the jack bank when I sign up for this castlelike university residence, perched on the slopes of Table Mountain, overlooking the vast Cape Town coastal plain—a hodgepodge of highways, cooling towers, factories, railways, and houses, all sprawling out to the sea. Fact is, I think coming here will be a reprieve from violence: from corporal punishment and youth preparedness marches and fistfights.

On the face of it, this place could not be more different from the part of the country I come from—the sweltering savannah. It's the farthest geographical point in South Africa from Skukuza, which is in the northeast of the country, near the borders of Mozambique, Swaziland, and Zimbabwe. That old place was dry and hot, earth-colored—brown and yellow and ochre, dotted by umbrella thorns. It was at the center of a war zone, on the main route for the African National Congress guerillas infiltrating the country with their bombs and hand grenades: on the weekends when I caught the National Parks Board bus back to Skukuza, we were accompanied by armored cars; the downtown department stores sported guards standing outside them, with rifles.

Cape Town, on the other hand, is a three-hundred-year-old coastal city of Mediteranean-style terra-cotta houses, cute Victorian cottages, and, downtown near the cobbled Greenmarket Square, elegant white gabled Cape Dutch–style buildings. The largest ethnic group in this city—the mixed-race, brown-skinned Coloreds—are descended from the eighteenth-century Dutch colonists, the Indonesian and Malaysian slaves that the Dutch brought here, and the San and Khoi nomads who combed these white beaches for clams and abalone. They speak a dialect of Afrikaans I find spicy and musical after the clipped, proper consonants of the game reserve staff village. In the central city, street vendors sell spiced curry pancakes, with recipes originally deriving from the villages of Java, Sumatra, and Penang. The natural environment, too, is more reminiscent of San Francisco than of Africa. The mountain slopes looking down on the city are a brilliant green as a result of the heavy winter rainfall; the pines in the houses' gardens grow out sideways because of the wind.

Nor is this university, founded in 1829, before a European had even set foot in the Kruger National Park, anything at all like my old boarding school. Backed against the mountain, on its lower slope, these redbrick ivy-covered buildings have no burglar bars on the windows or lattice security gates in the doorways. There are no perimeter fences; students are free to come and go as they please. I can walk off anytime I like, down to Rondebosch station, where I can catch a train to the city; to nearby Somerset West, where my Uncle Karl and Auntie Lois now live; all the way to Durban or Johannesburg if I had the money. There are no more prefects standing at entrance gates asking me where I'm going; in fact, there are no prefects here at all, only elected student government representatives.

The residence hall contains black, Colored, and Asian students. For two or three years, South African universities have been permitted to admit students from all race groups, and this college has been one of the first to take advantage of that policy. This in itself is somewhat exciting to me—apart from the occasional, awkward "interracial get-togethers" organized by the Catholic youth group during my high school years, during which the different race groups huddled together in their own corners of the church hall, I have not really had the opportunity to engage with nonwhite South Africans as equals. I am looking forward to hearing firsthand from them about the political issues that James and I have been discussing for five years: Why the uprising? Why burn schools?

Hazing is banned here. So is violence of all kinds: fist fights, jacks, thrashings. The guidelines for the residence I picked make this clear: any forced humiliation, nudity, corporal punishment, or sexual abuse of newcomers are grounds for expulsion. There are people to contact—names and room numbers—if anyone violates this rule. This is not what this institution is about; this isn't an army school, although of course we white men will receive our apartheid call-up papers as soon as we're no longer receiving deferments to study. Rather, the mission here is "to be an outstanding research and teaching university."

So, on the day Auntie Lois and Uncle Karl drop me off at the castle with my suitcases and boxes, I am convinced I am entering a refuge. Surely here, in this walled-off rectangle built in the style of a medieval Oxford college, with arches running down the outside passageways and a palm tree in the middle of each of the two bright green courtyards, I can focus on studying English, religious studies, and computer science. (I am not sure if, when I graduate, I want to be something contemplative, like a writer or a priest, or something practical, like a computer scientist in the mold of my father.) Surely here, in this shared wood-floor room on a top turret of this fortress, with the view out to the Hottentots Holland Mountains—surely here I'll be able to forget for a time about the questions life has been asking me.

Such as: how do I *really* feel about John and his jack bank? The thought of it fills me with a mixture of leaden, sickening dread and tremulous, excitement: on the one hand, a dry palate and a belt of repulsion squeezing my chest; on the other hand, that contrary strand of exhilarating eroticism—me pushing Waldo's head into Ronnie's bookshelf.

Am I going to stay in South Africa or flee into exile to avoid the army? If I do go into the military, what will I become there: The sissy who gets stripped and tied to a tree for cowardice? Or the tough sergeant who fries a captured terrorist on a running tank engine?

In the meantime, who am I going to love? Will I find a girl-friend? Who will I be in the world?

I can't avoid these questions forever: that I sense dimly, even at age seventeen. But these days, when, say, I go for a walk through the library stacks just across the central courtyard from my new home, it seems to me I can at least delay resolving them. The stacks here are filled with something like a million academic titles: monographs on South African butterflies; ethnographies of Kalahari spiritual dances. The newspaper collection on microfiche alone runs back to the Anglo-Boer War. Surely among so much ink, dust, and learning, among wood-floor classrooms with fifty-year-old oak benches and scholars standing in front of green and white chalkboards—surely here I can focus on something else for a while other than jack banks? Something other than how sex, race, and violence have twirled themselves up together in my unconscious like a triple knot.

The first problem, though, comes when I meet my roommate, Bill. An engineering student from East London, he reminds me, physically, of my old high school crush, Nick. He has dark brunette hair and lightly tanned skin the color of yellowood. His eyes are umber; his body lithe and defined from his running and rugby. Worst of all, it seems he's something of a nudist: he quickly explains he likes to sleep naked and wander around in the buff in the evenings. His perfect penis dangles down between his legs when he lies on his back. His nipples are small brown coins, about an elbow's length apart.

Bill's good looks are an instant, unwelcome reminder of one continuing dilemma: my erotic attraction to boys. But then my first week or so at college brings another familiar prod of what I'm trying to avoid. The head student calls the year's opening assembly of all residents. The common room fills with the various kinds of boys who live here: the white, private-school contingent—probably a majority of the boys come from the families of rich private alumni who seem to all know each other from polo tournaments and country clubs. The white lower-middle-class boys like me and Bill, admitted only on the strength of our scores in the matric exams. And, most notably from my point of view—since I have never sat next to a person of color in a formal business meeting—the minority of black, Colored, and Indian students.

The beginning of this meeting focuses on mundane issues: noise rules, litter, pub hours. Perhaps an hour or so into the gathering, though, a black man in a trade union T-shirt asks to reopen discussion on a resolution taken last year, when the castle inhabitants decided to lock the front doors during political demonstrations.

"Comrades, we have new members of the house," says this young activist. "I think it's only fair to tell them they might be in the library, sitting at a desk when a Boer comes in and beats them on the head. Or they could be running around the indoor track when the teargas comes in and burns them." He coughs into his hand, as if just the recollection is prompting a reaction. "If this happens, we should warn them not to come back to their home, for which they've paid fees. Oh no, we should warn them they'll find the doors locked, because we are too scared to protect our brothers."

Chaos erupts. Twenty boys are all trying to talk at once. In an instant, a division is laid bare: deposits of conflict liquidated. White students: "We paid for safe accommodations. How is it fair to expect us to fight your battles for you?" Blacks: "We paid, too, and by preventing us from fleeing the police, you are denying us our rights."

"Residents!" shouts the head student, struggling to regain control. "We have a proposal to reopen discussion on the locked-doors policy. Those in favor? Against?" At the latter a forest of pale fingers pushes up into the lamplight. Bill, sitting next to me, votes against the motion. He rolls his eyes and whispers, "Stupid *munts*." Perhaps partly because his comment is so offensive, I abstain from the vote. The motion is defeated.

Afterwards, I ask a senior what actually happens when a protest occurs. His answer prompts a familiar crowd of cockroaches to jiggle in my intestines: "The cops, they seal off the whole top of campus, hey. Then, when they get the *moer* in, they just go after students."

It is, of course, another version of the jack bank. Police clobbering students with whips and billy clubs. Back at the station, the electrodes, the hanging helicopter, the battering until they break the detainees. I feel my usual combination of sheer, naked terror and repressed fascination: a falling sensation, the intuition of tumbling downward towards a ravine. Part of me is certainly sorry the black students lost this vote—one less place for people to run. Another part of me, however, is relieved. Once James and I closed a piano room door on knocking prefects; now a proverbial drawbridge has been lifted against something scary and confusing.

The sense of safety is illusory, though, for a little piece of the outside world has lodged itself a few feet away from me. Back in our room, Bill spends the rest of the evening complaining about the black students. He says: "I wish I could be a cop, hey. I'd make them go back to classes the way they're supposed to." None of my platitudes about freedom of speech—beliefs honed all of the way down from Dad's BBC broadcasts to my chats with James about detention without charge—sway him. He is convinced blacks want to turn South Africa into one of the catastrophes that litter the rest of the continent. He's supported in this opinion by Stephen, his best friend, who's had the misfortune, as he sees it, of being assigned a lone room in an all-black flat.

"Disgusting," Stephen says about his flatmates. "They pee in the damn shower. I think they keep a witch doctor in the upstairs room—I'm always hearing foot-stomping."

Bill is in many ways decent and good-natured. He turns his music down when I want to study. He clucks sympathetically when I say I'm the only person I know of here from the Eastern Transvaal. He even invites me to join Stephen and him on their expeditions to a student pub down the hill called the Puss and Pint.

But after this initial disagreement about race politics, within a matter of weeks our relationship unravels. He tells his girlfriend, Denise, that she and I are both too liberal because we are opposed to beach segregation. In a discussion about the cold war, he proclaims that what's needed is an atom bomb dropped on Soweto. Worst of all, he begins to cheat on Denise. When he comes back drunk from keg parties with girls he's just met, he has sex with them in his bed. He probably imagines I am asleep. Out of Catholic propriety I turn towards the room wall, but the rustles and groans are enough to fire my sexual imagination and make my dreams of him vivid, painful, and electric.

This combination of violent machismo and sexual attractiveness pushes psychological buttons and winds me back in time. Now in my dreams Bill, naked, holds up an accounting ledger and a cricket bat—even though he doesn't play any cricket.

"How much do you want to put in?" he asks. In the dream I am mute: I have lost my voice as well as my physical dexterity. My arms are stones. I wake with a sore neck.

"Surely Bill isn't so bad," says Mom on the phone, when I tell her I'm not as happy with this place as I'd expected—there are pools of puke lying in the bathrooms after a pub bash; the guys throw napkins and polystyrene cups in the toilets. "It seemed so nice from the pictures. Is there someone you can talk to about a roommate conflict?" But I don't know where I could move, and I don't want to make things worse with Bill by complaining.

One Sunday morning Bill stumbles into the room, drunk and swaying. He vomits into the wastepaper basket—a sickly sweet aroma like the walkway below the rugby field, where the hobos live.

"Shit," he says. "Sorry." Then I see he has a nosebleed. "Got into a fight. Some queer trying to chat me up. Bloody hell. Told him I wasn't into that, but he just kept at it. Pathetic!"

That night, I am even more edgy and anxious than usual, getting up several times, tossing and turning. What is it about this revelation that makes me feel as if I have something stuck in my throat, as though my lips and mouth taste of tin? Later, in my sleep, Bill bangs my head against a compartment divider in one of the old school bathrooms, saying "queer" and "sick poofter"; then suddenly it's me beating him up, or someone else—the dream gets mangled. I wake again, my heart pounding. Which is the most profound nightmare: that Bill would one day notice me checking out his body and attack me? Or that I would one day, like Bill, make myself feel better by clobbering the weak?

That afternoon—a sunny summer day, pigeons alighting on the outside sill, a wet salt smell—Stephen stops by and the two of them joke about the incident: *Hirre, but you were drunk, hey.*

"He knew what he was doing."

I keep quiet and try to read *Othello* for English class. Soon the conversation floats to more familiar moorings. D flat, Stephen reminds us, is so horrible. Jeez, but what is it in the blacks' biological makeup that makes them stink so much? And they are so standoffish. They don't give him the time of day. How envious he is of the two of us for living in K flat. Everyone is so nice. Look at this view.

It's in the midst of all this that the impulse grabs me. There is nothing conscious about the thought process—nothing remotely like, "Bill doesn't like homos like me, so I must move in with the other despised people," or "My values are different from theirs." Just: "You have a single room, don't you, Stephen?" He nods.

"Would you like to swap? I'd love to be in a place by myself—to study, you know."

Stephen's eyes widen. To him, this is certifiable insanity. "Just don't claim I didn't warn you."

The next day, because my aunt and uncle picked up the suitcases and boxes the day after they left me here, I have to carry my possessions in my arms: like a refugee crossing a border; like an asylum seeker begging haven.

So now I live here in the bowels of this castle, in its twilit innards smelling of water and mildew. Stephen was right about one thing: it is indeed dark here. My room, which has a small window facing a sunken patch of grass below a narrow tar road under the mathematics building, receives sunlight for perhaps one hour a day, around noon. The rest of the time it's overshadowed by mountains and buildings. The light coming in has the dilute quality of a screened-in porch. Outside my bedroom door, it's downright dismal: here is the small portal with the neighbors' doors, the staircase up to the toilet, the shower room to the left, and then, in front, the entrance to the courtyard.

Apart from the darkness, it's not bad here. The black guys, my neighbors, wave hello, but for the most part they leave me alone: after the bustle of K flat, the privacy is comforting. The pee smell in the shower basin that so bothered Stephen is too faint to be annoying. Nobody vomits in this place; compared to K flat, it's a paragon of cleanliness and quiet. Music stereo drumbeats get muffled by walls. Century-old wood paneling soaks up spillover conversations.

Since moving here I've become even more of a social hermit than I was at boarding school. I have two friends, it's true: Louise and Alex, whom I sit next to in English lectures. But I don't really see them all that much outside of classes, other than our study sessions in the library and our occasional chip roll and Coca-Cola in the cafeteria together, in the racket of the scraping chairs. Here in the castle itself, I've become unmoored, adrift. More than ever, I have the sense of not belonging here, of not having anything in common with the other students. I have begun to take most meals in my room instead of in the dining hall with the other kids, boiling water in my mug with my portable electric element for ramen noodles. Lunchtime often coincides with the hour of the day when the sun comes in. As I eat my cereal with powdered milk, my tuna crackers, or my packet of nuts from the tuck shop in the entrance hallway, I watch the dust motes glow in the golden column of light, bright miniscule hairs and specks whirling in circles, spinning on air currents. Sometimes I ask myself if they might have any message for me—if they do, I can't decode the syntax.

What is it about the dining room I find so alienating? Although I haven't yet formally studied the concept of socioeconomic class, this is a big part of the barrier. To stroll across the parking lot to the girls' residence where the dining hall is located is to navigate a quarry of gleaming, silver BMWs; pert, red Jeeps with tires the size of roulette wheels; sleek, shiny Mazdas and VW Golfs that would have caused heads to turn in the old game reserve staff village—or even in the parking lots of the farm supply stores near my old school. Here, in the castle, the boys and girls whose faces I recognize from English lectures all seem to wear imported Italian or French sunglasses. They sport trim, elegant, brightly colored shirts and blouses, with tailored khaki shorts—I feel underdressed in my tatty Pink Floyd T-shirts and my ugly black boxer shorts. They went to schools with saints' names, with which they all seem to be familiar, even though they are located at opposite ends of the country: "Oh, yes! St. Stithians! Great place!" They seem to have met each other, over the years, in private game reserves or on educational tours of Greek archaeological sites. Much of their conversation revolves around international travel.

"What do you think of Venice?" they'll ask, over canned green beans and dried-out cafeteria chicken.

"I've never left South Africa," I'll admit. "I'd love to go, though. I hear Venice is gorgeous."

"Oh, it *is*. It *is*," they'll croon. "And Paris, of course—Germany, too. Germany's much more fun than it gets credit for. Cute architecture. And German food's surprisingly good, you know? Schnitzel and—oh my God!—spätzle!" Soon, as we eat our bland sago pudding and lumpy custard—pudding that somehow tastes exactly the same as the one I've been eating for the past five years at boarding school—the conversation turns to culinary delights I've never heard of: stuffed cannoli—which is better, ricotta or chocolate? Bagels and lox. Thai curries with coconut cream.

To me, they might as well be talking about mathematical string theory. Listening to them debate how the New York Metropolitan Museum stacks up against the Louvre, or the virtues of skiing versus skydiving, I feel corny, parochial, and unsophisticated—Crocodile Dundee in his straw hat, trying to figure out how to use an escalator. I'm too embarrassed to tell them about tourist buffalo meat pies. I do not yet think of my background as unique or interesting. Once when I accompanied a group of them to a film screening in town, they laughed at me for staring at the night skyline and for being astonished at a movie theater with five hundred seats.

In any case, I love the solitude. I still attend some lectures and tutorials—not strictly required in the South African system, but I don't want to fail varsity and have to go to the army. I call my parents once a week or so; catch the train to visit my aunt and uncle in Somerset West every month. I'm not quite Jesus in the desert, but on any given day I will probably spend three-quarters of my waking hours alone, reading and writing. I now read Orwell, Woolf, Yeats, Rushdie, Camus, Sartre, de Beauvoir—all the new names I'm encountering in English lectures. I write papers, reports, and poems; letters to James, to Gogo and Yaya, to Mom and Dad. I masturbate in the evenings—this too is a glorious luxury: for the past five years of boarding school I've had to hide away in public toilets. I keep a diary every day now, ever since a poetry tutor told me about how writers and intellectuals keep journals. I find it valuable to document the feelings that stir in my soul, the moods that drift across my consciousness like cumulus clouds across the Kruger Park savannah, mysterious in both their growth and their movements.

March 21, 1988. Last night the strangest thing happened to me. Okay. All right. It's very peculiar. But this is what it was. (By the way, I hope nobody ever reads this diary entry. I'd be terribly embarrassed. But then what's the point of having a diary if you're too scared to write in it?)

I went to mass at the Catholic Centre. As I say, I don't really know why I do that. I don't like that mass there, in the house that's so plain and boring. Give me stained-glass windows. Give me some high ceilings. Do I even believe in God anymore? Sometimes I wish I could see him, experience him. It is so difficult to keep believing.

Anyway, I was talking about last night. Maybe I was lonely. I called Mom and Dad in the morning, and Mom asked me on the phone if I'd made any friends yet in the res, and I had to say no, not really, not anyone I can actually hang out with. I mean, there is nobody actually here. She and Dad suggested more clubs and activities, things like that. They said I had to get out, so maybe I was trying to please her. I don't think Mom likes the sound of Alex and Louise that much, since I told her last week they were a bit "hippyish."

Anyway, I stayed afterward at the Catholic Centre for coffee hour and most of it was disgusting. I hate James, that self-important trainee priest, talking about how much he despises the permissive society. Yissis. He hates this, hates that. Black revolutionaries—acknowledges they have a just cause but says they are looking in the wrong place (Marxism) for answers. He wants them to pray until the manna falls from heaven.

He disapproves of sex before marriage, of condoms and birth control, even of wanking! Parrots the old bishops' line of the seed being meant for the soil. I wonder if he ever does it himself? I asked him once, and he said no, although I don't know whether to believe him.

But then I got talking to a girl called Jill. She was very nice. You know—beautiful. Dark hair, like Mom, and freckles. She seemed very kind. She's studying sociology. She reminded me of Denise, too, clever in that modest way. We talked and talked. Then we went out to the back of the Catholic Centre and sat on a step there. I told her I thought she was beautiful. It was true. I held her hand. She let me hold it! My heart was pumping. She said, "You're so nice." Then I leaned over and kissed her, and she kissed back, with her tongue. A funny feeling. Just turned eighteen, hey, and the first time I've ever kissed a girl.

I certainly wanted more to happen. I wanted to reach down and touch her breast. I need to have sex with a girl, don't I? But I don't know. Something stopped me. There was a wall, a block. I kept thinking one of the people would come out of the house and into the garden and see us holding hands like that. "Permissive society." And then something made me say, "Jill, I don't think God wants us to do this before marriage."

She looked at me as if I was nuts. We hadn't even done anything yet except kiss and hold hands! "Okay," she said. Just like that she let go, got up, and went back inside. I suddenly felt intensely embarrassed. Hirre, hey! What must she

think of me? Spastic! And I just wanted to hug her and tell
her how lovely she was, but I couldn't even manage that.
What will the weather be like on the night I finally lose my
virginity? Sometimes I think I should go to a bloody shrink.
But other times I think, how would I even begin to explain?

And staying by myself, of course, in that little room with the
bookshelf, the wooden floors, the beige curtains, and the study
lamp, there is no need for analysis. Lying on my bed at noon,
counting the cracks and watermarks on the seventy-year-old ceiling, eavesdropping on the conversations of the people walking by
on the road above me, I do not need to ponder how I'm secluding
myself in a fortress.

Religious studies is my most difficult class. Maths and computer
science are relatively straightforward, as long as you keep up with
the homework assignments and make use of the tutors who sit in
the classroom and help us integrate algebraic expression. I have
done reasonably well thus far on my tests. Dad is especially relieved
about this fact, given that he views a humanities degree as a waste
of precious time and money ("They say a BA stands for 'Bugger
All,' hey?"). English is, of course, wonderful—talk of psychoanaly-
sis, feminism, gender-bending in Shakespeare, Emily Dickinson's
revolutionary use of the dash to convey the fragmented nature of
thought.

In religious studies the picture is different. There, I sit in the
back of a modern lecture hall and listen to my professors discuss
God, Jesus, Mohammed, Buddha, and Zoroaster from a scholarly
point of view. Religion, so they claim, is a sociological phenomenon
defined mostly by the way it promotes social cohesion. Whatever
the details of a given belief system—whether its adherents believe
in a personal God; whether the participant is advised to pray,

meditate, detach from desire, or go on pilgrimages—organized religion tends toward maintaining existing power relations. Thus, men's authority over women; Brahmins over untouchables; Popes, bishops, and priests over lay Catholics and parishioners.

This is only the beginning—me, sitting on the blue upholstered chair under the pale buzzing neon lights. Christianity is only one of tens of thousands of religious belief systems in the world. Its cultural prevalence can be explained by Constantine's adoption of it as the state religion of the Roman Empire. The Bible, too, whether Catholic or Protestant, looks, from a scholarly point of view, more like a literary hodge-podge than a letter from an omniscient creator. Genesis is a recycled story from the Mesopotamians. Modern archaeological scholarship has uncovered no evidence of the Israelite captivity in Egypt. Even Jesus, the son of God and the savior, is a recurring narrative: in first-century Palestine, claims of messiahs who'd been killed and then raised from the dead were plentiful.

All of this is so disorienting it's as if I can literally feel my preconceived ideas juggling loose and rattling around

"But what about the supernatural?" I ask my religious studies tutor, an earnest, blond, woman in her twenties. "Isn't there any objective way to evaluate religion's claims? Can't we ever figure out which one's right?"

She smiles. She is probably only a decade older than me, but she seems a thousand miles away in terms of sophistication and clarity. How must it be to proceed through life with such supreme self-confidence? I have never seen her ruffled or confused. "No supernatural occurrence has ever been documented under scientific conditions," she informs me. "In America there are prizes offered by famous magicians for anyone who can show any suspension of the regular laws of physics. Nobody's ever won it. Resurrections, angels, a heaven just beyond the blue of the sky—if you ask me these are just prescientific explanations. What's interesting to me as a scholar is what they give people."

"Prescientific." In this, I hear: foolish, superstitious. "What they give people": what does religion give me nowadays, all wrapped up in books and ideas, kissing a girl at the Catholic Centre and then telling her it was wrong for me to hold her hand? I call up my parents.

"I don't know what to believe anymore," I tell them. Probably I'm not talking here about the prayers I sent up to God at the time of the jack bank—the moments I stood on the top floor of the East Wing classroom building and felt kindness in the morning sun. Probably I don't mean meditating with James in matric, on my bed in my boxer shorts, breathing in goodness, peace, and light and breathing out fear, worry, and confusion.

What I mean is much more literal: whether or not Jesus is the son of God. Whether bread in the Holy Sacrament becomes muscle tissue, skin follicles, and amino acid when the priest holds it up; whether wine acquires cytoplasm fragments and T-cells.

Perhaps, I sense the profundity of the change that's occurring. "I will not serve," Stephen Dedalus says at the end of the book I've just been assigned in English. I have it on my bedside table, but haven't read it yet; when I do I will feel I am reading, in some profound if indefinable sense, about myself. Dedalus will be alienated from culture, religion, and even family. Is this more or less the same thing as locking oneself away in a turret?

"You were the ones who gave me this belief," I tell Mom and Dad. "Please defend it now."

But they have no answers for me. "I don't know, love," Mom says. "This is always just what I've believed. You've either got faith or you haven't."

That night and for the rest of my life I skip Catholic mass. Back in my room, I hardly register the extent to which I've just, to use the metaphor Mom will share with me in a couple of years when she tells me about her own struggles with faith after Lisa's abuse, been willing to let go of a concept myself as spiritually solid: I'm no longer filled by a loving being—brimmed up, like trees with sap. Now I, too, am more like a poinciana pod—easily blown around by a berg wind until I find the right place to collapse, crumble, and germinate.

I don't really think of my outside window, the one facing the grass and the street, as being the sentry box in the curtain wall of the castle—the logical spot for the world to reach back in and demand my participation in it. So on the day there's a knock on it, a loud, insistent rat-a-tat on the glass pane, and I see the tall, dark-skinned, slender boy in the fitted jeans, bright white sweatshirt, and clean Nike sneakers standing outside, out of politeness I open up.

"Yes?" I'm my mother ready to send off a Jehovah's Witness. But this guy isn't intimidated by my brusqueness.

"Hey, man," he says, "we're neighbors! I live there." He points to the window to his right. "I hear you through the wall sometimes, moving around. But no one ever sees you, man. You're like a ghost."

These last words, which could so easily be reproachful, are delivered with crinkling eyes, as if he's on the verge of breaking into laughter. I could get angry and defensive, but the truth is, he seems the soul of good nature, at this moment. He is all friendly curiosity, written onto his raised eyebrows; his wide, dark eyes; his oblong head, unabashedly tilting to get a better view of my room.

"Well," I say, "I'm here."

I invite him in. It seems to be the polite thing to do, as well as what he's waiting for: the done thing. So he walks around the building to come back in the front. In my room, holding a mug of tea, Aubrey—for that's how he introduces himself—strides around chameleon-like, his neck leaning first one way and then the other. He is as tall and skinny as I am: probably side by side the two of us look like stick insects, one of us burnt umber, the other pale ginger and freckled. His frizzy hair is neatly trimmed, barber-style, as is his mustache and goatee. By contrast my shaggy brown locks curl out in all directions, like Diego Maradona's. In my plain black boxer shorts and my holey white T-shirt, I feel as dowdy next to him as I do next to the golf-playing crowd.

But as he looks around my room, his face shows no disapproval—just fascination and intrigue, then puzzlement, then mild bemusement.

"Poetry!" he explodes when he sees the T. S. Eliot collections. "I don't read that crap, man. I like novels with *action*. Forget long descriptions. Do you know James Hadley Chase?"

I do not—it sounds a bit like an upmarket automobile.

"Brilliant, man! You can't put his books down. Where I come from, he's the main man."

He pauses at my French impressionist posters.

"I see you artsy. Yeah, man—I'm seeing you're one of the fartsy ones! Me, I'm a commerce student, man! I like business!"

I nod to say to him: yes, you are different from me. Still, I am enjoying this Sherlock Holmes performance of his—now he's bending over the rubbish bin and examining the tuna cans and noodle tubs and saying something about how I obviously don't like cafeteria food. Certainly there is no one who has taken anything like this kind of interest in me since I moved here. There is something refreshing in his frankness.

"Hmm . . ." he says, but doesn't finish his thought. Then his eyes narrow, making him suddenly streetwise. "You moved down here to be with black guys. Why, man? What's up with you?"

What there is comes out all in a jumble: the meeting at the beginning of the year, where we voted to not reopen discussion on the door policy. Bill and the atom bomb on Soweto. Losing my religion.

The drunken night, when Bill punched a guy—the way I tell this story, it is just because Bill enjoys fighting: some instinct tells me not to bring the word "homosexual" into Aubrey's immediate line of vision. I mention the people in the dining hall with their tennis teas and their holiday houses on the Garden Route. At the end I say: "Probably I just don't like people very much. I learned a new word the other day. Have you heard of "misanthrope"? It means a loner."

Aubrey looks at me long and hard. Then he leans his head forward.

"Interesting, man, interesting! You really don't understand yourself, do you?" He pauses, waiting for my reaction, but I don't give him one. "You don't know who you are." He stops again, scratches his goatee. I shrug: what's this guy talking about? But then he continues: "You sound exactly like a black guy, man. The way you talk—your worldview—you're exactly like us. You're not a misanthrope. Crazy! It's just that you see things as we blacks do."

What do I feel when I hear these words from him? Almost certainly surprise: despite John's accusation, when I was in Standard Six, that I was a waste of white skin, and despite isolated incidents since then, such as the rugby team's flushing my head in a toilet in Standard Eight for wearing a yellow ribbon to protest detention without charge, no one has ever said anything like this to me. Quite possibly intellectual disagreement—by now I have read my introductory social theory: *But I receive white privilege, so by definition I cannot be black.* I certainly don't feel any sense of racial insult of the kind that will strike me, years later, as a possible reaction to this statement: *Gee, thanks. You don't seem black to me, either—just human.*

Instead, in that room, what I do begin to feel is pleasure, flattery: *I know something the other whites don't.* Beyond this, the hint of something even more imprisoning. *Oh, I see. So* that's *what's wrong with me.* A postern that seems to open onto blue sky, but in fact leads to a parapet walk.

Not that all of this occurs to me instantly that morning, with the curtains open, sitting on my bed, drinking tea with Aubrey. Now, flustered by the sheer strangeness of Aubrey's statement, probably I just shrug again and mumble something about how my neighbors have been very polite. The two of us make student' small talk: What courses are you taking? How do you like your tutors? And then, that evening, when his neighbors Dumisani and Brazzo visit him, he calls me over to tune with the gang and glug down bottles of Castle lager on his room floor while he stands at his window smoking Marlboros.

But over the weeks and months that follow, the notion that I'm at least in some sense a black soul trapped in a white body—that I have nothing in common with my fellow whites, that politically, intellectually, and morally I'm a misfit and belong better with this group of guys, my new neighbors—becomes more solid. It expands out into chapels and turrets and gains the heft of stonework. Each new friend I make is a brick in this self-protective edifice; every conversation with Aubrey and the guys is one more tile in the spire.

In this view of myself, the main point of difference between me and the rest of humanity isn't any longer the thing that John once noticed in me.

It isn't being English in an Afrikaans village, or being an ignorant country boy in the city. Rather, it's that there's something fundamental about my values that sets me apart from my own culture.

Of course at one level this delusion—for that is how I'll eventually see it, as less a grounded act of racial solidarity than as a strategy to avoid facing my emotional problems—opens up a vast new world for me. So here we are, the four of us, sitting around in Aubrey's room at ten or eleven o'clock on some weeknight in, say, May: the months and seasons will eventually blend together in memory. With these black guys I've stopped caring so much about marks and lectures. I'm developing some attitude; I've stopped being such a nerd—now, I skim textbooks in lieu of listening to professors drone on about linear algebra. Here, tonight, is where I'm really learning something: holding a bottle of beer in my hand, breathing in Aubrey and Brazzo's tobacco smoke, just listening to the ebb and flow of the discussion—out of consideration for me, they talk in English.

Brazzo's the alcoholic philosopher. Next to him, on the wooden floor, lies a circle of beer bottles as wide as a cafeteria tray—"Eish, *buthi*," he says to Aubrey, slurring his words only a little. "You should read your Frantz Fanon, my man, and your Steve Bantu Biko. The solution to the black man's problems will never come from imitating the white capitalists, *wena*!"

Aubrey: "You got no idea what you talking about. Money, man! It's the poor man's only revenge." Although I might have previously entertained the intellectual possibility of society's being fundamentally unjust, this is real, concrete, unarguable: living people who have been mistreated. Communism is an option to argue about here, not a demon anymore to be defeated. Black rage is taken for granted; the discussion is about how to channel it. I find all of this bracing and refreshing. To me it seems real and truthful. Something in this anger of theirs connects with me, too—cricket bats and nooses made out of sheets—and I find myself nodding and seething, agreeing: *Oh yes, the poor have been abused.* In my mind, a dormer window opens; a loophole expands.

Or, say, on a Saturday afternoon we're bored out of our minds. We've hit the common room together, but we don't like the TV the whites have on—a cricket match. It is as stimulating as watching palm fronds sway. Soccer, that's the D flat sport: I have taken to observing the guys play on the field below the castle, in the dense, foggy winter evenings, under the floodlights. Dumisani, in particular, is sexy when he takes off his shirt to reveal his well-shaped sweaty chest, although of course I cannot yet actually think those words, *Dumisani is sexy*—homosexual is still something I can't be. As in childhood I once cultivated an interest in rugby in order to fit in with Afrikaners, now I become something of a soccer fan to connect with these guys. I buy *The Sowetan* newspaper to be able to talk about the football scores. When a D flat guy scores a goal or successfully tackles an opponent, I cheer and jump up and down on the bleachers.

Now, in the common room with the cricket on the TV, Aubrey says to us, "Let's go drinking." He targets a rich Hilton boy, an old acquaintance. "Jerome, come on," he says. "You don't need your car today." Jerome hasn't heard what Aubrey said to the rest of us, so Aubs lays it on: "I want to visit my mother. If I have to catch public transport, I'll be busy all day, Jerome, up and down, in a minibus. Just for a few hours?" In Jerome's bright red Golf, speeding down the highway to Gugulethu, the four of us roar together at his successful bamboozling antics. Aubs—he's a born business student: he's already fleecing the customers. Besides, privileged rich kids like Jerome deserve to be fooled, argues Aubrey. The rich get their money from the poor, through colonial theft; deceit's the only way to level the playing field. *Yes, yes,* I say. Am I forgetting my own racial privilege? I haven't thought through how I'd feel if someone lied to *me.*

That afternoon provides other new experiences. Here we pass through a comrades' checkpoint: a few spare tires along the side of the road; a teenager holding a petrol bomb. They hold up their hands; we stop; but then they smile and wave us through when the guys explain our purpose. Aubrey claps me on the shoulder.

"Sharp, man!" he says. "You like one of us, now!" And that *feels* right, *seems* true. A shift has occurred: I am being made welcome in a new place. At the shebeen, the informal tavern, I buy the three of them a round of pint-sized Castle lagers. I laugh with them and dance briefly with the shebeen queen, a tall, plump, middle-aged woman who ululates when she meets me and clicks her fingers above her head. "Welcome here," she says.

"Welcome," says Aubrey's mother, a shack-bound housekeeper on the day we go to visit her.

Welcome. One night, sometime that spring, I come out and tell Aubrey about the jack bank—the first person outside of boarding school I've ever shared this with. Again, as when I explained to him on the first day about how much I hated the castle, by instinct I provide a filtered version of the story, leaving out my shower erection and John's paternalistic kindness, focusing only on the madness and horror.

"Eish," he says. He shakes his head, visibly stunned. "Eish, man. I'm sorry, *né*? Crazy."

He bends over and lights a cigarette. He is on the bed, me on the floor, the way the two of us so often seem to end up, on those nights we talk. There is something soft about him now. He sips a dumpie of lager. He moves across to put a new tape in the stereo—Whitney Houston or Brenda Fassie—and lays a hand on my shoulder. His face is thin and elongated, like that of a mantis. Although I've never been consciously attracted to him—Dumisami is more my fantasy—now, I have to restrain myself from leaning upward out of sheer affection and kissing him on the lips.

"Only a white guy could have done that," he says at last. "We blacks can be cruel, it's true." He branches off into the story of a township gangster who burst into a shebeen, grabbed a drug rival, and cut this man's living heart out of his chest in front of all the onlookers. "But we blacks aren't kinky like you whites, man. See, that *tsotsi* in the shebeen, he was defending his territory. Your guy—it seems he just liked it." Then he continues to tell me a story about how he lost a friend in primary school during the riots. The cops shot this friend. He, Aubrey, was the first to pick up the body.

"Eish," he says again. "I was so sad, *né*? The pain went right in here—" He puts his hand on his chest. "I really think those Boers, too, they liked hurting us."

A shared pain is a soothed one. Apparently we both know about broken skin: his back has been peppered with buckshot from the riot police, mine with athletics spikes. Aubrey reaches out his hand, offering me a tube of XXX Peppermints. I take one. I head out to the tuck shop in the castle portal; return with chips and chocolates.

As before, there's something comforting in this judgment pronounced against my race. I do not feel implicated: rather, I feel sustained and supported. If the punishments inflicted on me in childhood are due to my racial sensibility, then there are, or so my unconscious adolescent logic concludes, forty million black South Africans who share my suffering. If the problem John once saw in me was blackness, then I am united with a world stretching out in front of me as far as I can see.

A night during final exam week. I'm sitting in Aubrey's room avoiding reviewing for my literature final tomorrow afternoon. Although literature is my best subject—my math, computer science, and religious studies grades have been sliding with the expansion in my social life, but English has held because of my interest in it—I still need to look over my books and notes. Aubrey and I have been remembering all the fun we've had this year, and Aubrey has finally commented on how I'm the only one in our D flat cohort to not have gotten any sexual action.

"What do you do for sex?" Aubrey asks now. "I mean, I know the girls don't want to go home with you because you hang out with black guys." This, conveniently for me, is the gang's de facto explanation for why I never pick up women on club runs or she-been outings: understandably, I don't like black girls, and white ones are too racist to want to hook up with a white guy in a black group. "You must miss it, man. I mean, once you've tried the pussy, it's hard to go back to just the hand, don't you agree?"

A direct question. Part of me wants to avoid the query again. But part of me feels a pulsing need to take a hammer to a corbel.

"Actually," I say. My palms sweat. "I've never, you know, gone all the way with a girl. I've done a lot. But not—penetration. I suppose you could call me a virgin."

Aubrey's eyes widen.

"*Yissis*, man!" He leaps up from his bed and leans over me. "Nobody is a virgin at your age. Tell me the truth!"

"It's true, Aubs. You've seen me this year. I think I need some help." I begin to explain to him about Catholicism forbidding sex before marriage. Then there was the problem of partying with the D flat guys. And he's seen how shy I get talking to girls.

"Incredible," Aubrey says then. "There isn't a black man in the country." He pauses, apparently lost in thought. "You're interesting, man. I like that you tell me these things. I like that you're so honest, man." Later: "No, man, you just haven't had the chance. Maybe your standards have been too high." At last, after sitting around for maybe fifteen minutes, he says: "But you got to know what it is, man! You can't go through life a baby—crazy!" He reaches for his wallet at his bedside, heads to the cupboard, and pulls out jeans and a cotton shirt. "Come on, man! We going to find some *girls*!"

I try to plead my need to look over the crib notes for *Portrait of a Lady*, but Aubrey will have none of it.

"Who knows if we'll even see each other next year, man?"

On the train we sit in the third-class compartment, which on this weekday night is full of nurses on their way to work, aproned housekeepers off to clean office buildings, and street sweepers—only a few party-goers like ourselves. Aubrey walks over to a group of nurses and begins chatting to them in Xhosa. I may be, in Aubrey's estimation, an honorary black man, but I still haven't learned more than a word or two of this language—*molo,* hello; *nyo kanyoko,* your mother's vagina. As Aubrey chatters to these women, pointing back in my direction—when he does so, one of the nurses, who's wearing the white veil of a head sister, roars with laughter—I still have no idea what he's saying. Aubrey returns.

"What was that all about?"

"See, man, that may be part of why you're a virgin. So many girls like that, thinking they're better than us."

We get into town. The first place Aubrey takes me is a liquor store, where he buys us a six-pack. "The first time I did it I got drunk," he says. "I was fourteen. It was with a girl from a shebeen. It helped—gave me some confidence. Then, when things get going, nature takes over, *wena*! Trust me on that one." This sounds good to me. I would like nature to take over at some point for me too, so I can find women's bodies as sexy and desirable as Aubrey does—so I, too, can kiss and fondle them in shebeens, disappear into bedrooms or bathrooms with them, and then laugh about it.

We sit in Greenmarket Square, in the center of town. On a weeknight the place is deserted except for the tramps, so it is easy to sit on one of the concrete benches and hide the empty tins in a paper bag. When the hobos come up and ask us for change, Aubrey shouts, "*Voertsek!*" meaning "Get lost!" They stumble off, cursing us.

"Just ignore them," Aubrey says. Where did he develop this sublime self-esteem? "Drink up, Glen," he says, even though gulping down as many beers as this in public is illegal. I wish I could be as assured in the world as he is.

When the six-pack's done, we enter the pub off the square, where we have drunk before. Here, Aubrey strikes up a conversation with a middle-aged blond woman who somehow reminds me of my alcoholic Aunt Lois: she has the same lined face, puffy chin, and affectionate but despairing eyes.

"You wanna fuck her?" he asks me when this woman goes to

the powder room. "Older women, man—they're great to help break in a guy. And they like young dick."

But I cannot stomach the thought: it would be like a lion bringing down a wounded antelope. It is just that she's so much older than me—a mismatch.

"Okay, okay, man, I understand. You don't like the older ones. Me neither, honestly."

We go on to the next pub, up the street that leads to the foothills of the mountain. And the next, and the next. It gets later and later: midnight rolls by. In one bar we meet a pair of olive-skinned mixed-race girls. One of them, slender and boyish, I find somewhat attractive. I tell Aubrey I think I'd like to go to bed with her. He high-fives me. "Yes!"

He pulls this young woman aside, leans in to talk to her; she giggles and turns away. He gets out his wallet: now she actually clouts him hard on his left ear with her palm.

"Hey, what you do that for?" he shouts. But her friend looms in front of us, plump and formidable, with two giant breasts pressing out of a red halter top. "I want the two of you to leave, or I'm calling the manager. Prostitution is a *crime,* I say."

"You were going to pay that girl to have sex with me?" I ask when we're back on the street. The idea seems outrageous. We were in an ordinary bar, the kind my dad might visit for afterwork drinks. People come to places like that for meals. "You can't just offer a strange girl money for sex, Aubs!" Although I've stopped going to mass and have intellectually rejected the idea of a creator god, the Catholic instincts vanish much less slowly: women need to be respected, the way that Jesus treated Mary Magdalene. The body is a temple of the Lord.

But Aubrey replies: "*Bra,* what the hell do you know? You are the one who asked *me* for help. You're a kid, man! You've lived your life in a Boere-village with kudus. Let Aubs take care of you tonight, man."

And I do. This is it, this is the core of the matter: he, black, is in the driving seat. In my whiteness I am missing an unnamable kernel. Can I learn it from him? Both of us want me to. We keep drinking: more and more pints, maybe eight, maybe ten. The night dissolves into that incoherent drunkenness where time disappears and all that's left is a collage: neon, salt wind, asphalt. At one point we walk all the way to Sea Point, two miles away, to find a hooker bar Aubrey's patronized with some of the rich boys. "They'll see you're white and they'll be all over you, man. You better just have sex with one of them. I know they're whores, but, man, you need to get started." But in that suburb of high rises, silent now, facing out to the quiet sea, cargo and oil tankers in the distance, Robben Island, where Nelson Mandela is confined— here, we get lost. Where is the bar, after all—behind St. Elmo's Pizza? The shops and restaurants are an abandoned movie set. On our return trip into town, we stumble along, our arms on each other's shoulders, singing "Flashdance, What a feeling!" A police car slows next to us, asks us for identification. When the policewoman sees our student IDs, though, she turns protective and maternal.

"Isn't it exam week? This is how you spend your parents' money, hey?" She seems, at this moment, just like my Auntie Merle: kindly and no-nonsense. Something about her manner shames me. There is this reality, too, isn't there? That our castle-residence on top of the hill isn't just a snare, but also a privilege.

Mom and Dad: in a day or two I'll be catching a flight back to them, to Lisa and David, in the game reserve village. What would my parents say if they could see me now, so dissolute and desperate? But the image of them quickly disappears as the cop moves off and we stride, singing, down the street again. Surely there are no real solutions for me there, in that tiny village with the impala dung and the glossy starlings.

"That cop was nice," Aubrey admits, later. "Still, police, you know—they'll pick on guys like you and me. They see a black man and a white man together and they think drugs. Racism, it never ends, man." He's worked up from the alcohol. "It's like the air, like this city, man, these buildings around you the whole bloody time, you can never get out of it, man, it's like they're gripping you." As he says this, perhaps it's the drunkenness, but somehow I see it, what he's talking about: the whole city is a fortress, a giant trap holding us in its jaws. There are armored cars, this minute patrolling the highways and townships, vehicles as large as houses, with soldiers' rifles all pointing outward, and prisons, hundreds of them, with activists in handcuffs and lawyers with taped-up mouths. Razor wire, so much of it, around all the middle-class houses. Aubrey in the shack he grew up in, and now locked away with me in our faux medieval quadrangle. And I'm in another prison in the midst of all this. Now, bumbling down Strand Street, past the shuttered shops and the empty office buildings towards the taxi rank, the answer seems both clear to me and yet obscure: if I look left there will be some trap door with a route out of the labyrinth, but when I turn my head, it's gone; now, stumbling forward, there is nowhere to go but deeper.

On Adderly and Strand streets, Aubrey breaks away from me a last time. He corners a prostitute on the corner: a tall, regal Colored woman in a skin-tight black dress, stockings, and a full-length leather coat.

"Darling!" Aubrey says. "Listen, darling, we need your help. This boy, he needs a lay—hasn't had one before. Look how cute he is!" She smiles at me obligingly.

"But we need a student discount."

To my surprise, she runs up and hugs me. She feels and smells nice: wonderful, really, sweet, warm, perfumed, her breasts pushing up against my chest. There is a minute in which I *am* going to have sex with her. It is going to be relaxed, comfortable, like sitting on Aubrey's floor.

But then as quickly as she's embraced me, she lets me go. "Sorry, boys," she says. "Got to make a living." Even between us, Aubrey and I can't muster her fee. And sitting in the taxi with Aubs, driving back down the highway with the sea of lights below us, so drunk I don't even know where to tell the cab driver to go— somewhere on this ride, I'm just a bit relieved.

Back home we stumble across the car park and knock stupidly once or twice on the door to D flat. "Open up!" says Aubrey— until we push and it gives and we laugh at ourselves.

"Next year!" says Aubrey then. It takes me a moment to realize he's talking about my virginity. But, although there is indeed a next year—that afternoon, despite my hangover, I somehow do all right on my English—it takes much longer than that for me to find a way out of my defenses; longer to demolish all the moats, baileys, and barbicans I have built to protect myself from the obvious.

Black Boys of My Youth

How does Eshu come into the picture? I am talking here, of course, of the mischievous West African trickster god with the black-and-red two-sided cap who provokes so much strife in the old legends because the villagers, looking at him from different directions, cannot agree on his hat color. He's an orisha with a thousand faces, a god of multiplicity, ambiguity, and confusion, a god of possibility, radical and otherwise. Beloved from Nigeria to Cuba, from Haiti to the northern jungle coastlines of Brazil, Eshu is said to be a difficult but good teacher: he exposes your foolishness with his pranks, but he does it for your own benefit. Looking back on my years immediately after moving out of D flat and the hilltop castle; reimagining those times of experimentation, of sincere but unarguable idiocy, it seems to me that Eshu must be the puppetmaster-deity who steps in to take the place of the ones who have so recently been deposed.

Not that I know yet who Eshu is, or any of the replacement gods who are about to step onto this stage: Marx and his postcolonial disciples; radical feminists; queer liberation icons. I am still many years from developing an interest in traditional African magic, folklore, and mythology, from buying the candles in New York bodegas with their layers of colored wax. To the extent I've invoked the trickster god at all in my life, the process has been entirely accidental. At ten years of age, naked with Dirkie Coetzee on the edge of the black workers' compound in Skukuza: *Tokoloshe!* I yelled that night, tossing a stone on a corrugated rooftop. *Tokoloshe,* Eshu: the prankster god goes under many different names. But this child's plea can be ignored by the orisha: he focuses his educational attentions on grown-ups.

But even in my early years of adulthood, I do my best not to engage with Eshu-like excess and rebellion. After those drunken expeditions with the D flat crew at the university, I spend the three-month vacation with my parents back in the game reserve, two thousand miles away—far from prostitutes and revolutionary checkpoints. With Mom and Dad, Merle, Ian, and the old crew—sundowners and Sunday backyard *braais;* the Verhoefs stopping by for cane and lime juice; and Linda, my parents' new housekeeper, hanging up the washing—with all of them, I revert back to a younger self, compliant, asexual. I peruse *Reader's Digest Condensed Books* instead of *The Metamorphosis* and *Pride and Prejudice.* In the mornings Mom and I go for runs together and drink *rooibos* tea; at night, after my summer job helping Dad develop a database for the citrus farm that's located on the edge of the Kruger National Park, I chat with Lisa, now going into matric, and David, entering Standard Seven, about pop bands, teachers, politics—small talk that does not especially lodge in my memory. Much later, after I have already left South Africa, they will both mention this time as a period when I seemed particularly wrapped up in myself and oblivious—as if the center of gravity of my life has really shifted elsewhere. (Unknown to me, David has already begun to sniff glue and thinners to cope with the cruelty of the school. Lisa has moved on from her wild early flings with boys to a girlfriend she's successfully keeping secret from Mom, Dad, and me.)

Two main things will stick in my mind from that visit. First, there are some awkward moments between Mom and me when the conversation gets around to the change that has happened this year in my religious beliefs.

"I'm sad you don't have the support of your faith anymore," she tells me. "I went through a bit of a difficult time myself when you lost your Christianity, my Glen. But then I got better and realized that God loves us not matter whether we see it or not."

What am I supposed to say? I now identify as an atheist: I give as much credence to this love she's referring to as I do mermaids. Years later, when I reach a more metaphorical understanding of religion, I will comprehend what she means emotionally by this statement, that my fundamental sense of being does not need to shift with a change in dogma. But now her insistence on talking to me about a religion I've left behind seems merely irritating.

The second recollection is how boring computer science is: programming mainframes to keep track of grapefruit sales, orange truck invoices, and employee paychecks is about as intriguing as listening to Afrikaans country music on the radio.

"I'm not sure this career is for me," I tell Dad.

"Computer science isn't all so dull," he replies. "Remember, this is just entry level." I don't yet decide to cancel my computer science courses for my second year, even though the truth is that these lessons have been boring me almost as much as Dad's citrus weight/price ratios: there is something soulless and technical about this profession that makes me look at my watch every ten minutes and wish for the day to be over.

A therapist would tell me I'm ducking a coming-of-age conflict: "Mom, you make me uncomfortable when you assume I should have the same beliefs as you do. Dad, enough pressuring me to become a computer scientist." But all I'm aware of, at nineteen, is how suffocated I feel in this world. Greeting my parents' maid, Linda, who lowers her eyes whenever she encounters a white person, I feel like the Buddha secluded in his garden. Swimming in the whites-only pool while the gardeners trudge by in their blue overalls in the glaring heat, shopping in that store with its shelves and freezers where Aubrey, Brazzo, and my other new friends wouldn't even be allowed to set foot—doing all of this, I feel both guilty and angry. My real life feels half a country away.

Back in Cape Town I join an artists commune in the student ghetto of Observatory. Dad gives me a small monthly allowance in lieu of residence room and board, an amount I supplement with loans, odd jobs, and the saved income from my lemon-analyzing gig. In Obs I rent a tiny monklike cell at the back of a house inhabited by Alex, Louise, and a third girl, Janine. My plan is to study hard and raise my grades: Aubrey's lost his financial aid as a result of partying too much the previous year, and I worry I'm headed in the same direction if I'm not careful. I picture a much more sober college career for myself than the previous year. Can't I just be a normal nineteen-year-old—work hard at my classes, maybe take one of my female housemates on a date? But even here, Eshu comes into play. The *tokoloshe* goblin pricks at his pupil's weak spots until he pays attention to them. He dances and shakes his head—in traditional dances, the trickster god often twirls a silken scarf. His repetitive motions, those mock whips, flicks, and darts—they are there to remind us of what we'd prefer to overlook.

"Why are you so square and uptight?" ask Alex and Louise, on the night we hear about a countercultural party just down the street. The coolest performance artists will be there—oral activist poets, radical graffiti artists. Why wouldn't I want to come? Alex firmly replaces my preppy-looking, blue stone-washed shirt—picked out for me by Aubrey on a day we walked together through a flea market—with a home-dyed potato print T-shirt belonging to her painter boyfriend, Ian. She musses up my hair, tells me I should grow it. Then we're at the party with dreadlocked white boys playing Bob Marley and Joan Baez in the back courtyard, naked body painting in the corner, and a red bowl of hashish cookies standing on the kitchen table—surely placed there by agents of the great divine mischief-maker? Eshu is the orisha of unpredictability, of loss of control.

"Nothing bad will happen," Alex assures me, when I express my trepidations about the hashish. "It's exactly like having a glass of wine." So I try one. It's good: sweet and buttery, with a slightly leafy aftertaste. When nothing happens, I eat another, and eventually a third. An hour or two later I'm high as a bateleur over the savannah, lying on my back on the cement of the courtyard, looking up at the orange neon sky and talking to complete strangers about sex before marriage, and how glad I am not to be burdened anymore with that whole religious hogwash, about the girl I kissed at the Catholic youth center, about the sex worker Aubrey once tried to buy for me on Strand Street.

"I liked her smell," I say. "It reminded me of lilies. Her skin was much warmer than I expected."

"Man, you really need to get laid," says a shirtless Colored Rastafarian. He nods back to the perimeter wall, to where a short blond woman is letting one of the dreadlocked musicians paint round Earth Mother globes around her nipples. But I still don't want this. I'd rather be, say, this rastafarian's girlfriend—would like to run my finger around the inside of his bellybutton and taste his treasure trail on my tongue. I wish he would take off his shorts and let me shave his testicles before painting them. But even high, I'm much too scared to ask him.

Other incidents bother me. One night Ian, Alex's painter boy-friend, bumps into me, stark naked, in the kitchen. Ian has a per-fect body: muscled, with just a dusting of hair on his chest, and—I can't help glimpsing—a long circumcised penis hanging over a pair of well-developed testicles. These guys who come and visit in this commune aren't in the least bit self-conscious about their bodies. They go to nude beaches, skinny-dip at the university pool after midnight, attend Woodstock-style rock festivals where every-one ends up stripping off and lighting up spliffs. Tonight, Ian hasn't seen me for a while—I've been in the library or computer labs while he's been visiting Alex and the girls—and he shoots out his hand in greeting: "What's up, man? Good to see you!" The touch of his skin thrills me. He smells vaguely dusty. After he's made small talk about classes and the Tiananmen Square demon strations in China, and after he's said good-bye and returned to Alex's room, I masturbate compulsively, imagining what it's like to be Alex, with Ian's body right next to me.

Another time two male friends of Louise's crash at our pad for the weekend. Louise has had a fling with one of them, Richard, a brooding, skinny, strong-featured guy with brown spiky hair. Rich-ard and his friend do more drugs than I would have believed could be safely consumed by the human body. They smoke up an entire salad bowl of weed—this is, of course, the unregulated developing world, where you can buy a pound of the stuff for the price of a steak. They swallow mushrooms and methamphetamine, and sniff long lines of cocaine powder. They put Bob Marley on the stereo and do a jerking, marionette-like dance whose intensity disturbs me. When Richard takes a break from his reverie, somehow he and I end up on the kitchen floor together, me drinking tea and him sipping from some Brazilian herbal concoction with rumored psychotropic properties.

"Oh, man, *moffies*?" Richard asks. How has the subject of ho-mosexuals come up? I won't remember: all that will stay with me is what comes next, the story of how he was hitchhiking shirtless to some music festival in ragged denim shorts, when an elderly man in a Mercedes offered him drug money for a blow job and he said yes.

"It was *lekker,* man," Richard says. "I enjoyed it as much as I liked being with a girl, really. There's nothing wrong with being gay, I reckon. It's just a different preference, you know?"

I nod in agreement: but of course I don't know; I still have no idea; a tightness in my solar plexus still grips me. Long ago, John held up his penis for me, his face nakedly contemptuous: *Do you want this?*

Now, when I see myself in the bathroom mirror, tall, thin, and gangly, with the remnants of teenage pimples on my chin and cheeks, I wonder who I am. Somehow, I've wandered off the hiking trail into a forest with tree shadows and gulleys. And others? How do they see me? Once at the Labia Cinema, the arthouse in Cape Town, I leaned over to Louise.

"Would you ever have sex with me, just to help me break through the barrier?"

"Sometimes you worry me, Glen," she replied then. She is the calm one in the household; she loves listening to jazz and blues and watches movies on the VCR in the lounge while the others party in the courtyard. She is pragmatic. She does well in school, bakes bread or goes running when she's upset. "Sex should be relaxing. Watching you talk about it is like watching a raw-haunch pony."

I last only six or so months in the commune. Over time it gets to be too much: as when I roomed with the racist engineering student, the stimulation pricks at too many painful places. That winter, I move out of the commune and sign a lease on a tiny bachelor pad in the inner city with a view of Table Mountain. In the mornings I catch the bus to school—on sodden windy days, the double-deckers sway in the southeasters and the passengers moan

and scream. Aubrey starts visiting me again—he never particularly enjoyed hanging out with the white hippy crowd—and for a
while it looks like that old friendship is headed for revival: the
two of us go out carousing, as in the old days: once we end up
drunk on a Taiwanese container ship, where a tattooed sailor
pulls a switchblade on us, and we run.

Still, there's something false and empty now about these hunts
for girls, booze, and trouble. My heart isn't in it anymore. I sigh,
"Not tonight, Aubs," when he suggests another expedition to divest
me of my virginity. "Reading a good book by Bellow." When my
doorbell rings unannounced I don't answer it. He no longer stops
by. I disappear into my shell, a ghostly figure picking up mail in the
front portal of the apartment complex.

For a few months, I replay my early time in the single room in
D flat: a solitary existence punctuated only by classes and the occasional dinner and movie with Aubrey or a trip back to the old
Observatory house for tea and cookies with the girls. This time
the feeling of looming change is even more palpable. I'm aware of
it on my long walks up Adderly Street, to Tamboerskloof and
around as far as Signal Hill, as high up as I can go, until the metropolis spreads out in the dusk like glowing crystals. I can sense
it in the music I listen to, the writing I recite to myself when I climb
the mountain contour path alone at sunset. My favorite literature
and poetry all express a sense of exile, of being on the cusp of
metamorphosis:

> *No longer at ease here, in the old dispensation,*
> *With an alien people clutching their gods.*

Is this just what I always do to gear up for change? Drift for
weeks or months on nothing but the texture of my own consciousness.

"Are you sure you're okay, my love?" This is Mom, on the phone from Skukuza. God help me—she has always known instinctively when something major is going on.

"I'm fine, Mom. Of course, yes. Why wouldn't I be? Just busy. Alex and Louise are well, thanks. Oh yes, Aubrey's fine, too." She and Dad think the bachelor pad is just to get more work done. They know there was a lot of partying in the last place and I was worried about my marks: of course they have no idea about the bongs the size of tennis shoes left on the living room couch.

In September, on a whim, I attend the "purple rain" protest against what will turn out to be the last whites-only elections. I sit near the side of the demonstration so I can dash away down a side street when the police fire the teargas and water cannon; still, it's exhilarating to be in a whole crowd of people crying for liberty, singing "We shall overcome" and "Justice for all."

"We want to be free!" yells a butch-looking, heavyset woman in a United Democratic Front T-shirt. She is probably a lesbian, but in 1989 I wouldn't know a dyke if she rode her motorbike over my legs. To me she's just a strong woman, asserting herself against the blue-uniformed representatives of the police state lined up on the sidewalks. Still, the words resonate. *Free:* I, too, want to lose my straightjacket. *Overcome:* that is what I want to do over the frightened growling in my stomach and the recollections of hardboard rectangles.

That November at a corner store I buy the freshly printed *Vrye Weekblad,* an antiapartheid weekly that specializes in exposés of the Afrikaner establishment. On it I see a photograph that seems vaguely familiar to me: a handsome man with graying hair combed in a side parting. A memory buzzes to life. The headline states: "Bloody Trail of the South African Police." Alongside it: "Meet Commander Dirk Johannes Coetzee, commander of an SA police death squad. He tells exclusively the gruesome story of political assassinations, poisoned cocktails, foreign bomb blasts and letter bombs."

Coetzee: the surname is common enough. I read, horrified, the unprecedented testimony about human rights lawyer Griffiths Mxenge, stabbed to death after his dogs were poisoned. Vusi, an ANC member, kidnapped from Mozambique, drugged, shot, and burned while Coetzee and his buddies sat around drinking beer and eating meat, the ashes thrown in the muddy, green Komati River, which briefly runs along the border of Kruger National Park.

And then suddenly it hits me.

Roger that.

"Yes, it's Ben Coetzee's brother," Dad confirms when I call him. "Ben and his family had some idea what was going on, but they didn't know the details." Apparently Ben has been encouraging his brother to take this step—resign from the Security Forces and then share the truth about them with the media—for much of the last decade.

I admire Dirk Coetzee's integrity in coming clean: as a result of this interview he has had to flee for his life, into exile in London. I also value his brother Ben's—and by extension his lone liberal Skukuza friend, my father's—commitment to truth. Still, the main feeling I get from hearing this news isn't relief, but rather distaste, horror, and implication. Blood brothers with Dirkie makes me a blood nephew of Dirk's—he who apparently gave an imprisoned and thirsty activist Kool-Aid laced with poison and shot a screaming woman during a house raid in Botswana. The Rocco de Wet I idealized as a kid turns out to be more of a modern-day Eichmann. Going back to Skukuza this year for another summer stint writing citrus estate algorithms is even less appealing than before.

But then Eshu comes to my rescue again. He will do this reliably over the next couple of years, every time I'm seeking out some way to leave neurosis, repression, and conventionality. An old friend, Colleen, calls—she was my catechism teacher in matric. She now works at Rapid Results College, a correspondence school in Johannesburg. They need a debt collector, someone to chase down African peasants who've fallen behind on their tuition payments—a morally unpleasant job, to be sure, but someone has to do it. Am I available? I am—I need the money—and even this seems better than C+ programming in the middle of a literal and metaphorical burial ground. Then, a day or two later, I receive a letter from Stephen, the old friend of James and mine from high school; he was a day scholar, he was never part of the boarding school scene, but we often sat with him at break. Stephen is in fact going abroad this summer. Do I happen to know anyone who's available to housesit a one-bedroom flat in Braamfontein, a short walk from downtown? I do.

Dimly, somewhere I register that Stephen's flat is a mere four blocks away from Hillbrow, the epicenter of gay South African life. Incoherently, I recognize that there's something special about all this: for three months, I am going to be entirely anonymous and will be able to be whatever I like without even my Cape Town friends asking after me.

What exactly prompts me, just before I climb on the northbound Translux bus to the knotted-ribbon highways and tall mine dumps of South Africa's largest metropolis, to call the gay counseling help line listed in the Yellow Pages? It's the first time in my life I have requested mental health assistance.

Perhaps it's the self-help book, *How to be a Happy Homosexual,* I come across in a bookstore—its being there is another Eshu-style trick—and slip surreptitiously into a brown paper bag. All I'm going to do is read it for curiosity's sake, or perhaps to laugh at the pop psychology. At R 2.50 it costs nothing—the price of a pencil eraser. But despite myself, I find the words in the book intensely thought-provoking. In 1989, it says, any gay man who chooses to remain miserable or involved in a sexual relationship that has no appeal to him is lashing himself to the Inquisitor's rack for no good reason at all.

"I'd like to make a comment," says the phone counselor I speak to, after he hears all the gory details of the boarding school hazing. "It's not even clear to me your boarding school abuser was gay. He might have just been a straight guy who hated sissies, you know? And was trying to encourage you not to be one. In any case, you shouldn't judge a whole community by one crazy individual. Most gays you'll meet are really perfectly normal."

These words, so self-evident in hindsight, strike me with all the force of an epiphany: Of course. John is one thing, homosexuality is another. I can be gay without having to become John: without hooking up telephone cranks to copper electrodes. I don't, after all, have to become Aubrey, Brazzo, or anyone else: I can be myself. I can create a new life that suits me as an individual. Now my chest feels more open than before. My feet, resting on the smooth parquet wooden floor beneath the phone stool, feel more substantial.

It's a Friday night in Hillbrow, Johannesburg. I'm hanging out with a girl called Nikki, the daughter of Colleen, the woman who got me the job with the correspondence college. Nikki is a lesbian. From the day we met at the Rapid Results College main office, Nikki, an intelligent, charismatic social worker who's also something of an antiapartheid political activist, apparently sized me up as being a member of the family—and probably a closet case in need of a rescue mission.

"We should go out sometime, hey? I can show you some places in town. I know what it's like to be on your own in a new city."

In a gay bar called Connections—a favorite spot of hers—I told her I thought I might be gay. Maybe it was just the normality of all of this, the matter-of-fact, relaxed way same-sex couples were kissing each other, holding hands, embracing, and talking and laughing. I *might* be like her, with her Wits University lecturer girlfriend, sitting around a circular black table, drinking gin and tonics. *Could* be like these men listening to the Village People and P. J. Powers on the jukebox, laughing at the cute, blond bartender.

"It's possible," I say. "I don't really know."

She clinked my glass.

"Of course you're gay, Glen!" Her tone brooked no disagreement. "Even my mom recognized it when she was teaching you catechism! Who were you fooling?"

After that night Nikki and I went out together several more times on the gay scene—to Connections; to a coffee shop called the Three Sisters; to a disco in the party district in Melville. I enjoyed meeting several more of her queer friends: a middle-aged lesbian couple, living with their son in suburban Germiston; a male pal from her social services agency, who seemed to develop a crush on me. Unfortunately he wasn't my type.

But one thing didn't happen: I didn't meet anyone to go home with. Until physically consummated, how could I be certain of my sexual orientation? Perhaps this homosexuality was just one more self-delusion.

In the weeks that followed, I tried to get it on with someone, but I am as shy about gay sex and dating as I was in the straight clubs and shebeens of Cape Town. When I see guys I find attractive, I clam up, look in the other direction, go to the bathroom, or pick up a copy of *Exit,* the gay rag. Nikki has teased me about what a nervous nelly I am, saying I'll never get laid if I act like Scarlett O'Hara. But who is it hovering at the edges of this narrative, chortling at the main protagonist? For trickster deities, the point is never about making it easy—hooking up with some pleasant white boy who has a lot in common with me. Eshu upsets hierarchies and dynamites complacency.

So tonight Nikki and I are in a different bar, called Skyline—an overwhelmingly black gay bar, the most famous such hangout spot on the African continent. Red lights above us color the whole main room, with its white walls and its pink floor tiles, an incandescent magenta. From the verandah the downtown skyscrapers are visible: macho *injongas,* butches, stand around hip-hop style in studded silver belts and wife-beater vests and chat up femme *skesanas* in plain slacks and shirts. There are only a few women here, which is why Nikki seldom frequents the place. She merely wants to show it to me so I'm aware of all the local entertainment options.

When we come in, we take a table at the far end and sit talking about race, perhaps the obvious topic: my year in D flat, the purple rain protest in Cape Town, segregated places like my home village that I find culturally suffocating, Dirk Coetzee. Then, without warning, *he* pulls up a chair to our table: a trim, handsome Colored man who introduces himself as an off-duty police officer named Dylan.

"Can I buy both of you drinks?" he asks. Nikki nods and thanks him. He's cheerful, friendly, and confident. He buys the two of us more gin and tonics, then sits and makes small talk about my studies, Nikki's job. Soon, he lays a hand on my back, as I've seen other men do to each other, leans in close to me with his body, pecks me on the cheek. It's the first time anyone has tried to pick me up. I thought I would be nervous, but I'm surprised by how good and natural all of this feels. *You and I are both going to be okay,* John once said, meaning, of course, something different— but maybe I will be?

"Your friend's cute," Dylan tells Nikki. He winks at her. She laughs. "He's new on the block," she replies. "He needs to have sex with someone—you should take him home." This isn't just her trying to be helpful, like Aubrey, Alex, and Louise. It's also the ethos of the time: to be antiapartheid is also to embrace anti-Calvinist sexual ethics. When he heads to the toilet, Nikki says, "You should have fun."

I do in fact invite Dylan home with me. He is nice enough. The two of us kiss, fondle, and masturbate each other on the leather couch under the window with the view of the empty bank offices. The recollection of my first sexual experience will forever be imbued with the image of bright white fluorescent bulbs, black metal filing cabinets, and abandoned wood-composite reception desks. Later, I'll remember the astonishing ease. *Trust me,* wena, *when you get to a certain point, nature just takes over.* Now, my skin is as sensitive as a record player's needletip. The hard need in my groin is an unambiguous message.

So is this when a switch flips in my brain and I begin to develop a more or less exclusive sexual attraction to black men? A neuron pathway, twisted to register this as sexy—this pale beach sand set off against soaked driftwood? But no, in fact I'm still not caught up in the spell. That night, after he leaves, I'm plagued by anxious dreams. John thrashes me for not polishing my shoes. I'm ill and hooked up to a respirator. Probably some old angry Catholic god has it in for me, is going to punish and kill me—I feel queasy. When Dylan calls to ask if I want to go to the movies, I chicken out: "Sorry, but I'm leaving in three weeks for varsity, and I don't want to get emotionally entangled."

But the fetish pixie's whirling: the wind that will blow me towards the black boys of my youth whistles through the concrete canyons. A few days later, I leave my office at the correspondence college to see a dancing crowd coming down Bree Street: De Klerk has announced the release of Mandela and the unbanning of the liberation movements. The whole country is celebrating. On the television back in the apartment, people crack open champagne bottles from Soweto to Durban.

Nine days later, I join the rest of the planet in watching on television as a gray-haired Mandela proclaims on the balcony overlooking the Cape Town parade: "Today the majority of South Africans, black and white, recognize that apartheid has no future." I do not realize it, but here, too, the future is beckoning me to come along with it. Political freedoms will lead to unprecedented personal possibilities, and vice versa.

Soon after my return to Cape Town I mention to a few people hanging around in the student government offices that I'm interested in joining a gay group on campus—preferably one with an antiapartheid flavor. At the very least, as a result of my Johannesburg experiences I have begun to identify with the lesbian and gay community intellectually: I want to be part of the networks Nikki has exposed me to. A woman takes me downstairs to the cafeteria to meet a tall, thin, amicable young man named Stephen Garrett. He's with a group called the Organization of Lesbian and Gay Activists (OLGA), which aims to both mobilize the gay community behind the push for democracy and persuade the liberation movements to endorse gay rights. OLGA has been talking of restarting a defunct LGBT group on the university campus.

"Let's start a club together," he says. "But also, why don't you try out an OLGA meeting?"

When I do so I encounter a relaxed, racially mixed gathering in a white stucco Victorian house near the university, with wooden floors and a living room fireplace—much like my old artists commune. The house belongs to Ivan Toms, the country's first jailed conscientious objector. Literature lines the shelves: *Our Lady of the Flowers, Death in Venice, Best Gay Short Stories.* Toms himself is a stocky blond intellectual in his thirties with an engaging way of leaning forward to listen intently. Our small talk revolves around how extreme homophobia in white South African culture predisposes white gay men to take a stand against conscription. I am about to obtain a political understanding of the jack bank: how it feeds upon itself, like a bush fire, but how it also contains within itself the seeds of its own destruction.

"*Ja*, we gay boys sense early on that the military doesn't like us," Toms says. "If we have half a grain of sense, we realize we have to fight against the entire system."

Should I be an antiapartheid revolutionary? At the OLGA meeting that evening the chief item of business is the aftermath of the De Klerk and Mandela speeches. OLGA is expecting that soon the major political parties will issue calls for submissions from the public for what we'd like to see in a new South African constitution. Mandela's African National Congress has expressed some sympathy for gay rights, chiefly as a result of the contributions to the liberation struggle made by open gay men and lesbians like Ivan Toms himself; Sheila Lapinsky, a heftily built Jewish lesbian in her forties and an OLGA member who spent several years under effective house arrest; and Simon Nkoli, a Johannesburg pro-democracy activist prosecuted for treason. As a result of all this, they hope that gay and lesbian equality might be enshrined in a future bill of rights.

"Do you think you might be interested in working on this?" Sheila asks me. She wears a red South African Communist Party T-shirt and appears to be the group's leading spirit: in the meeting she used phrases that impressed me, like "intersection of sexuality and gender" and "antibourgeois ethics." "It should be interesting work," she continues. "Who knows—we could even launch a domino effect! You young people are always saying you want to change the world." Of course I'm not much more, this evening in 1990, than a twenty-year-old child. I've never had a boyfriend; I've never held a permanent job or filled out a tax return. Yet I'm being invited to help make South Africa the first country in the history of the world to ban discrimination on the grounds of sexuality. Somewhere, invisible, on a hill slope, the *tokoloshe* goblin shakes his beard: Sexuality can give you power, can make you feel whole and important.

"Sure," I tell Sheila. "Of course I'd love to."

A few weeks later, Stephen Garrett and I organize a launch party for the Gay and Lesbian Association of the University of Cape Town. Maybe forty or fifty young women and men gather in yet another one of those beautiful but dilapidated Victorian houses. Again, something trendy and countercultural plays on the hi-fi set: Bob Dylan, perhaps, insisting we don't criticize something we can't understand. Across the oceans, Zimmy may have long ago found Jesus and John Lennon's aorta may have been perforated by a well-aimed bullet. Here, on our green foot of a continent, though, the times are still very much a-changin'. And tonight, among all the women and men at the party—the college dykes in tie-dye T-shirts who balance my chakras and talk to me about feminism and democracy; the thin blond law student who instantly steps into a leadership role in this new organization, talks about constitutions and by-laws and methods of balloting membership—among this throng of young, energetic queers, there's someone special: Bradley, a short, elfin-looking Colored man with thin, dark hair, a narrow face, and a protruding chin.

Why does Bradley capture me so immediately? He is, after all, an unlikely candidate to serve as successor to the D flat guys and be the next link in the chain of a developing interracial orientation. Bradley's an unabashed Europhile—he's studying French at the university and he loves Balzac, Godard, and burgundy. In fact he plans to join an older "friend" in Europe the next day, for a holiday. Having just turned twenty, it does not occur to me to ask Bradley for more information about this mentor. Who is buying the ticket for this reunion on the Champs-Elysées? What is expected in return for the more or less indefinite accommodation Bradley seems to enjoy on his friend's nearby wine estate?

"You'll have to see it," Bradley insists. "It's beautiful."

What I do notice, however, is how exquisite Bradley is: caramel-complexioned, with moist dark eyes and thin attractive fingers. We french-kiss—surely even *pain au chocolat* has nothing on this smooth sensuality, this sweet, warm, delicious taste of saliva.

"Don't leave me alone," Bradley says, when the party ends. "I really like you. I want to be with you." And now, in a replay of Nikki in Hillbrow, Stephen and Peter and the remaining clump of New Age dykes overhear what Bradley says. They nod, yes, sure, you really should go home with him.

"Do what you feel," says Stephen, with a shrug.

"What's wrong with you?" asks one lesbian, laughing at me.

Are you still battling with your apartheid hangups? That's her real question. This is what we believe, even if we don't admit it—to say no to sex across the color line is to still be suffering from racial prejudice. The sign of a liberated sensibility, on the other hand, is the willingness to miscegenate. Tonight, Bradley and I hardly need a full-blown position paper to desire sex with each other. Soon we're in his car headed west, my seashell hand curled around his loam-ridge knuckles, the neon orange streetlights flipping by and over us, coloring us persimmon.

And that night on the wine estate, beneath the skylight and the walls laden with big grinning masks—probably there's an Eshu in there somewhere, complete with hanging cowry shell necklace—is simply wonderful. Bradley is a gifted lover, sensitive, intuitive. As we spoon together under the sheets, his touches are moths of affirmation fluttering up and down my body; his kisses are ghost shadows of wholeness that penetrate my chest cavity. Fact is, I feel I haven't really been touched gently like that since I was a child and my mother tucked me under the eiderdown. Since then it's been John's hand, or James and me lying on our boarding school beds in our invisible cages. Deep down, I've longed for something exactly like this: this simple reassurance, this uninhibited tenderness. How could I have needed it for so long and not even realized it?

In the morning the smell of wet-spicy dust and freshly doused grape leaves drifts through the bedroom windows. Sprinklers chug in the daylight.

"Bradley, do you think if things were different here—" I ask as the two of us make the bed and dress again in our party jeans and shirts, "you know—if you weren't off to France, if you lived in Cape Town, would you see me again?"

"Are you joking?" Bradley asks. His face and chest are thin. By daylight there is something solemn and grasshopper-like about him. He is skinnier and frailer than he looked with his clothes on. But he smiles. "You're wonderful, Glen. I'd do more than see you again. I'd love to be in a relationship with you!" He hugs me before putting on his shirt. I feel, of course, a tiny stab of fear at this. A *relationship*: On the one hand, Dad bringing me cold Milo for breakfast, the multicolored vitamin tablets lined up on the composite kitchen tabletop. People caring for each other, supporting each other. On the other hand, John, embracing me one moment in the showers and then balling a fist. Pleasure and danger; possibility and pain—these are, in fact, the two sides of the trickster's cap. Still, this morning, with Bradley, something about the sincerity in his voice and the kindness in his face let possibility win over anxiety. A rectangle of delight in my chest expands outward.

But of course he's sweet-talking me. Of course this is still an Eshu prank, an educational exercise. His estate-owning "friend" is a sugar daddy; that delicate spiderweb of bone visible on the back of his hands is in fact due to the late stages of HIV infection. He is headed to Europe to access first-world health care. In a week or two, all of this will be explained to me by a colleague from the gay and lesbian student group who knows Bradley. When I hear this I will feel all the shame and anxiety I experienced after Dylan all over again: the edgy trembling, the psychosomatic diarrhea. I'll meet with a counselor, take an HIV test, and eventually figure out that with the protection we used my risk is close to zero: I'll process the sense of betrayal in the fact that my transcendent sense of union was based on omissions. But right now I've been bitten. A coffee-colored hand has touched my face and made life seem good. Kisses and embraces have satisfied intractable longings.

And then it will all seem a bit like this, won't it—my life over the next two or three years? Like a magical encounter, no less romantic for being short-lived: a game, a merry-go-round, laughter behind the protea bushes. A period of unprecedented empowerment, an unleashing of stored-up intellectual, emotional, and physical energies. An outpouring of hope and passion that will later seem to mirror that of my society—that brief fling with the prospect of love and togetherness between the races.

So here I am, then, sometime in the middle of 1990. I already look significantly different: my hair is trimmed short—within a month or two of coming out, I cut off my scraggly locks and replace them with the look I like from the gay bars, spiky, inch-long orange hair, with large silver earrings. I'm sitting around a kitchen table with my new OLGA comrades, Ivan, Sheila, Sheila's partner, Julia, and Derrick, a human rights lawyer. Others, too, drop in on this group from time to time—perhaps they're here this Saturday afternoon, perhaps not: Hein, Ramsey, Derrick's boyfriend, Niezhaam.

Today we're writing a constitutional brief on lesbian and gay rights for the African National Congress. Derrick has penned an early draft of the argument, but now we're all weighing in on the logic. If we get this right, perhaps we can shape the future. We splash out thoughts like paint slops.

"Can you add something to the section on history to address the counterargument?" I ask. "I mean, there have also been well-known statements by ANC leaders that this is a trivial issue. Can we say something about how gay rights aren't luxuries?"

Sheila, Ivan, and Julia all nod. "Good point," Ivan says. "Glad you're here," nods Sheila. All I've done is parrot my university professors: they are always handing me back my literature papers with red-ink comments like, "Discuss the opposing point of view." I still know nothing about politics; nevertheless, my heart swells with pride.

Early signs from our informal outreach to members of the ANC's constitutional committee are positive. The committee is chaired by a man called Albie Sachs, a survivor of a car bomb set by cronies of Dirk Coetzee, my childhood police-lingo instructor. Albie's a known supporter of lesbian and gay equality and speaks with immense authority, partly because of his history in the movement and partly because of the trials he has survived. Here, too, the sense of miraculous beneficence continues: as if there's a charm in the air, something lucky and golden in the sunlight. Does Eshu like to upend norms and play with assumptions? While he and the other orishas aren't exactly pancontinental queer icons, he clearly does have an anarchic, gender-bending streak: in Dahomean dances, I later learn, his part is typically played by a woman with an attached phallus.

Politically, what has in fact happened is that we've simply been fortunate enough to be active at a unique historical opening. The African National Congress, influenced by a decades-long alliance with socially progressive antiapartheid movements, is willing to adopt left-wing European liberalism. Just as importantly, there are too many other competing national dilemmas for this particular stand to attract any organized opposition: the country is worried about white secession and tribal battles, not about gay men getting married in the future or lesbians holding onto their jobs. However, this is not the way it feels, on the day human rights lawyer Albie Sachs visits OLGA and tells us our prospects for victory are excellent. On that day, again, there's a hint of beguilement in the breeze, a suggestion of sandman's dust in the lamplight.

"Apartheid tried to tell everyone what to do, how to be," Albie says, sitting on the couch in Ivan's living room: all the chairs, tables, and floor spots are filled with listeners. "The essence of democracy is that people should be free to be what they are."

Albie, middle-aged, wrinkled, with thinning gray hair, wears a bright red shirt with what looks like peacock motifs printed on it. One of his shirt sleeves dangles limp and empty; one eye is blind—motionless, with the eyelid drooping half-closed. As I watch Albie tonight, it's hard to decide which seems the greatest providence. He has survived an entire vehicle exploding beneath him, the thunder of the dynamite, glass and shrapnel flying into flesh. How does he now talk so calmly about peace and human rights? Then there's the nondiscrimination clause itself, which goes beyond anything that currently exists in places like Amsterdam or San Francisco. Soon, it seems, gay couples in New York City will be looking with envy at their counterparts among the stark neofascist Pretoria buildings and the mud huts of the Transkei.

But that isn't all. This evening, as I sit leaning against a wall, I'm stunned by what seems to me perhaps the biggest miracle of all—the transformation that's occurred in me. Just a decade ago, after all, I was sitting on Dirk Coetzee's lap with hyenas yowling in the distance.

That year I stop asking for academic deferments for my military service. This is what the papers say, the ones I crumple into a rubbish bin: "You must appear at Bloemfontein train station" at such-and-so date and time. I imagine a chilly highveld morning with frosty steam coming out of my mouth: power lines on the distant ridges; a restaurant serving greasy bacon and eggs. "Refer to the reverse side for permitted personal items." But now, these commands no longer seem incontrovertible. As an auxiliary to the memoranda of understanding and the preconstitutional negotiations, army functionaries are holding talks with ANC guerillas about new, volunteer-based platoons. *No, sir, no deposit*—this time I won't go back.

At the university I join *Varsity* newspaper, a left-wing publication with a long connection to the antiapartheid movement. Here I get to experience for the first time the public limelight, and somewhat to my surprise, I find it suits me. In the first month or two, for example, I'm quoted in the front page about gay rights on campus. As part of an activities fair, both Muslim and Christian groups have been distributing pamphlets denouncing homosexuality and abortion. This is hate speech, I opine. The university should remove the offending literature.

This statement elicits a good deal of outraged mail to the paper. But for others, I'm an exemplar. Alex and Louise, their boyfriends, people from English class—these folks all come up to me in the cafeteria and slap me on the back.

"Good for you," they say. New members of the gay student group thank me. At that moment, am I aware of the figure I must cut? Standing somewhere in that omnivorous ruckus and clatter of the dining hall in my jeans and my newly purchased Freedom Charter T-shirt, inspired by my new OLGA comrades: these are the years when perhaps a third of the campus wears T-shirts supporting the minimum wage, an end to violence against women, the scrapping of the draft. The truth is, it matters little to me, at this moment, whether I am advancing the cause of gay equality, let alone free speech. Deep down, all I want is for the police to confiscate these brochures I experience as potent miniature thrashings.

In *Varsity* I pan a community Shakespeare production in Athlone—me, spreading my literary-critic wings. "As dismal as the streets the theatre stands on," I proclaim. "We have to do better at providing cultural services to the historically disadvantaged."

The director I'm criticizing, an old friend of my erstwhile down-town landlord who forwarded me free tickets, is a Colored lesbian in her forties with a lifetime of experience bringing culture to the Cape Flats. What exactly makes me think I know more about the cultural needs of the mixed-race working classes than she does? It's true I didn't much like the show, but something else, too, is going on. There's something thrilling about flexing my intellectual muscles, about saying, "Look at me." And the review indeed provokes all manner of interesting chatter in my Shakespeare tutorial. "How do we make Shakespeare relevant to Africa," my teacher wants to know? This is the same professor who, when I wrote a paper about heterosexism in the bard's comedies, commented: "I'm not sure I entirely agree with your conclusions. But South Africa's going to need queer critics, you know. Have you thought of carrying on with a masters?" In fact, after my fourth year in school, I will be offered a scholarship to pursue a Ph.D. at the university: an opportunity I will turn down in favor of an activist-academic job in the Institute of Criminology, examining homophobic human rights abuses.

In a collapsing right-wing police state, gay is cool; queer is avant-garde. It's a way for people like me to enjoy the best of both worlds, to leverage apartheid privilege, such as my elite taxpayer-funded education, and still be part of the new clamor for inclusiveness. At parties I'm now a social magnet. Women and men will scoot across batik-covered couches to ask me whether I think homosexuality is a western imposition. I happily play the expert. I talk about the Balobedu rain queens near where I grew up, who take multiple wives and whose sexual ambiguity is presumed to be at the root of their prowess with the thunderstorm spell. I ask the questioner if Christianity is an import from Europe, and if so, whether this, too, should be banned.

For much of the past seven years I have been a recluse, locked up in a residence bedroom or piano studio. Now I feel knotted to a generation. One Saturday afternoon I represent OLGA at a United Democratic Front meeting—an umbrella group. Dullah Omar, a human rights lawyer, the chair of this meeting and the probable future justice minister, makes small talk with me afterward and inquires after my pending project at the Institute of Criminology. After I write several successful articles for a Johannesburg gay paper, its American expatriate editor, who's returning home to take care of a sick family member, offers it to me for free if I want it. I decline because I'm not ready to accept the responsibility. This, for me, is something brand-new, this being on leaders' radar screens, being so engaged with the wider community. I can talk to people; I can speak at conferences and argue my points and win a resolution at a student congress. There are limits, though, to this political passion. As a criminology researcher, I'll squander away my time reading novels with criminal justice–related themes; I'll chitchat with the department secretary and fail to fundraise. I'll organize a phone-in weekend that attracts only eight or so respondents. In truth, I talk a good talk, but when it comes to the hard slog, mundane details, and legwork, I'm not much of an asset to a social-change movement.

The one thing I do throw myself into is pursuing my black boys. Looking back on this time, it is these young men who seem to me the all-important background score to my adventures, the leitmotif from the orchestra pit that reveals the ongoing vulnerability of the hero-protagonist. It is the personal that is opened up by the political: the emotional drive that both undergirds and is enabled by my activism.

The pattern goes something like this.

It's a Friday night. After gluing captions on the front page of *Varsity* or attending a political meeting, I catch a train to a club called Caesar's in Long Street. It's on the second floor of a nineteenth-century mansion: elaborate iron lacework on the upstairs balcony; big, dark windows. The doorman nods to me as I hand over my money. I'm almost certainly wearing my signature outfit: bright-checkered clown pants and a psychedelic rainbow-colored T-shirt. I think of this gear as bright, sexy, ethno-tropical. Really, though, I've the aspect of a harlequin, a picador-jester—surely I'm not to be taken seriously among all these polished club kids. As in Johannesburg, the *injongas* dress in designer jeans and gold chains; the *skesanas* in stonewashed Levis. Flamboyant *moffies*—Colored drag queens—parade in wigs, sequins, and sti-lettos. But nobody laughs at me for my absurd look: it's so unusual to have a white regular that I'm granted a mascot's leeway.

The music's deafening. Tomorrow my ears will ping. This ca-cophonous racket, these flickering strobe lights—it's a realm where boundaries meld together and the mind is emptied. *Every-body, everybody.* That's the megahit of the time, our incantatory hymn. And it's only a slight overstatement of the group of people, in that wonderland of spin shadows and glitter, that I will want to share communion with.

So: Bradley's successor, Mark—I meet him there, on the dance floor. Mark's a plain-looking, somewhat plump man in his twen-ties, dressed in tweed pants and an ordinary shirt. But what I like about him is a certain boy-next-door charm: he has a mustache, smiles a lot, and uses down-home rhyming slang like, "Safe like a *duif.*" In Mark's case, "next door" is a tiny two-bedroom tin-roof house in the sprawling Colored township of Athlone where he lives with his sister and brother-in-law: children running around outside; laundry flapping above a small rectangle of sand and grass. Mark works in a household goods factory near the inner city. Sis-ter looks after the kids; brother-in-law's a rookie cop. Mark invites me to have supper and stay the night. What's extraordinary to me about this experience is how safe I feel, how at home. On the shelves are Mark's high school trophies. This could be me, couldn't it?

Our affair doesn't work out, though. Stupidly, one afternoon a couple of weeks into the relationship, I leave a bunch of flowers at his factory. It's an impulsive move: I'm in town, shopping at the Salt River Fruit Market, just down the road from his workplace. I see the bright white carnations. I leave these blossoms with the secretary for him at the factory front office. "For Mark's family," I tell her, "to say thanks for supper." It's romantic and yet it's not; I'm pushing the boundaries, yet giving myself cover. A day or two later, there's a note for me at the residence hall front desk: "How could you have done that, Glen? I could have lost my job! Please don't contact me anymore." On the phone his sister says, "You have to respect his decision, Glen. You'll find others, hey?"

And indeed I do. After Mark, there's Ramsey: a guy in his thirties from OLGA. Ramsey and I go on a couple of dates to the movies, a night drive to Signal Hill. We head back to my residence hall and fool around in my room. After this first love-making he says, "I've never been as excited about anyone as I am about you." He has had so many bad experiences with men, and he can tell I'm different—kinder and more genuine. I know there's something I really like about Ramsey—the way he erupts happily over a movie line, the gentle way he touches my forearm. With him, too, there is something healing. But now, the speed at which he's falling for me disconcerts me. I don't know how to slow him down. While I'm eloquent talking about anticolonial politics or sexual policing, I still have a child's incapacity for clear statements of feeling like, "I need to ease off." So now I do what will get rid of him.

"Actually," I say, "I'm not really sure I'm all that attracted to you, you know? There is an age difference."

Something in his face caves in. His jaw drops; he looks at the floor; he sighs before getting up and saying, "It's okay, really, no need to apologize, Glen." My room door behind him slams shut. Is it a coincidence that soon after this he drops out of OLGA? He has opened a vulnerable part of himself to me and I've jacked it.

Siphiwe, a student I meet at a political gathering, has a public sex fetish. He likes to lie flat on his back, on the floor of a toilet stall in my residence bathroom, while I penetrate him between his thighs. He explains that this form of intercourse is called *uku-soma*, thigh sex, a practice encouraged by King Shaka in the days of the Zulu Empire to promote intimacy and brotherhood between his warriors. When we lie doing this Siphiwe says we're being Afrocentric. The ancient bush *impis* would have to do it silently, too, for fear of giving away their battle positions. Maybe so, but I soon tire of this tawdry theatricism, the discomfort of calves and feet jammed between plumbing and cubicle posts, and then, before I know it, I'm failing to return his phone calls, telling him I'm not interested when I bump into him on campus. And then I'm on to Mandla, Kevin, Gavin, Sizwe, and Charl.

In one way or another, all the black boys from those two years are like this: something is always wrong with me or with them. In some part of my brain, clearly I'm longing to feel at home with them. It feels good to nestle in two strong arms on a Sunday morning. It's fun to head to a supermarket, to skip the cafeteria and cook spicy tomato pasta or lentil pie; to make love on a bed, couch, or carpet. Chests and tongues are pleasurable—there is something deeply soothing about reaching out, in the early hours of the morning, for a closing hand. But still there's some brake in my mind, some mental obstacle. What do I still fear—athletics-spike stigmata? Perhaps this dancing fetish-goblin's stardust has only a limited efficacy. Perhaps, like Cinderella's pumpkin coach, this dark, smooth skin with all its juju power of oppositeness—of *not*-John-ness—eventually reverts to plain old epidermis-dermis, with deposits of an entirely inanimate pigment called melanin.

James calls from Pietermaritzburg. Recently, he, too, has come out as gay—when the two of us informed each other by phone, we giggled at the shared five-year masquerade: "I had my *ideas*, hey . . ." Now, though, he has a warning for me. The long-distance phone line crackles; it's hard to make out his words, but I get the gist. "There's been staffroom gossip, hey, back at school about an article you wrote. *Ja*, they can't believe it—you some kind of gay spokesman. Everyone wondering if your folks know."

Mom and Dad. I've been deliberately avoiding thinking about them in the middle of all this. I still talk to my parents regularly, of course; I love them. But there has been a part of myself I have kept from them. We talk only about classes and friends. What will two devout Catholic savannah dwellers, with their bird-watching binoculars and their mammal identification books, make of a life dedicated to sexual exploration and social activism? Still, it is too cruel and disrespectful for them to learn about me in a newspaper passed to them in the Pick 'n Pay. It is time, now: I have been living in the shadow of half-truth for too long. So one winter break I go back home to the wilderness.

When I step off the airport shuttle, Mom is too delicate to criticize the earrings and hairstyle, even though she's visibly surprised. "You look different!" she says. With my last transfiguration, the hippieish hair that sprouted in all directions, they took several weeks before they asked me, "But why?" This time round, though, I don't wait long. That evening, after Mom's in bed, when it's just Dad and me in the TV room, I say, "Dad, there's something I need to talk to you about." He is always the one I've wanted to talk to about the weighty issues—his opinion will carry Mom.

At first he replies, "Let's talk tomorrow, hey? I'm getting ready for bed." But then when I retire to my own room, he knocks on the door.

"I'm not going to be able to sleep wondering what this is about."

We sit in the lounge, on the fluffy cream-colored couches, beneath the watercolor of the kudu stooping down to drink at a river and the painting of a herd of wildebeest kicking up dust under Mount Kilimanjaro.

"So what's going on?"

I take a deep breath. "I'm gay, Dad. I don't think I've ever, in my life, been sexually attracted to a woman. Also, I've become something of a gay activist. I'm being quoted in the newspapers and stuff. I thought it's time you and Mom knew."

Initially, Dad is crestfallen, particularly about the news of my being a six on the Kinsey scale—no hope for an eventual metamorphosis. He sighs, "I always thought you were just a late bloomer with the girls." I ask him if Mom has ever guessed: he says no, not as far as he knows. He confesses: "Honestly, this is like the first act in a three-part tragedy. The next thing I'm expecting to hear is that you're dying of AIDS." I've sprung this all on him without the slightest warning—he is having to process it in the moment. But soon he gathers himself. He hugs me. "Of course we're going to accept you the way you are, Glen. That's the important thing. How could we do different? You're our son."

Next morning, Mom calls me from the office—she now works as a secretary in the tourist information department.

"I just wanted you to know, Glen, my love, that we love you no matter what," she says. Dad has told her, of course. She is simply unable to contain herself until five o'clock. "I really want you to understand this, Glen. You'll always be welcome here. This is your safe place, where you belong. This is *home*. Do you know what I mean? This is where you can be who you are."

Home: have I been wrong about her and Dad, about this place? Perhaps there is more enlightenment here than I give the environment credit for—in this tiny village that has only just desegregated the swimming pool. That evening, Mom and I go for a walk. We wave together at the old Afrikaner uncles and aunts sitting on their porches; we watch the warthogs play in the sprinklers on the rugby field. It's just like old times—except, of course, that everything's shifted, like one of those kaleidoscopes that fall into patterns that only seem like the previous ones.

I ask her if she ever guessed about my sexuality. She confirms Dad's impression that no, the thought didn't ever really cross her mind as an issue: there was the example of her own father, who didn't have a girlfriend until he was twenty-eight. "What's it like to be an activist?" she wants to know. I tell her about the fascinating people I've met, about the ANC Constitutional Committee and Albie Sachs. She's intrigued. This is all alien to her, of course—talk of car bomb survivors and constitutional clauses—but there is no fear or judgment; she's genuinely motherly and curious.

"It seems you like all these people, which makes me happy."

We walk past Merle and Ian's house; I ask about Lisa and David, away at boarding school, and Lorna and Ian. By way of friendly chitchat, Mom updates me on Marriage Encounter, a program she and Dad have been participating in since the early 1980s. It has helped them to improve their communication and treasure their love, she says.

"You should try it one day," she says, and then she realizes her faux pas—as a program sponsored by the Catholic Church, it's unlikely to welcome my relationships.

"I wonder if gay couples could attend a Marriage Encounter weekend?" She catches herself: "I suppose they wouldn't." She continues to think aloud: "It isn't really fair, is it? I imagine that's what all your activism is about." I nod. Again, have I underestimated her? How much does she sense about the last eight years—about how she and Dad progressively disappeared from the center of my life, after the jack bank? How I couldn't help feeling angry at them for sending me there? Everything sexual I left out of my account of John and his bullying—sex is a secret I've been keeping from them, for as long as I can remember.

"It must be hard to be a gay person in Skukuza," she says, as we double back past the squash courts, towards the corner house where uncle Dirk Coetzee once pressed my thumb on the walkie-talkie. "You must feel alone." I nod. She has always had an astounding ability to know what I needed: *I'm sorry, Neels, but Glen and his dad went shopping in town, so he won't be able to keep his three o'clock appointment.* Can she still do this?

We cross in front of Merle's a second time, then head down the hill and past the church with the fever trees where we retreated from the lions, the school where a principal lectured me about drawing the crucified Jesus, the turnoff to the tourist camp where once, long ago, Dirkie and I threw pebbles. At last, she asks me, "My love, is there a special man in your life? You could bring him to meet Dad and me, you know—I think we'd really be open to that. I suppose that's always what a mother wants, isn't it? To see her children settled."

Is there someone special in my life? My mind, now, is a collage of a dozen or more black men. Sizwe, in the Skyline bar in Johannesburg, during a conference I attended—he cruised me in the hallway outside the bathrooms, and we ended up in his cheap hotel room. Clinton, the visiting African American exchange student. Mandla, who broke up with me in Kirstenbosch Gardens.

"I just don't know what exactly you want from me, Glen," Mandla had said, on the lawn below the proteas with the view of the city, and with the picnic I'd prepared for him as a votive offering. "It seems you're trying to pull something out of me, spiritually. You're digging in me."

Homosexuality is one thing, interracial dating is another, and promiscuity's a third. And as for this *chi,* this god I only dimly realize I'm hoping will resurrect me from my whites-only crucifixion—how to explain all this to the woman who taught me about Jesus?

Can a god, spirit, or orisha scatter all the jack bank dollars deposited in me?

Can an investment of a hundred kisses cancel out six blows of earned interest?

But of course this isn't what Mom's asking, now. She in her floppy cotton hiking hat, smelling of suntan lotion and insect repellent. Mom is wondering about sons-in-laws and Sunday picnics and game drives with a new family member.

"Not really, Mom," I admit. "I've still just been getting to know guys. But maybe I will, hey, one of these days?" To myself I wonder: if I did, would I be able to invite him here to barbecue with Merle and Ian in a backyard? Would we be able to walk hand and hand in the staff shop? Would we stand any chance at all of being able to unite two worlds—this one, so placid, wild, and beautiful; that other one, increasingly my stomping ground, so imbued with life's exuberant but frightening uncertainty?

Equals

There's something proverbial about the way we meet. Love at first sight, the look of recognition across the classroom floor where we're having our activist workshop, that instinct flickering; *Hey, I think that one might just be different.* Sure, this moment's probably familiar to me before it happens. A dozen Hollywood films, a shelf of my maternal grandmother's old Mills and Boon romance novels: the pivotal second when a bolt in the protagonist's brain goes snap, and the playboy with the pastel-colored lounge suit and the Clark Gable cigar—suddenly he's not so cool, casual, and debonair anymore. Suddenly he's *really* interested in a girl. He's visualizing mountain walks. Sitting in that workshop, the first thing I think when I see him is, *Cute.* And he is that—short, chest muscles pressing out against his T-shirt, dark-skinned, dressed in tight-fitting jeans and expensive sneakers. The next thought, *Really smart,* and there's no question on this count, either, as he bounces on his toes, smiling, nodding, and listening, filling out goals, objectives, and guiding principles on a white newsprint sheet. What does he think of me that morning, sitting around on plastic chairs under the overhead light? Hardly the dandy. Later I'll hear what he remembers thinking: *Why is that boy wearing those red-and-black baggy shorts that look like they've come from a charity shop castoff bin? Eish! These white intellectuals dress badly. But a handsome guy, né? I like his legs.*

We're at the October 1991 national lesbian and gay conference in Johannesburg, planning a strategy for getting a sexual orientation clause into the Bill of Rights. The meeting's in a hall with big windows and wooden parquet floors. I have a vague sense of nurses wandering around in their green smocks, the sound of cars below, fast food and corner barbers and sidewalk domino games when we step outside the building. OLGA, my organization, has sent up a minibus full of activists from Cape Town. There are folks, too, from Durban and Pietermaritzburg. The biggest group, however, is GLOW, Gays and Lesbians of the Witwatersrand, by far South Africa's largest, predominantly black gay organization, which sponsors township shebeens and has at least a thousand members. Among its most prominent leaders, and the facilitator of the workshop I'm in right now, is *this* man, according to the program I'm holding, Cecil—this sexy twentysomething guy leaning into the microphone at the center of the room, saying: "Comrades, order please. Comrades, please quiet down."

His good looks derive mostly from his strong physical features: an emphatic bone structure that I will later recognize, after I have left the country, as distinctively black South African: small round head; clearly defined jaw; and an attractive framed-up haircut. As I watch him he bounces, yo-yo-like, on the balls of his feet. He is like a kid making up for his smallness with his sheer vivacity. "Comrades," he says, springing again and waving his arms in something of a windmill motion. A hush falls. Not only is he lively and humorous, but he has a sense of authoritative command. He smiles a beaming, toothy grin, which relaxes the group. Before long, as the workshop unfolds, I find myself backing up his political positions, even when they're contrary to the ones I usually take.

"We need every sector to pull its weight," I say, in response to a question about the correct balance between social services—housing, employment, parties, and so forth—and political lobbying of the kind my own gay and lesbian organization has been focusing on. "None, by itself, can be successful." When did I ever believe that? I have always said that at a time of such drastic political change, civil rights is the first priority.

"Yes, right!" Cecil says, from the front of the room, beaming. "And the same must be true of the regions; *iGoli* and the Western Cape, they each have their strong points. If you just have a lobbyist working by himself—that victory, it can be taken away like that!" He snaps his fingers, his whole body twitching as he does so. He grins at me again. Even though, technically, he's putting down my political organization, it doesn't occur to me to quibble with him; he is altogether simply much too amiable.

"Great workshop," I say afterwards, as we shake hands. "I really learned a lot."

"Me too!" he says. Then, after a minute or two of small talk: "What are you doing for dinner?"

We go out and get something to eat in the city—pita sandwiches, fried chicken, salad—and engage in get-to-know-you chitchat. This, too, has something of a foreordained quality to it: what the Czech writer Milan Kundera means when he says love stories are composed of marvelous coincidences. *Oh, you like Biko's essays too?* Both of us are social democrats: "I do not care about capitalist this and communist that," Cecil says, and when he does so I'm pleased: in activist circles, these distinctions are much more important than religious ones. Friendships have dissolved over the technical question of whether the Soviet Union is a corrupted socialist state or a form of state-controlled capitalism. These shared values between Cecil and me bode well—and all in all, as we eat together, I'm confirmed in my initial impression of a smart, articulate, and charismatic man, gorgeous, only a year older than me, with whom I really have a significant amount in common.

"Do you want to visit a friend of mine?" he asks, when we're done.

And isn't there something perfect, too, about the confident, seamless way he, the home boy, orchestrates the tryst that follows? The two of us stop by the house of his friend, a thin, sandy blond intellectual active in GLOW. After tea, biscuits, and repartee about committees and activity rosters, Cecil's friend makes a tactful exit to go grocery shopping. We are left, just the two of us, in the small house with the mattress on the floor in the guest bedroom—condoms and water-based lubricant thoughtfully left out on an end table. Abdullah Ibrahim's *Manenberg* plays on a portable stereo. Incense, masks, and candles—all the accoutrements of romance, twentieth-century African-style—are laid out for our union.

The sex is terrific: sensual in that unique way that sex becomes when emotional chemistry is added to physical. "I really like that," Cecil says, when I rest my hand on his naked thigh—a pale cloud silhouetted against a dark night sky.

"Mmmm," I moan when he runs his tongue down from my belly button.

"So good!" we both cry—and we aren't talking about Abdullah's silken, soaring virtuosity on the piano, nor about the rusty orange quality of the evening light falling through the window, although we certainly could be: if someone overheard us, they'd think we might be.

We spend most of the rest of the conference and the accompanying pride festival in each other's company. Two other memories

adhere from that first weekend together. One, we're having breakfast somewhere. (How is it possible I remember so many restaurants from that period? I am still a student living on loans and
summer jobs, and for as long as I'll know Cecil his financial situation will be worse than mine, since he works in HIV prevention
counseling and community organizing.)

Still: we're in some Steers or Wimpy Bar, eating baked beans
on toast or cheap, greasy bacon and eggs. I ask him where exactly
he lives.

"I am in a gay Soweto commune," he replies. "There is an older
couple, Thomas and Dube. They are having me there, too, to help
around the house. It is sort of a family, you know? It is very nice."

The news of this bona fide queer African commune fires my
curiosity and gives Cecil the exotic aura of a social pioneer—a
John Humphrey Noys of the black working class.

"What do the neighbors think?" I want to know. "What are
your cultural models for this? How do you handle conflict?"

"Well, are you not the cultural anthropologist?" Cecil says, smiling again, putting his hand on mine, now, in full view of all the
other diners. "You will just have to come see for yourself. I will
volunteer to be your study object. You are welcome to analyze me."
How I love this flirtatious offer! He seems as open as a wheatfield.

The second recollection is from the pride festival. The two of
us are standing at the OLGA stall, talking to Josie, a young, blond
South African lesbian who's returned from exile in San Francisco. Marchers mill by: leather daddies, Zulu gumboot dancers,
dykes on bikes. An erotic photographer waves to us: he had earlier enquired about having the two of us pose for him, and we
turned him down. Now Josie teases us.

"I see your cruising was successful, Glen," she says and winks.
Now, Cecil and I find ourselves united in a kind of knee-jerk ter-
ritorial outrage that, like the breakfast conversation, inadvertently

reveals where we're headed and signals the profundity of the connection we've made.

"This wasn't cruising," I say, offended.

Cecil lays a protective arm around my back.

"I like this guy," he says. "We are special to each other. You can even say we love each other." He winks at Josie as he says this and smiles—he is not altogether serious. Still, he isn't purely joking, either. There's no doubt this is still nothing more than a no-strings escapade—fourteen hours of road lie between our home cities; if you added up our years of life we'd be in our forties, barely be middle-aged. But something in the way we stand together, on that field, arm in arm, the drag queens singing behind us on the makeshift stage by the bluegum trees, me leaning forward to kiss him so naturally—something within all this suggests we mean something to each other.

But now, for the next three months or so, my memory enters a black hole, suggesting to me that in fact the two of us are initially very sensible and rational with each other—we recognize the limitations of our three-day romance in the midst of a political gathering; we know that everyday life is different from pride marches, music festivals, and carnival parades. We carry on with our respective responsibilities. I wrap up my honors degree in African studies and get ready for my first full-time job, as a criminology researcher examining the policing of sexual minorities, a position I've obtained as a result of my activism. In accordance with my pending status as an employed person, I move into a beautiful ranch house on the slopes of Table Mountain, with an interracial lesbian couple called Patti and Jeanelle.

Cecil and I must stay in touch, though, because when I fly back to Nelspruit for Christmas and buy a used blue Peugeot from a friend of my parents—I'll now need good transportation around Cape Town—on the way back I meet up with Cecil in a Melville music club. This is the first actual date I will remember with him: a thick fog of basement smoke, heavily made-up women sitting on the laps of the plumpest and oldest businessmen—prostitutes plying a weekend trade. We talk some more. As before, we discover or construct near-identical predilections. How can we both love anguished, talk-heavy French movies? How do two people develop such specific parallel loves for the smell of dust in the first minute or so of a tropical rainstorm?

When the band gets on the stage, Cecil and I join the dancing straight couples, and even after what must be the intervening months of handsome Xhosa *amadoda* and luscious Colored guys dancing at Cesar's in Cape Town, I find him sexier than ever, exploding with energy, his fashionable Adidas sneakers glowing a spectral pale green on the dance floor—miniature yachts tossing and bobbing on a black sea. When the band covers Sonny and Cher's "I Got You, Babe," he flips his arm and index finger forward in my direction. As he dances I see that twitch again I so love in him, coming from somewhere around his tailbone. At some point we both need the bathroom. Now he rolls in after me, as sure of himself as a wave. He locks the door and proceeds to embrace me and run his hands up and down my spine—hungry, defiant, lustful. I, responding to his passion, draw my tongue around the curve of his ear; suck the pulp of his lobe between tooth and lip. Something about being with him must make me feel invincible, because when someone knocks on the door, we merely chuckle. "Busy!" I say. "Leave us alone!" Cecil shouts. When we reemerge we hold hands.

Why are we doing all this? What exactly are we falling in love with, the two of us? As we field surprised stares and shaking heads and stride for the club exit, we overhear a suited businessman: "Think it's a bloody homosexual bordello, hey?" There's not a thought between us of the possible consequences—newspaper headlines, embarrassed political organizations, policy research jobs compromised before they begin.

Yes, of course this is youthful foolishness and immortality—invincibility. Yes, this is out-of-control hormones, love and lust gone berserk, just the way they are supposed to.

But for me, at least, there's more here, simmering in my unconscious, more in the happy way I rub Cecil's head and the small of his back, as we emerge together into the wan luminescence of the car park. I may not be aware of it, but there's a piece of wood from John's cricket bat stuck in my brain fibers; a jack bank deposit still earning interest: there is a part of me that *wants* one of these party-goers to get upset, so that I can fight my way back to dignity.

And with hindsight it will seem to me there are other ways, too, in the opening months of 1992, that I still show the scars of the jack bank. There is something mothlike and self-destructive about my relationship with danger, a way in which I'm both attracted by it and repulsed. Even now, almost a decade after meeting John, few things—certainly not death or illness—petrify me more profoundly than the thought of being imprisoned. When I'm driving to Cecil's on the N4 highway—my first road trip in my new vehicle—a cop stops me for speeding. My hand shakes so badly I can't flash the headlights, flick the indicators, or direct my foot to the brake pedal. Afterward, the anxiety is so intense I have to stop to vomit. When I hear about a draft dodger, like me, picked up by the military police and taken to a disciplinary camp, I develop nervous diarrhea; my sinuses inflame; I call in sick with a low-grade fever.

Still, the concept of violence also exerts a seductive power on me. In Cape Town I begin to order sadomasochistic erotica through a friend who owns an under-the-censors book business: I pick them up from her downtown Cape Town flat in brown paper parcels, like rough diamonds. In fact S&M isn't a staple of my sexual fantasy life—there are beaches, rivers, and summer camps there, too; school classrooms and urban construction sites and long royal medieval banquets. But still, there's no doubt this darker sexual material stimulates a special part of my brain, connected to my abuse memories. In the pictures and stories in gay leather magazines like *Drummer,* I see the B-grade sexual footage from my recollections displayed with a campy, light-hearted touch. It's a relief to see cartoonish Johns trying out their hangings and their electroshock in contexts that are clearly humorous and consensual. In the same way, I enjoy nihilistic literature that allows me to scratch at my psychic scabs without actually being pulled into a whirlpool: Conrad's *Heart of Darkness,* with its enigmatic horrors; *Lord of the Flies,* with its pig sacrifices.

But in 1992 I don't have to go far to find myself presented with reminders of John and his insanity. Those days, the early 1990s, are ironically some of the most blood-soaked of the apartheid era. Later, commentators will describe them as the vicious snaps and spasms of the dying racist Rottweiler. At the time, though, unable to see the relative peace that awaits around the corner, they strike me as an amplification of all the madness that has filled my life until then, a jack bank expanded into so many asset classes and financial derivatives that its power seems all but absolute.

Thus, in the immediate aftermath of Mandela's release and the Pretoria minute, when the African National Congress suspends its armed struggle and announces its intention to negotiate a new constitution, the rate of killings in South Africa quadruples. A turf battle expands between Inkatha, a Zulu nationalist movement informally backed by the police, and Mandela's ANC. During the bad months, three to four hundred people will be slaughtered every weekend: hacked to death by rampaging warriors wielding assegai spears and knobkerrie clubs, or shot or burned in retaliation by revolutionary comrades.

It's as if John's spirit has infected a whole country. On those glorious romantic afternoons in Johannesburg, that December before my criminology job, Cecil and I hang out in Stephen's apartment. Stephen is the high school friend who rented the skyscraper flat where I lost my virginity; he has since moved to new digs in the trendy countercultural suburb of Yeoville. While Cecil and I visit the cafés, cinemas, and traditional magic shops in Hillbrow, though, the rest of the country swelters in an orgy of sadism. Children's arms get chopped off in front of their horrified parents. Women and infants are forced to swallow laundry detergent. Through all this, there is talk not just of police complicity but of an ominous "third force," composed of the likes of the killer who once sat me on his lap—operatives who no longer even listen to the government but are determined to thwart democracy.

In our small group—Cecil, Stephen, and me—I am the one who cannot tune this out. I am the one whose eyes are pulled toward the big blue screen, who flips the channels to see abdomen hackings and ambulances transporting hand grenade victims.

"Don't watch that, babe," Cecil says, coming back from the fridge with a Sprite or a Fanta. "I have to be coping with that all the time, in Soweto. Now that we are on holiday together, let us think of other things."

"*Ja*, turn off the TV, hey," says Stephen, my friend from high school—a day scholar, he never experienced the dorm bullying the way I did. He lacks this fascination for darkness. But I leave it on as long as I can, keep watching the numbers and statistics and the chattering, bewildered analysts.

When there's good news on the reports—the signing, say, of the Declaration of Intent at the Convention for a Democratic South Africa—I'm like a head-over-heels teenager. "It's going to happen!" I tell Cecil. "We're going to have peace." At such moments I feel like I live in the most wonderful country.

But when national tragedy strikes in the form of pub patrons mowed down by machineguns, I'm shrouded in glumness for hours.

"You are a real news addict," Cecil remarks. "If I were spending as much as you with the newspapers and radio I would be going crazy. You have to be living your life, *wena.*"

But now, in Johannesburg, when the two of us say good-bye outside Stephen's flat—it's time for me to start at the university—he holds me tight and kisses me between my eyes: "I'll miss you."

Every few hours on the way home, I try to call him from pay phones, but he's not available. From Beaufort West and Laingsburg I mail him two postcards.

"I love you," says the first one.

The second: "You make me buoyant."

Back in Cape Town, a week or so later a neat white hand-addressed envelope arrives in my mailbox, replete with a small red inked heart under the postage stamp.

> Dearest Glen,
> [This is what Cecil writes: not "dear" or "darling," but "dearest," as if none could be more valuable. General news follows—about a search for a new job; about his health and well-being. Then it comes:]
> I can't tell you how much I love you, boy! From the core of my heart I would say it boldly. . . . My goal is to keep you as my priority, my aim is to have you in life—for I adore a person quiet like you. . . . If [any people] seem to attack me I know where I would turn and lay my head and if I cry out for help you will always be there. . . .
> Luv from Cecil
> XXXXX

The letter is on lined stationery, of the kind given away at conferences by financial sponsors. The advertising slogan at the bottom, just below that long line of kisses, is printed in neat, large blue letters: TOGETHER, WE CAN DO MORE.

From the core of my heart I would say it. No adult peer has ever expressed such committed love for me like this, in blue and white, in writing. Holding Cecil's letter in my hand in my bedroom, standing under the red drape I hang on the window, beneath the Miles Davis portrait—all of this is slightly surreal, like seeing the ocean for the first time after reading about it. *Together we can do more.*

I am all shivers as I pick up the phone.

"Hello, Cecil speaking." That voice—full-timbered, even across a thousand miles of copper wiring.

"It's Glen, Cecil. I got your letter. It was wonderful."

"I meant it, babe. I did." And when we establish, later in this conversation, that both of us really want to go forward into life, from this point on, together—"Two of us rather than one," Cecil says, "each one picking up the other when he falls down"—I feel as happy as a dolphin.

Cecil visits Cape Town. He catches the bus—I buy the ticket and send it to him. He stays at Patti and Jeanelle's. From the living room we watch the sun set over Table Bay, where my Dutch, French, and English ancestors pulled into Africa in small wooden sailing ships. We look southwest, to the distant townships that are full of his ethnic cousins, the Xhosa—Cecil's own background is Zulu. Again we have a wonderful time hiking, seeing movies, making love on the mountaintop and in the bushes behind the gay beach. We own the city: we kiss on the downtown parade, in front of the Rastafarian street performers and the women in *burqas* selling curried rotis. We are a force of nature, the embodiment of our own political beliefs.

But after ten days it's time for him to catch his bus back to the land of gritty urban health projects, electricity pylons, and mine dumps. "Your life, it is much better than mine," he says, as we wait at the bus station—traffic whizzing by; the big Intercape sign and the logo for Standard Bank. "I am ashamed to be having you visit me, you know. It is nothing like this. Maybe I should be the one to come here."

"No, Cecil!" I exclaim, genuinely horrified. "How can you say such a thing? We're a relationship of equals. There's no 'better' or 'worse.'" He nods reluctantly before hugging me good-bye. We part, smiling. Do I even realize I'm bamboozling him into accepting an intellectual absurdity? Does it even cross my mind I am denying a basic social fact?

It isn't, of course, that I lack an intellectual awareness of how many more opportunities I enjoy than he does. I'm not blind to the loveliness of the green pines, the clear sunlight, and open vistas of my house compared to the view he describes from his place—a dusty, potholed street; towering electricity pylons; a small rubble-choked stream separating Eldorado Park, where he stays, from nearby Chiawelo. Rather, it's that I'm emotionally committed to assigning equal value to his circumstances and my own. My life has advantages, to be sure, but so, I'm adamant, does his—perhaps that sense of human warmth I imagine to be common among poor people.

The rigorous reciprocity I insist on dictates that if I played host to him in Cape Town, he must now do the same for me in Soweto. The opportunity arises when I get invited to give a paper at a government HIV prevention conference in Johannesburg. Dube and Thomas, the couple with whom Cecil used to live, have broken up, so Cecil is now living alone with Thomas, the older man. Since Cecil's original offer to be my anthropological sample, the security situation in Soweto has worsened considerably.

"I am not sure you should come," he says to me over the phone. "It is a bit crazy here at the moment."

But I have none of it.

"How can we be partners when I can't come near your home?" I ask him. "We can't allow these things to hold us back. If we do, then the other guys have won." My logic must be impregnable, because he replies: "So long as *you* are comfortable, babe. Of course."

He meets me at the Greyhound rotunda by Park Station and together we catch a minibus down Golden Highway past a prison, a shantytown, and Baragwanath Hospital, all square and red-bricked in the distance. The newly built First National Bank soccer stadium has naked bulldozed earth around it, construction tape still lying in the dust, and hollow concrete drainage pipes. Skinny dark-skinned children, barefoot and in rags, run around just outside the metal barrier on frost-blackened grass.

"See," Cecil says, pointing, a smile playing on his lips— "Soweto's national flower." The scrappy shrubs along the sides of the road are plastered with plastic supermarket bags: huge green, white, and yellow blossoms stuck to twigs or lodged between branch forks. He lets out one of those exuberant laughs of his. "See, Glen, this is not such a nice place." But the truth is, I fall in love with this stark urban landscape: the march of the gigantic power pylons, four or five rows of them, down the grassland dale right below the backyard of the simple two-bedroom brick house. The slushy puddles; the interlaced footpaths that seem to have people on them, walking and chatting, all hours of the day—the unemployment rate in these areas being upward of 60 percent. In the ugliness and desolation of all this I find a purity and frankness. The grime and desperation are visible here, and thus, or so it seems to me, manageable—the direct opposite, perhaps, of my pristine home village with its disturbing secrets. Besides, if I disliked this, the majority class and culture, what would it tell me about myself as a South African?

And so, for the moment, I play the slum tourist, someone thrilled—although of course I wouldn't admit it in so many words—with the authenticity of the suffering I see. Although I've certainly spent time in townships before, here, in this mother of racially segregated conurbations—a sea of two million maids, mine workers, lawyers, gangsters, and herbalists, in which I certainly seem to be the only resident white man—here, I persuade myself I feel more at home than ever. Cecil and I sit at the two-person table in the living room and eat breakfast cereal, maize porridge, and tomato gravy, just like any of the other married families around us. We play Yvonne Chaka Chaka and UB40 on the stereo; we dance and read the paper.

He gives me the sightseeing tour, such as it is in these days: Kliptown, where the Freedom Charter was signed; Tutu's old house; an Orlando Pirates and Mamelodi Sundowns game at the stadium. Throughout this, he's again uninhibited about expressing physical affection in public: holding my hand at the Kliptown taxi rank; kneading my calf muscle through my jeans at the soccer game, while around us the straight guys let loose their piercing township-style wolf whistles, index and pinkies splayed between their teeth. To the neighborhood ladies, he introduces me as his *umyeni,* his husband—they slap their hands over their mouths, say *"Hau!"* and burst into friendly laughter. When Thomas, Cecil's housemate, glumly shuffles through the house in his pajamas and slippers, ignoring my "Good morning" and "How are you?" Cecil reprimands him in Zulu until he nods hello.

"Please excuse him," Cecil says later. "It is nothing personal. He is just sad about Dube."

I succumb to optimistic thinking. I look past these minor danger signals—Thomas's hostility; the continuing reports of nearby conflict—and focus on what's good. By the time I head back to Johannesburg Airport, I'm infatuated not just with the kindest, gentlest, and bravest of young black gay activists, a man who cooks for me, hugs me, and demands respect from his neighbors, but also with what seems to me a warm, friendly, close-knit, happy place where people will make room in their midst for an interracial gay couple.

Now, back in picturesque Cape Town, I'm dissatisfied and restless. The beauty of the city grates on me. Those exquisite Hottentots Holland Mountains in the distance, a jagged line of rock—I can do without them. The magnificent cala lilies that grow in grassy ditches—I want to pluck them out and throw them against the thatched, old-world English-style pubs, which now seem symbols of the city's colonial insularity.

As the conflict worsens, so does my guilt and frustration at being removed from it. At Boipatong near Johannesburg, Zulu nationalist migrant workers hack to death forty-nine African National Congress protesters. At Bisho police kill twenty-eight. In London two security operatives are arrested trying to kill Dirk Coetzee for speaking to the newspapers. Then, on the very train that runs near Cecil's house, hooded gangs run demented with meat cleavers, hacking some passengers while prompting others to throw themselves to their deaths. The Institute of Criminology, with its attractive whitewashed cottages behind the clipped hedges of the university swimming pool, has never seemed so much like a tearoom behind the glass doors of an abattoir.

"Are you okay, baby?" I ask Cecil on the phone. In fairness to myself I do issue the sane suggestion: "Do you want to move here? We could be together in the Cape." But Cecil's just found a new job working as a youth educator near his home.

"Your job is finishing in December, honey," he points out. "How will we live? Anyway, this is one of the safer parts of Soweto."

Again I'm willing to be mollified—am prepared to construct a version of reality that minimizes the jack banks. Even with hundreds of deaths, statistics are on Cecil's side. And then there is that magnetic composure he's always radiated—if he says he's going to be fine, I believe him.

But the ennui grows. "I hate Cape Town," I tell a new friend,

Gerda. "It isn't real. It's like being in one of those kitsch tourist paintings." On the phone to my parents I note: "This city just doesn't have an edge." Do I notice the implications? *Give me a deposit of four, sir.* To be near violence, even to volunteer for it, is to feel alive and vital.

The year winds up. Despite myself, I pull together a basic research report for the institute, but after this I have nothing planned. By now my father has resigned his game reserve job. He and Mom live with David, now seventeen and in his matric year, in a spacious, leafy two-story suburban house just a few blocks from my old boarding school. In the afternoons they walk their dog past windows I once stared out of. Now, I wonder what to do next—my main objective is to be nearer Cecil. He certainly doesn't have room for me to move into Soweto with all my stuff, but I'd like to at least be somewhere close to him. My parents, three hours away, are the practical option.

At this time Lisa, my sister, lives in Cape Town. Two years ago, she moved here to study computer science. For the past twenty-four months the two of us have had a friendly, but ultimately superficial relationship: she did some computer work on the student newspaper at the time I was there; once or twice, at her suggestion, we joined a mutual friend for walks on a beach. She knows the basics about Cecil—knows I really like him and am thinking of moving north to be closer to him—but we do not go into any detail on each other's private lives. (Years later, after I've left the country, when Lisa comes out to me as a lesbian, I will realize what a lost opportunity those two years were to build a closer relationship.)

On this day, though, visiting her in her Tamboerskloof flat, I'm not thinking about *her* life. I'm here to get her perspective on the issue that's preoccupying me: is it a good idea for me to move back in with Mom and Dad until I find another job? She has more recent experience of them than I do.

Lisa brings me *rooibos* tea in a mug, just like Mom makes it.

We sit in her living room, with a green carpet floor and plain leather second-hand furniture. She is older now, casual in a studied, geekish, butch way—short, blond hair; jeans with holes in them; computers strewn all around the living room, in various stages of disassembly—it reminds me of my father's study. It is always nice, I reflect, when Lisa and I are together. I should see her more often.

"What do you think, Lees?" I ask her now.

Lisa pauses. I will always remember this moment: her, standing in front of me, at the full-length window, a sunlit pale muslin curtain moving in a breeze. "I think you should follow love, hey," she says. "If you don't, you'll always wonder what would have happened."

She's right, of course. At least she's correct based on the information I've given her, which is stripped of at least one relevant detail I haven't come to terms with yet: the self-destructive ribbon of jack bank recollections that runs from my amygdala down to my heart tissue. An only dimly understood need for connection, community, and refuge. What, I'll wonder later, prompts Lisa to take such a strong stand on the need to pursue love? Perhaps she has her own love preoccupations this morning—by the time I get around to asking her about it, she will have forgotten.

In any case, now, at the end of 1992, her suggestion is the persuasive one. I decide I'm ready for this—for my parents' acacia thorns and papaya trees, for Cecil's mine dumps and electric pylons—however the cards may fall. I pack up my belongings and ship them home to my parents. Then I organize a farewell party, call Cecil to tell him I'm coming to visit and job-hunt with him for a few days on my way home.

"Eh, I am looking forward to seeing you, babe," Cecil says, over the phone. If he expresses any reservation this time about the wisdom of staying with him, I won't remember them.

On the N1 highway—the towns sliding by, the telephone poles

flickering past, film seams clicking through a projector—not for a second does it occur to me I might be driving backwards rather than forwards; that by pushing into this future, I might be headed back into the past.

Frankly, I'm surprised at Cecil's demeanor when he meets me downtown, so he can guide me down the maze of roads in the Soweto area. "Welcome, babe," he says, but his heart doesn't seem to be in it: there is a tiredness about him. His shoulders slump. His smile is faint. Has something happened? But he denies it: "Eish, it's this new job, sweetheart. Always one more thing to do, *né*? Busy, busy, busy."

And back in Eldorado Park, with my car parked in his driveway, at first it's like old times. We make love in his bedroom. His new boss calls—I continue to tickle Cecil while he chats on the phone. Cecil giggles and pushes me away, but only half-heartedly; only gentle fingertips pressing my shoulder—he is still mine: *I would say it boldly.* It's fun, back in that simple bedroom with the white translucent curtains and the people walking by in the summer heat. The two of us make a tuna salad. He rinses my car.

But from the next day on he's self-absorbed. He truly is busy with his work: he leaves early in the morning and comes back around sunset. I buy *The Citizen* and *The Sowetan* at the nearby convenience store. On the living room floor I circle job advertisements, of which the pickings are few—a couple of teaching jobs where an education degree is desired; sales positions with no guaranteed income. I make phone calls from the beige plastic-covered rotary phone in the entrance hallway—an act that causes Thomas to straggle out again in his dressing gown and complain about the phone bill, which I say I'll pay in due course.

"You should not be here," he tells me. "There are few jobs in Johannesburg. And anyway, it's dangerous for a lone white man."

I think: what a sourpuss. I imagine: he must be so jealous of Cecil's and my happiness. I don't consider the possibility he's just sincere.

The job hunting takes only an hour or so. The rest of the day I'm mostly bored, listening to talk radio on Cecil's small bedside set, reading novels, cooking dinner for Thomas and Cecil—tomato sauce and *pap,* corn porridge. I'm not confident enough to drive to town on my own to see a movie. With Cecil at my side, I'm more than ready to claim citizenship in this black metropolis. On my own, though, I'm afraid of falling prey to a gang of criminals.

One afternoon Cecil's job requires him to go shopping, and I join him. At some point we're together downtown, around the Joubert Park taxi rank, clutching shopping bags. This is one of the most dangerous parts of the city—crowded, tin-shack and park-bench poor, free-wheeling, a place where gangsters lounge in front of crowded laundromats, their floppy cotton hat rims low over their eyes. Dusty white minibuses, at least two hundred of them, park three or four deep on the street; drivers whistle and call out the names of their destinations. But I feel comfortable here, with Cecil. This is vital and pan-African. "Maputo!" calls out one driver. "Harare! Nairobi!" yells another.

I stop to buy job papers at a newsstand, because the selection is better than back in Eldorado Park. I take out my wallet, pay with a ten-rand note, put the purse back, and the next thing I know Cecil has a tall young black man in a white shirt and checkered brown tweed pants by the collar. It lasts a second or two. He raises his right arm, fist clenched, as if to clout the guy. I didn't know Cecil's lungs had such force in them: *Msuno kanyoku, ugogo wakho is-febe!* Your mother's cunt; your grandmother is a bitch. Then this young man hands my wallet back to me. All the money is still in there, along with the First National Bank credit card. I hadn't even realized it was gone.

"Sorry, *baas,*" he says, surreally, using the old *apartheid* form of racial deference. I nod, still too shocked to formulate a response. Is this what the pickpocket's implying—that Cecil's protection amounts to a way of allowing me to move in the country as I please, like an old-style colonialist?

Back in our homebound minibus—we left the car at home to avoid parking hassles—Cecil berates me for my foolishness in flashing money in a well-known crime spot.

"That *tsotsi,* he could have had a knife. He could have been stabbing me." Cecil points, through his T-shirt to his solar plexus—to the warm chest I so enjoy reaching out and touching in the morning when I'm half-asleep. "Everybody, Glen, we all have to take care of each other. If we do things without thinking, we can cause problems not just for ourselves but for others as well."

"Sorry," I say. "I just didn't know."

"It's okay, baby," he replies putting his hand on my leg. "Just be more careful in the future, *né*?"

Do I listen to what he's saying? I should be making notes and sticking them on our room door, on my manila job record folders, on my arms and legs. I should be *thinking—really* thinking. Whose responsibility is it to make me feel comfortable in the world? But in some youthful corner of my heart, I still think Cecil, and by extension his community, can grab life by the collar for me and stop the swing of a cricket bat.

Cecil's work schedule becomes more flexible: some mornings he makes phone calls and does paperwork at home, then catches a minibus in the afternoon to see clients. Soon I begin to accompany him to work to print out copies of my résumé and cover letters. After doing this, I hang out until he's done. In the sparsely furnished activities room of the youth project, with its concrete floor, I sit on a plastic chair for hours and read novels or play with some of the younger children—games that don't require a shared language: rock-paper-scissors; chase-around-the-chair. I page through the teen magazines that lie on a corner table. I glance at the newsprint lining the walls, with handwritten self-help slogans on them: "We don't know what the future holds, but we know Who holds the future." For the most part it's boring. Cecil, to my right, busy with prepubescent orphans and street kids released from reformatories, has very little time to chat. The corrugated iron roof creaks in the heat. The small grassy backyard is filled with litter.

It smells of recent construction. Every time I come back from the yard, or from a trip across the street to the convenience store to buy chips or Coke, it hits me anew: the sharp odor of freshly dried white paint. Newly set concrete—its dust seems cleaner than regular dust, somehow, sweeter. Soft, vaguely earth-scented putty around the windowpanes. Is it coincidence that the smell of the place is both so distinctive and at the same time so similar to that other spot, years back, where I experienced a terrifying violence? The two-story dormitory building with metal walkway shadings below the windows, shadings that, like this roof, cracked and ticked in the sun. But the comparison doesn't strike me until much later. How many new buildings are there in the world? As I sit on my chair, a single blue-and-white plastic fan shakes its meshed-wire head at me, blowing out its tepid breath.

Sometime during those days I meet Cecil's boss, a lean, solemn, heterosexual Zulu man who knows about Cecil and me and who's cool with it. He wears glasses, jeans, and a plain shirt, and spends lots of time on the phone in the office talking to potential funders. According to Cecil he is good at paperwork, wins grants and secures licenses and keeps track of details: his desk is full of envelopes, forms, and letters. When I shake his hand he says, "Very pleased to meet you." To my later shame and consternation— the reasons for which will soon become clear—I don't retain his real name. Nhlakanipho? Nkosiphendule? I hope it's some long, difficult combination of unfamiliar vowels and consonants, so that my forgetfulness isn't entirely self-incriminating. For now I'll call him Musa, meaning mercy.

I feel superfluous in this place. I am not needed. While the ability to make computer printouts is a tremendous advantage, doing so feels like an imposition—there are floppy disks, paper jams, a forced bathroom break for Musa so I can sit in his chair, the phone ringing and bringing him in before I'm finished. The only thing that keeps me here is my uncertainty about how to get home via minibus—that, and the thought of Thomas with his gray hair and pimply skin, asking me how long I plan to stay. From Musa's office I borrow a Zulu dictionary and memorize words. I really do need to learn an African language. To fully connect to my country, and to be in any way a meaningful part of Cecil's world, I need to be able to understand what the people say.

It's maybe my second or third afternoon there. The day is late: rose-orange sunlight falls in through the windows; for some time I have been bugging Cecil to go home. Back at his house, the last night or two, he and I have in fact been talking about my possibly staying for a while in town with my friend Stephen or picking up the original plan again of driving to my parents' house.

Now, at first when the child runs in, I don't realize anything untoward is going on. Just another kid in rags running to Cecil. More excited chatter in Zulu suggesting, based on what I've learned the last few days, more street fights, police cars picking up vagrants, someone stealing money to buy sniffing glue. All these stories have been, of course, yet another reminder of the vast treasury of pain that surrounds me here. But this is not what I think at the moment. Rather, what goes through my mind is something along the lines of: *God, with all these clients, will Cecil and I ever get home for supper?* At that moment, I still think of the suffering as an unwanted distraction from my life.

Initially, then, I'm incurious about the argument that quickly erupts. Through the excited shouting, Musa, who has joined the fray, barks out some kind of order. Almost all the kids in the project—maybe ten or fifteen of them—leave together now, out the front door. But some kind of further conflict breaks out between Cecil and Musa, a clash in which two older male youths get involved. One of these guys breaks away and begins to close and bolt windows. Cecil shrugs; says something along the lines of "okay"; shakes his head. Musa gathers some papers, then disappears into the passageway behind his office, where he has a small bedroom with a floor mattress and a stand-alone clothes closet.

"Eish," Cecil says when he joins me. "The thing is, Glen, they are saying the Inkatha are coming. I am telling Musa, you and I can go home, but he is saying no, we must stay here with the place, he is going to his girlfriend's."

Inkatha. Although Cecil's demeanor is matter-of-fact, the implication sinks in like a dumbbell: this is our nightmare scenario. Inkatha is the group that, with the help of the police, has been terrorizing the rest of the country. Spears rupturing esophagi. Eyeballs gouged out. To me they seem the heart of this country's mad, evil violence—the grand reserve of the jack bank.

On their way here. A chill descends. Where my brain goes first isn't to the existential issues—Why am I repeating personal history?—but rather into the practical sociopolitical calculations. This neighborhood is overwhelmingly ANC-supporting. The Zulu nationalists will reasonably assume anyone they find here is an opponent. Regardless of what Musa says, we need to get out. Cecil's ANC T-shirt is like an invitation to assassination—perhaps Musa can lend him a nonpolitical one? But Musa is the one saying we should stay. And even if we do get out, the fact is, I'm a liability for Cecil, too. If the murderers really do have a police escort, there's a chance some burly Afrikaner might still pluck me out of the fray.

But Cecil, obviously a communist or gay for being with a white man, would get it three times as hard from the *impis*. I feel even more useless.

"Close the curtains," Musa says. "Tight, with no light coming through." We obey him.

One early instinct—upon remembering it, later, the embarrassment will rise in me—is in fact to be enraged at Musa for keeping us in the place. Who does he think he is, this bland, bespectacled functionary? He's not my parent. He should not, by virtue of his organizational position, make life-or-death decisions for Cecil and me. This place is dangerous—as a youth project it will be associated with left-wing activism—and we shouldn't be in it.

"What's he thinking?"

But Cecil's on Musa's side. "He is a Zulu. He can pass for Inkatha. He is the one who must be going outside now. Anyway, he is worried about his girlfriend." There is nothing I can do: in these situations one must trust the locals. I have chosen, albeit only briefly, to try to live in this Soweto environment: now I must defer to these men.

Musa leaves. I pace the length of the building: the main meeting room, Musa's small office, his bedroom, and a toilet. Although at some level I realize it's futile, I continue to run through the potential scenarios, plan for them. The doors are indeed sturdy—large green-painted metal frames with triple steel bolts that sink into drilled cinderblock holes. It would take a battering ram to get in here. Bars are soldered onto the windows. A breakin isn't going to occur in the thick of a street battle, but what perturbs me more is the possibility of a petrol bomb, tossed in through the gaps. I notice the stacks of papers, the posters on all the walls, Musa's office with its printed spreadsheets. Kindling. If the place catches fire we will be forced to choose between burning to death or being chopped up at the exits. My mind loops back to James in that music room on the day the school hall burned down.

I begin to take down posters and stuff paper in the metal drawers of Musa's desk.

"What are you doing?" Cecil asks. He seems visibly impatient with me at this moment—doesn't even look me in the eye. He is sitting on the office phone, talking away again in clicks and consonants that separate me from him. When I explain about the possibility of fire he clucks his tongue.

"Try not to worry too much, *né,* Glen? Do not overreact. We are just being cautious. And leave the papers—you are just giving us more work, babe."

I am losing him. I sense it now, without being ready to articulate it to myself: we are drifting into alternate realities. I leave him on the phone. In this eight o'clock blackness—there are no street lights in this part of Soweto, and most of the other houses, like this place, have been darkened—I lie on Musa's mattress. I don't believe Cecil. Nobody is acting as if this is nothing. "It's not so bad," my father and uncle said, just before the jack bank. "Just keep your sense of humor." When I go to the toilet, Cecil puts down the telephone.

"Try not to flush unless it is the brown stuff, hey, babe? We will try to make it as if we are not here."

The silence drags, punctuated only by Cecil's soft drone. How many hours is he glued to that receiver—one, three, four? This is my core experience that night, the fundamental recollection that stays with me: lying on the bed alone, with Cecil talking nearby. Every movement outside causes my heart to race. When I get up and look, there's nothing: a shadowy figure hobbling by on the street in the darkness, the gleam and creak of two moving bicycle wheels. The fact that not everyone's feeling compelled to hide indoors provokes a moment of peaceful reassurance; but this haze of calm lasts only a minute before, back on the bed, the dryness in my throat and the hand-tingling start up again. I shiver in the heat.

I run into the office.

"What's going on?" I ask. "Should you really be talking like this, Cecil? Won't people hear you?" I pace up and down, pick up Musa's papers and put them down again.

"I am worried about Musa," is all Cecil says to me now. "He isn't getting to his girlfriend's. He should have been arriving there a long time ago."

"But I need you, Cecil." This is all I say to him. Can I explain to him about boarding school, about how John has planted a sliver of metal in me that has made me more than usually scared of life? Can I explain about the profound contradiction: how part of me has courted danger, deliberately daring something like this to happen—*give me a deposit of four*—while another part of me, at a moment like this, is simply petrified? But I am years away from figuring out the paradox. At age twenty-two, I still think myself an undamaged person living an adventurous life.

"Soon, babe," Cecil says now. "I must just call a few more."

Is this the moment our relationship begins to end—when whatever cord has still been holding us together unravels? How do I look when I ask him these things? My hands visibly shake, as they do with the traffic cops. My thighs wobble. I sit on Musa's desk. Likely, I look at my most skinny and neurotic, my most vulnerable and weak—an overgrown twelve-year-old-boy stepping forward to receive a beating. In a different mood Cecil might reach out and hug me, but now he's concerned about other things.

What I *could* say, that night in the youth project: *Cecil, I'm not being a normal, nervous white kid. This is actually reminding me of some stuff that happened when I was twelve.*

What he *could* reply: *Okay, Glen, but this is why I can't focus on you. Musa's at* risk *here. We are in a safe haven—he is not.*

But we do not say these things. The fact is that—although the memory will perturb me in hindsight—now, this evening, I don't recognize, even slightly, the seriousness of Musa's absence. Probably, to be honest, I think: *African time*. Musa has just run into some friends. This is my image of Soweto ambiance: Cecil and I will set out on a given Saturday afternoon to drop by at X's house. On the way there we will bump into A, who wants to talk to Cecil about GLOW business. We will duck into the living room of C, another shared acquaintance, and end up having a beer. Then P and Q will happen to knock on the front door. This is, quite possibly, the world's most social culture. So now I imagine Musa in a living room, holding a beer. Do I really think this, or is it just that my self has shrunk back to being a ravenous pinprick of need, the way it was on the night of the mock hanging?

Later, I do hear a scattering of distant shouts—glass smashing somewhere. There are car noises—police vans? But there are no rifle thunderclaps, no anguished ruckuses. It is like a distant bar fight. When I tell Cecil he nods again—in the middle of talking— and says, "Do not worry, Glen. If they are here, we will know, *né*? It is not something that comes quietly." Surreally, Afro-pop music briefly emanates from one house, then hushes down again. The whole neighborhood sinks back into silent torpor.

Eventually the anxiety exhausts me. Too much sweating and trembling with nothing to do and nothing outside to respond to. The heaviness of the heat. The fan turned off so as not to make a noise. Incredibly, I fall asleep—my body trained, perhaps, all of those nights ago in the Standard Six dormitory, to slip into uneasy, alert slumber. At some point Cecil joins me. My hand flails outward, a panicked dove; it slaps him on his neck.

"Hey, hey," he says, laying his hand on my shoulder. "Just me, Glen. Relax."

When I try to cuddle with him, he says, "Too hot," and shifts away. At some point, briefly, I actually try to make love with him— start rubbing his chest the way I do when I'm in the mood; I'm desperately trying to draw out of him some calming embraces.

But he says, "This room, it is belonging to Musa," and rolls out of reach.

I must fall asleep again, because suddenly it's first light—a silver-jade haze pressing through thin green curtains. Upon seeing it my relief is immediate and overwhelming. We've survived the attack, if there was one. It isn't Inkatha's style to butcher all night: after an hour or so they go back to their political bases in the miners' compounds. A rooster crows nearby: a common occurrence in African townships, I love it because it evokes the best memories of my childhood, mornings in my maternal grandparents' house on the farm estate with warm fresh oatmeal. I get up. Outside, on the street, the first housekeepers and office cleaners head to work—I wave at one, who returns my greeting with a rather confused look. Cecil wakes, too.

"We are fine now," he nods and dresses. But when he patches a call to Musa's girlfriend, his boss is still absent.

"This is really bad," Cecil says. "I am worried now." And now even I begin to be concerned about Musa. Why wouldn't he have called?

Outside, on the main road and the minibus taxi route, we do see some signs of a fight—smashed bottle glass; a teenage boy with a blood-stained bandage on his head, to whom Cecil talks briefly. But what's most stunning to me is the absolute normality— the houses that look exactly as they usually do, the swept yards, the uniformed school children. From the debris it looks like a friends' brawl.

But no: "They came here," Cecil confirms as we head home. "Their numbers were too small, though. The comrades, they fought back, né, and they chased them away quickly! It was good." For a moment the old romantic illusion reestablishes itself, of Soweto as a safe place, protected by collective revolutionary activism. But if I'm thinking of creating more adventures for myself on the front-lines of a tribal political war, my hosts are having none of it. Unknown to me, one of the many conversations that took place last night over the phone lines was between Thomas and Cecil.

"Yes, we have decided you must stay in town," Cecil confirms, when we're back at the house, the three of us eating breakfast. "It is not fair to your parents that you are here with us. Or to your friends. I have to be here, Glen. It is my house, my job. But for you it is too dangerous. What will all your Cape Town comrades say if you are injured here?"

"But I'm an adult, Cecil," I try to protest. "We've been okay."

"If things had been a little different, we could have been killed." He shakes his small head and frowns at me: recently I have not been comprehending anything. "It is crazy. Anyway, we can still be a couple if you are in town. Maybe even a better one."

Thomas nods: "Absence makes the heart grow fonder." Do I even notice what has happened—how Cecil has abandoned the primary romantic bond to form an alliance with his housemate? At age twenty-two I still have little sense of such subtleties or the risks they imply to attachments. What I do realize, however, is that I've run out of leverage when it comes to my living arrangements.

Fortunately Stephen has a daybed in his living room. I park my pale blue Peugeot outside under the green, leafy oaks of the city: a different universe from tin-roof youth projects and women carrying water down muddy footpaths. Stephen is gone during the day—he is studying actuarial science at the university. Perhaps he has a job, too—I don't remember. Now, I sit around. I make only the most perfunctory efforts at job hunting. Technically, these are the last six days I live in South Africa as someone committed to long-term residency in the country, but this week, it's as if my brain is leaping ahead of itself, avoiding anything that could imply geographical commitment—figuring out some pathway to a quieter life. What I do instead of mailing out CV's is read, watch, and listen to news reports. A Commonwealth group pronounces South

Africa the most murderous country in the world. The ANC protests a 4 billion rand army slush fund that may have been used to fund political massacres.

I call Cecil a couple of times a day. Often Thomas answers; he's become much more gracious since I'm no longer living there. "I will tell Cecil you called. No, no, he is still very concerned about Musa." When I reach Cecil: "Eish, babe, it is bad. Nobody has heard anything. The police, they are useless, they care nothing."

The fact that Musa may be dead or injured is still too much for me to absorb. "Maybe everything is okay?" I ask Cecil. I try my hand at gallows humor: "Maybe he has a secret girlfriend, and they've eloped to marry on Lake Malawi?"

"No, Glen, not that," says Cecil, less than amused. And deep down of course I know this is impossible: not that serious, authoritative man who double- and triple-checked every window bolt.

Cecil comes and stays over one night in Stephen's living room. The three of us watch television together: we laugh at cricket and at the chatter about Madonna's book, *Sex,* photographs from which have been banned. Apparently the most offensive one showed the Material Girl ejaculating from a sunscreen bottle. We guffaw at the unintended apartheid undertones of the controversy—Cecil says the government wants to make sure white people use their sun protection factors correctly, so as to retain their superior complexions. This is what it's like, in the midst of madness: there are spells of humor, sanity, and intimacy, when it seems things can still work out. But the next morning Cecil leaves early, scouring Hillbrow Hospital and the old clinic where he worked in the city for news of Musa. I stay in bed.

Why do I not join Cecil? It is not as though I'm busy with other responsibilities. Rather, I choose to keep my distance. When Stephen and I are alone, we make fun of Cecil for trying to be Magnum, P.I. or Starsky and Hutch—surely, even with a corrupt and biased police force, it's better to advocate for someone in the detective branch to take this case seriously? What can an ordinary civilian do except endanger himself? But when we suggest this to Cecil, he's adamant. Musa's friends and family all agree: telling top detectives will only make it worse. There is the black perspective on matters like this, and then the white: blacks know they cannot trust apartheid institutions. Despite the balding headmaster and the ineffectual redhead teacher-on-duty at the boys' dorm, I apparently don't share Cecil's skepticism. Do I notice that I've now mirrored Cecil's defection to Thomas with an allegiance switch of my own?

Perhaps six days after the attack, I call Cecil's house. He picks up.

"Hello," he says, breathing heavily. He is distraught: I can hear it from just that one word that comes out a sigh. Cecil is so seldom this way—bubbly animation being his default setting—that I'm instantly quiet myself: slow-moving, alert.

"What's wrong, Cecil?"

He takes perhaps a second. Throughout this conversation his words will come out crawling like this, stones thudding down a hill. In this moment I suddenly sense a depth of pain I haven't encountered before: certainly not that evening in the project, when he talked on the phone. Too late I see his vulnerability.

"It is Musa, Glen." He's almost whispering. "He is in the hospital." Another sharp breath—it is as if his chest is tight, as if he is a kid not daring to breathe during a prefects' meeting. Cecil mentions the name of a township medical facility—probably it is Baragwanath, but maybe it is another place, Leratong or Natalspruit. "I am going there now, Glen. That night—the Inkatha, they kidnapped him."

Prompted by my questions, Musa's story stumbles out, jumbled and broken. It's a short conversation: soon Cecil draws it to a close, citing exhaustion. "I cannot tell you everything. It is too hard." Only later will I get more details from him. When I do so, this is the story I'll reconstruct and reimagine:

It's early afternoon again, that day the child came to warn us. After locking us up in the youth project, Musa moves purposefully, focused on getting to his girlfriend's house. The streets are emptying. People are scurrying indoors. At the corner store the owner rolls down the metal hatches. Musa's girlfriend is only fifteen minutes away; he has no overnight bag or toiletries—his exit was a quick one. He can move well; he heads to the nearby main road, the double-lane asphalt roadway with the minibus taxis and the roadside hawkers; the litter, potholes, traffic robots, and towering street lights clustered like flowers. The hawkers are gone— illegal street sellers vanish at the first sign of trouble. But cars still drive by, insulated from the panic. The woman and child in the ubiquitous Omo washing powder billboard smile at each other serenely as always.

Does Musa hold out his index finger for a minibus? Let's say not initially. He's a fit guy. He can get to her alone. So he jogs. At some point, though, he gets impatient. It is still some way to her place. Where are the Inkatha guys? Maybe they're headed to her neighborhood. He needs to get to her quickly: the thought of her alone, at home, with those thugs smashing windows and trying to kick down doors—this horrifies him.

So he notices nothing abnormal about the minibus that slows next to him. A white, dusty Kombi, just like twenty thousand others on this nation's roads. Women and men crammed tight onto tatty plastic seats. The driver whistling and shouting the name of the destination: "Orlando Diepkloof!" Musa jumps in. He crouches by the sliding door. "Just a few stops, driver!" The minibus pulls off.

Now, he tells the other people in the taxi of the coming *impi*. He stirs up a conversation—Inkatha—horrible. Maybe someone even says something obnoxious and offensive about, say, the un-circumcised King Zwelethini, still a boy from the other tribes' point of view. Does the driver have a small IFP sticker on his dash-board that no one has noticed yet—a beaming Prince Buthelezi holding his scepter?

Nor does anyone observe the driver's wrong turn, at first.

"Just getting petrol," the driver shouts back at the first question—although if anyone looks at the gauge they would notice it's full. But then, in a minute, his foot slams down on the accelerator; he begins to whirl around corners and through stop signs. Now something's wrong. Women scream. Musa shouts something at the driver. But before they know it they are through the gates of the nearby miners' hostel, screeching to a halt in the clearing be-tween the parallel tin-roof dormitories that stretch out for hun-dreds of yards. "ANC!" shouts the driver. And in a blink the minibus is surrounded by mine workers—blue overalls, some with scars on their arms and faces—who pull the door open, tug out Musa and the other passengers, pin arms behind backs, tumble people into the buildings. Where will they imprison them?

"I do not know these details, Glen," Cecil says, when I ask him. "Of course I cannot ask Musa. Terrible, né?" Again he seems on the verge of tears.

Some storeroom, then, let's say—an empty one. A tight room—people thrown in, bound up with rope. Angry shouting: *Como-tsotsis!* Communist gangsters!

Of course the women are punished first. This is logical, isn't it? This is what always happens in the realm of the jack bank—the weakest are always taught the most severe lesson. Perhaps the driver repeats some of the jokes the women told about his politi-cal faction—comparing Gatscha to a horse's behind! Maybe these men are sick of Sotho chicks making fun of their foreskins.

"I do not know what happened to the women," Cecil says. "Musa does not know either." Are we really so ignorant? Three hundred furious men, separated by apartheid policies from their wives and families. Just three or four women, all presumed from a hated enemy faction.

"Musa," Cecil continues. "Musa was one of the lucky ones. He was telling them all this time he is Inkatha. In the end, a miracle—they believed him. Now he is bad, Glen—his legs, face, and ribs, they are broken. Horrible."

Horrible, yes. But Musa—How would it have been? Six days. Hands tied above his head. Knobkerrie blows, over and over again, on his head, jaw, rib cage. Who would have been there, torturing him? Some Zulu John, aflame with outrage. "Your comrades killed ten of us!" Blood flowing out of Musa's mouth. A ghastly cracking where the blows land.

At some level, of course, this is all not that important. It's just one more horror story in this collapsing country, in this world full of villainy since its history began to be recorded: Jesus on his cross. Mustard gas and Zyklon B. Soon, in Rwanda, severed Tutsi Achilles tendons to stop detainees crawling away during the hacking breaks. Since at least Voltaire modern human beings have known about their inhumanity; since Hannah Arendt we've registered evil's tedium. There's nothing extraordinary about Musa's experience. For me, though, a moral choice. A closed feeling in my chest, as I listen to Cecil. A cold numbness fanning over my body, like it did on those long-ago afternoons when John would sit next to me.

Running—that is what I did before. What will I do to handle the malevolence in the universe this time?

"I am going now to the hospital," Cecil says. "I have to see Musa." A pause. "Do you want to come?"

I can hear the sadness and grief in Cecil's voice, his need for support. Regardless of my irritation for the night on the telephone and the Soweto eviction, I still love him. I need to be his boyfriend. To Musa I need to affirm his courage: "Cecil has been looking for you for a whole week, Musa. We didn't forget about you." I need to hug Cecil, to show I'm proud of him.

I also need to become blacker. This half-decade yearning for a dark-skinned community of refuge—for all its foolishness, it can lead me out of terror and into convalescence if I only take it seriously enough. *Community*—the word implies reciprocity. The purpose of life, it suggests, isn't to avoid agony or duck the jack bank, but to band together with others against it. To find in solidarity a fragile but sustaining redemption.

Finally, of course—I cannot leave this out of the roster—at this moment I owe it to Musa. Whatever the wisdom of his decision to go to his girlfriend's house, the fact remains he gave up his room, that afternoon, for my protection. *A white man like you shouldn't be outside.* A deposit of jacks made not in his own account but in mine.

"Well," Cecil asks, "are you coming?"

"Will you get me?" I'm playing for time, now—I know this isn't practical. Cecil is an hour and a half away by public transport. If he ferries me around all day he won't get anything else done. "I really want to see Musa, babe." This, too, is a lie: he must sense it. I do not want to be reminded of my trauma. I do not want to feel Musa's pain, and by extension my own.

"But I don't know how to drive there. Is it dangerous if I get lost?"

"It is okay, Glen, really. Don't worry. I cannot come for you—I am too busy." We say good-bye and hang up the phone on friendly terms.

But it's not genuinely all right. Really, he sees through my ploy; he understands the cowardice of my decision. A week or so later, in an over-the-phone breakup conversation, Cecil will say: "I do wish you had come to visit Musa that day, *né*? It would have showed me we were equals, as you always said."

———

Next day Stephen needs his daybed for another guest. I am an unemployed ex-researcher: I have no money for hotels. It seems as though I'm out of accommodation options for Johannesburg. Also, I need a break from slashing *impis* and stories of angry torturers: I feel ready for different horizons.

"Going home, babe," I say to Cecil. "Come visit me, soon." I drive the three hours down the highway, across the highveld grasslands and cornfields and down the lush Crocodile Valley into the subtropical savannah landscape of my childhood: aloe vera and acacia scrubs on the hill fingers; tea, banana, and citrus plantations in the bush hollows. My parents' big white two-story house is shaded by jacarandas, bananas, and poincianas. It has a pool, a vegetable garden in the back, and an orchid garden on the side verandah—David, in his final year of high school, has taken up flowers and vegetables; under his care the place has become a cornucopia, an Eden, blossoms hanging in all the windowsills; fresh pumpkin, corn, watermelons, and strawberries on the kitchen table.

Mom and Dad are overjoyed. Mom, in particular, has been a bit troubled about my visiting this "boyfriend" up in Johannesburg, even though, to keep her from worrying, I've given the two of them only a carefully filtered report: Cecil lives in "southern Jo'burg"; Cecil's friend is "missing" rather than kidnapped and tortured. Mom runs out in her shorts and blouse and gives me a big hug. Here she is again, warm, loving, protective, wearing her violet perfume—and then Dad and David arrive, too, and the family's barking new golden Labrador, Tshane, and their Swazi housekeeper, Nora. After the night in the youth project and Cecil rolling away from me, this is all so much like old times I cannot stop the tears welling up: this is a kind of home. Mom serves apricot chicken and brown rice for lunch, or perhaps it's macaroni and cheese: at any rate, what matters is that it's familiar food and with every bite I feel more myself. It feels so comforting to be there that even the breakup with Cecil, which comes within a week or two, doesn't bother me as much as I expected it to.

"I don't know if this is really working," Cecil tells me over the phone. He says he wants to think about it and decide where to go: then he abruptly stops returning calls and letters.

"Just let it go, my love," Mom tells me. "You'll meet other guys."

And so I do let it go. I am now in an older reality, what feels in some ways like a more grounded and solid one. I commiserate with David: a thin and angst-filled teenager himself, my brother clucks sympathetically and makes me tapes full of brooding alternative rock. At age seventeen, he is already a music fiend; he is full of names I've never heard, like Lloyd Cole and My Bloody Valentine and the Pixies. He, too, says nothing to me yet about his own love life. I assume girls in the picture, secret flirtations and crushes, but in a few years he, too, will come out of the closet, giving Mom and Dad a home run in the queer baseball championships. They will, in fact, handle the news with extraordinary grace: within a few years they'll be founding a Parents of Lesbians and Gays support group and sharing their story during lay sermons from the pulpit at their Catholic church.

For a week or two I laze around the pool and watch *Matlock* reruns, then get the idea of placing an announcement in the paper advertising my services as a private tutor. The process of breaking down an argument for a constitutional committee is in the end not that different from helping a fifteen-year-old unpack a word problem. Since the town is no intellectual or educational powerhouse, I'm quickly swamped with business. Boys and girls, wearing the familiar uniforms that James and I once did—gray trousers, white shirts, and blue blazers for the boys; plain turquoise dresses and navy jackets for the girls—sit around Mom and Dad's teak dining room table under the wildlife paintings, work hard under my supervision, and achieve ten- and twenty-point increases in their exam scores. This is the most fun I've ever had working. It's better than researching human rights abuses and certainly superior to calculating citrus yields. I laugh with the kids; find ways to help their homework make sense to them. Although I don't quite register it yet, I am in fact discovering my future vocation as a teacher.

The urge to take a break from South Africa and try out life in another country grows slowly. It begins, unsurprisingly enough, as a continuing reaction to watching all the news reports of the Afrikaner Resistance Movement smashing an armored car into the constitutional negotiations room at the World Trade Center; the racist paramilitaries who blow up the athletics stadium of my old boarding school when the administration decides to admit black students. Every weekend, or so it seems during this time, there is another drive-by shooting at a bus stop or a machete attack. Now, when I watch such reports I am more than ever on an emotional rack. On one side sits my love of South Africa, my family and friends, James, even Cecil, whom I still remember fondly. On the other, the jack bank: cruelty, fear, and power. Now, when I see people being burned alive or hacked on the television, I'm instinctively in a nearby hut. The terror, now *my* terror: the skin at the back of my neck a taut, thin drum.

The impulse grows. *Leave this whole mess behind. There are places on earth where, whether through wisdom, good fortune, or merely the capacity to export their aggression elsewhere, deposits of brutality won't earn this kind of compound interest. An existence where dividends are paid in money, art, books, or whatever you want them in—not in electric shocks or jacks.*

I don't specifically decide to emigrate. On the day Mom and Dad drive me to the bus to Johannesburg Airport—green backpack on my shoulder; $2,000 in tutoring savings turned into travelers' checks; a ticket to New York via Amsterdam and London in my money belt—on that day, my plan is just to travel the world while I'm still young. I'll see what pans out in London or New York. I'll try to teach English in Spain, hop on a fishing trawler in Alaska. I hug and kiss Mom and Dad good-bye at the petrol station on the Johannesburg Road. I wave from the window. Do I even cry? Does my mother? On later visits back, we'll both be in tears for these farewells. But today, at the end of 1993, I don't think anyone's imagining the decades of geographical separation of eight thousand miles. The scratchy phone calls via AT&T or Internet Protocol from mornings into afternoons. The homesickness; the days I gaze longingly at my photobook of South African scenery and yearn for granite kopjes, the smell of rhino dung on the back of my parents' pickup, the taste of Appletiser sodas. One day in New York City, I calculate for fun how long it would take me, if I could walk and sleep on water, to make it home: just under a thousand days and nights, three years of watery emptiness.

A month or two after I arrive in New York City, where I'm staying with a friend I know through human rights circles, I'm sitting around a table with a group of expatriate South Africans, black and white, whom I've met at the embassy. They're musicians, journalists, writers, restaurant waiters—young bohemians of the kind the city seems built for. *Rent* has come alive around this dining room table in a two-bedroom Jackson Heights walkup. The topic's the annual green card lottery—a program under which the U.S. State Department awards fifty thousand residence permits a year to immigrants from nations traditionally underrepresented in migration flows. These men and women are trying to persuade me to enter. They have, they say, a lawyer who can help them tilt the odds. For $50 he can ensure it's all done correctly, the stamp and the paperwork and the zip code.

"He's a cool *ouk,* man. I've met him—a Colombian or Venezuelan or something."

I examine the instructions. To me it looks as though this lawyer is going to charge $50 for nothing more than seeing whether these people followed instructions as simple as those for opening a milk carton.

"No, look, see, this is all you do—no need for a lawyer. Just seal it"—I demonstrate the gesture with tongue and hands—"and drop it in a post box." On the way back to the subway stop, I mail my application for the heck of it: why not?

Six months later, I've obtained a temporary visa extension to teach English in a job-training program in Manhattan and moved into a two-floor, dilapidated-but-beautiful Brooklyn brownstone apartment, about half an hour from work. I share this place with a Swiss musician and a Jamaican painter, and my plan is to live and work here for a year before returning to South Africa to pursue a career in teaching. Even in this short time, my life has become unrecognizable, however. Instead of talking about the newspaper crime reports or the debate about land reform, the conversation in our Brooklyn commune revolves around Brazilian film festivals, poetry readings at St. Mark's Bookstore in the East Village, the latest exhibitions at MoMA. I go for walks at night, fearless, through the streets of Greenwich Village, lined with their gay bars and porn shops. I still cruise black guys in the bars and clubs: in the Two Potato; on the Christopher Street pier. Most find me intriguing and exotic on account of my foreign accent; I land up in elegant apartments over Christopher Street and in grimy squats in the meatpacking district, with a cheap battery-powered alarm clock ticking on the bedside table, and the sweet smell of crystal meth still clinging to the curtains and blankets.

There are days, certainly, when my overall sense of privilege in this city feels surreal to me—morally deadening; a kind of beautiful sleepiness. Moment to moment, I admit it's simply lovely: the breezes off the East River in my apartment on lazy summer afternoons; the jazz trumpeting out of the Village Vanguard on Sunday mornings, when my friends and I go there for the free brunch. Yet when I count time in weeks and months rather than minutes, it sometimes seems to me I'm merely heaping up earthly delights and avoiding life's most significant challenges. Back home, people stand for days in line to vote in the country's first elections. President Nelson Mandela, a living hero for the world, holds up his fist below a battalion of fighter jets spewing out smoke in the colors of the new South African flag. In April 1994, the nondiscrimination clause for which Cecil, I, and all our comrades fought comes into force as part of the interim constutition: two years later, South Africa indeed will become the first country in the history of the world to ban homophobic discrimination in its bill of rights.

The U.S. government envelope arrives on a Saturday morning at the brownstone, forwarded from the friend I lived with when I first moved to the city. At first, when I open it, I have to read the words on the letter inside several times to absorb their import: out of millions of applicants, I have won a green card in the 1994 DV-6 visa lottery. I have the right, now, to permanently reside in the United States, and in time to become a naturalized American citizen. I need not go back to the Republic of South Africa. I can now, if I choose to, join the peoples of the rich world who are, at least to a greater extent than their third-world brethren, insulated from the instability and the violence of jack banks: kept at least at arm's remove from death squad leaders, crocodile rivers, shacks with starving children, prefect-sadists.

There's no party for me in the brownstone or in any of my favorite queer Manhattan hangouts. In the beginning, I don't even know whether I want to mail in the next set of application forms, those required to take advantage of the offer and formalize my legal transition. Walking along the Bay Ridge promenade, below the Verrazano Bridge; sitting on the steps by the lions at the entrance to the New York Public Library—a library that exceeds, by a factor of at least ten, any such institution I could even imagine before coming to this country—doing all this, I can see a kind of rough vision of my life if I stay here.

Coffee shops and restaurants: will it be Laotian in Chinatown this Saturday or Uighur food on Brighton Beach?

Universities, more of them in this single city than in the entire country of South Africa. I have a sense that I might want to study something for myself this time round—go back to graduate school, to my first love, literature and writing—leave maths and computer science behind me, along with new constitutions, national lesbian and gay rights conventions, and high-powered political love affairs.

Those forms lying on my kitchen table at home turn out to be easier to fill out than I expect them to be: name, date of birth, proof of high school education. Steam rises from the manhole next to the blue U.S. mailbox on the corner of Houston and Broadway, where I drop off the envelope. A Turkish immigrant on the sidewalk is selling cardboard cups of coffee and toasted cinnamon raisin bagels, with cream cheese. The street-cleaning truck that drives by as I close the hatch of the mailbox has both of its circular brushes revolving at full speed, whirling discarded polystyrene cups and chip packets into suspended garbage bags—scraping from the visible world its filth, detritus, and rottenness: only a partial sanitization, to be sure, but a necessary one for the street to be worth walking on.

Biographical Note

The author teaches creative nonfiction at Susquehanna University in the green, hilly Amish country of central Pennsylvania. He lives in an old Victorian house in Sunbury, Pennsylvania, with his partner, Peterson Toscano. He frequently spends weekends in New York City.

His parents, Pete and Dee Retief, still live in South Africa, where his father now manages a growing Internet telecommunications business. His sister, Lisa, lives in Cape Town with her wife and two-year-old son. David lives in Cape Town, too, where he works in computers. Glen typically manages to get back to South Africa to visit them every year or two.

James Stroud lives in Cape Town, where he makes a living as a wildlife painter. Glen and James still maintain a long-distance friendship.

The author is no longer in touch with John, the prefect who invented the jack bank.

Author's Note

The book you have just finished reading is a memoir. Once upon a time, it seems, as a culture we knew what this meant for most writers: something along the lines of the Merriam-Webster definition, "A narrative composed from personal experience." We knew memoir wasn't fiction, it was testimony—an author standing behind a story, saying these are my memories. But we also understood it wasn't factual autobiography. There would be a process of *composition*. Frank McCourt used a visual metaphor: autobiography is photography; memoir is painting. In order to be art as well as truth—to allow the reader to enter the story and not just encounter the facts of it—memoir must engage imagination as well as memory.

So, then: the book you have read is a good-faith memoir. The incidents dramatized here—the lion attack, the jack bank, my grandfather's pedophilia, and the Inkatha scare and kidnapping—are real recollections. They happened to me, not to other people. The cast of characters you met are genuine human beings, even if the versions of them you met over the course of this narrative were necessarily just limited glimpses.

That said, I took some liberties in this manuscript—license I consider to be implicit in the process of composition. I reconstructed dialogue from my recollections of conversations and from my general sense of how the people in my life talked. To sharpen the haze of forgetfulness, I did a kind of scooping from the pot of memory, ladling out the ingredients to spice up individual moments. So, to a real memory of a school lesson about the natural bounty of the Kruger National Park I added, say, on the bicycle ride home, a family of warthogs playing in the sprinklers of a rugby field. On our lunch table I set down a bowl of macaroni and cheese. Were those features there that day, or another? Truth is, I don't know—but the key fact is that these warthogs were frequently there during my childhood, running around in that exact way, and that macaroni and cheese graced our midday meals at least once a week. So it feels legitimate for me to write them in.

Another latitude I permitted myself is that of the educated best guess. Some memoirists like to include their readers in a kind of forensic investigation, saying, "I'm about 80 percent sure the policeman who showed me how to use the walkie-talkies was Dirkie's serial-killer uncle. This is a memory that came back to me, though, only in flashes, after I saw the newspaper article, so, memory working the way it does, it's certainly possible I'm imposing a face from my nineteenth year of life onto a memory clip from my tenth." Much as I admire this investigative style of writing, it just isn't my thing—I prefer to take an honorable stab at the truth and run with it.

I took two main liberties with this story's timeline. The first is really just an example of the "educated guess," namely, when my memories are hopelessly jumbled—did the mock hanging take place before or after the incident with John and the telephone crank?—I've picked the most likely sequence and then told the story that way. Second, I've been willing to combine different scenes together for the sake of artistic economy so long as that didn't affect the essential truth of my narrative.

It's hard to fact-check a memoir of events that took place several decades ago, on the other side of the world, but to the extent possible, I've done so. My parents confirm the general accuracy of my game reserve memories. Lisa gives her overall blessing to "A Man of Extraordinary Taste," although of course her memories of the time described in it are very different: most notably, she recalls the abuse having begun perhaps a year or so before I have any retrospective recollections of anything being amiss. James backs up my memories of boarding school, including such specific details as the cricket bat beatings, the pillow slip filled with athletic spikes, the electric shocks to boys' genitalia, the jack bank, and so forth. Like me, however, he can't vouch for the precise sequence of the events or exactly who instigated which depredations: for example, he recalls the mock hanging as dating from a different year of our high school, meaning that neither John nor Greg would have been involved. This is something that makes no sense to me given both what I recall about my betrayal of André and also about Greg, John's friend, being present.

Anyone who lived with me through my OLGA years should hopefully be able to recognize the clever, angry young queer activist with a major fetish for black guys. The Gay and Lesbian Archives in Johannesburg drew my attention to only one small factual error in my recollections of the history of the gay and lesbian rights struggle, pertaining to what Albie Sachs said during his visit to OLGA. Upon receiving this reminder, I duly re-remembered this meeting and corrected the story. I would love to be able to check my recollections of Cecil, Musa, the kidnapping, and the Inkatha attack, but Cecil has declined to respond to my e-mails and phone calls pertaining to this topic.

Some names and identifying details in the story have been changed; in other cases I've left out surnames and/or identifying details. As for the people who are named—what can I say to you, to all the friends, family, tricks, boyfriends, and acquaintances who helped shape me? It's common knowledge that if you portray someone you care about as entirely positive, the reader will smell the public relations lie and mistrust the book. Make the portrayal even 90 percent positive, and the person concerned is likely to focus on the remaining 10 percent. So sorry if, by writing this, I've hurt or embarrassed any of you. I was simply being true to my experience. I continue to believe in memoir as a social act. If no one is ever willing to break the protective silence of what goes on in individual lives, how will we ever learn from each other?

Glossary

ANC	African National Congress, the main antiapartheid liberation movement
Ag	exclamation of annoyance, pronounced "ah-ggg," like a throat-clearing
amadoda	men
assegai	short, traditional Zulu spear
baas	boss; expected submissive form of address for white men by black adults during the apartheid years
bakkie	pickup truck
bangbroek	scaredy-cat
berg wind	hot mountain winds that blow down from the South African plateau to the coastal plain
bende	gang
blikbrein	tin brain
blind one	a mean trick or con
bogs	communal bathrooms
boffin	brainbox; clever kid

boerewors	traditional farm-style sausage
boomslang	tree snake
braai	barbecue
bulletjie	little bull
Colored	mixed-race South African
cooldrink	soda
dagga	marijuana
doek	literally, "cloth"; often used to describe black women's head wraps.
dominee	reverend
donner	beat up
doos	cunt
dumpie	340 ml beer bottle
duif	dove
eish	exclamation, pronounced "eh-sh"
hau	exclamation, pronounced "how"
hinne	slang corruption of the Afrikaans word *"Here,"* meaning "Lord"
howzit	hello
impi	Zulu military battalion
injonga	active homosexual male
ja	yes
jack	a blow usually administered to the buttocks with a cricket bat or cane; "finger jacks" are blows to the fingertips, usually with a heavy ruler
kaalgat	literally, "naked hole"; nude or unclothed
kaalkop	bald head
kaffir	highly derogatory term for black people
kief	cool; groovy
kleinbaas	"little boss"; expected submissive form of address for white children by black adults during the apartheid years

klipspringer	small antelope that lives on rocky hillocks
knobkerrie	club with a round knob on top
koeksusters	literally, "cake sisters"; two strips of dough twirled together, fried, and soaked in syrup
Kombi	A VW minibus
kopje	rocky hillock
kys	roughly, "romantic commitment" or "the state of being romantically involved with someone"; to ask someone the *kys* means to ask them to go out with you.
laatie	chap, boy
langarm	a folk dance where the couples stretch their right arms out and up
larney	rich person
lekker	nice, cool, or tasty, depending on the context
lekkewaan	monitor lizard
matric	twelfth grade
meneer	sir
miesies	missus; expected submissive form of address for white women by black adults during the apartheid years
moer	beat up
moer in	furious
moffie	faggot
muntus	derogatory term for blacks; a slang corruption of the Swazi *umuntu,* meaning human being
né?	isn't it?
orisha	West African divinity
ou, ouk, oukie	guy, chap, fellow, dude, all depending on the specific context
pap	corn porridge
paraatheid	readiness

prefect	a twelfth grader with the responsibility of enforcing the school rules; unofficially permitted to administer corporal punishment
recces	reconnaissance soldiers
SADF	South African Defence Force, the apartheid army
shebeen	informal tavern
shongololo	fat black African centipede
skivvy	a younger boy who serves as the slave or servant to an older boy in boarding school
skesana	passive male homosexual or femme
skoffel	literally, "shuffle"; a dance
slimkop	brainbox; egghead
soutie, soutpiel	slang for English-speaking South African; literally, "saltie" or "salt dick," a man who stands with one foot in England, another in South Africa, and his genitalia hanging down in the ocean
spruit, spruitjie	dry riverbed
stompie	cigarette butt
SWAPO	South West African People's Organization, the main group fighting for democracy in Namibia
terries	terrorists
tokoloshe	mischievous goblin from indigenous Southern African mythology
togs	sports shoes
trekboer	nomadic farmer
tuck shop	snack shop
varsity	college
velskoen	big, flat sturdy shoe of untanned hide
viooltjie	African violet
Voertsek!	Get lost!

voorhuis	portal or entrance hall
vroteier	literally, "rotten egg," a children's game, similar to the American "duck duck goose"; one player runs around a group of seated children and drops a ball of tissue behind an unsuspecting player who must then catch that person before he or she gets back to your spot
wena	you
windgat	cocky or arrogant fellow; literally, an anus that's full of stomach gas
Witwatersrand	greater Johannesburg area
Yebo	Yes; also, "hi" or "hello"
Yissis	a slang corruption of the Afrikaans name for "Jesus," used as an interjection